The Colombian Peace Process and the Principle of Complementarity of the International Criminal Court

Kai Ambos

The Colombian Peace Process and the Principle of Complementarity of the International Criminal Court

An Inductive, Situation-based Approach

Springer

Professor Dr. jur. Kai Ambos
University of Göttingen
Head Department for Foreign and International Criminal Law
Chair for Criminal Law, Criminal Procedure,
Comparative Law and International Criminal Law
Judge at the Provincial Court (*Landgericht*) Göttingen
Platz der Göttinger Sieben 5
37073 Göttingen
Germany
kambos@gwdg.de

ISBN 978-3-642-11272-0 e-ISBN 978-3-642-11273-7
DOI 10.1007/978-3-642-11273-7
Springer Heidelberg Dordrecht London New York

Library of Congress Control Number: 2010927684

Cover design: WMXDesign GmbH, Heidelberg, Germany

Printed on acid-free paper

Springer is part of Springer Science+Business Media (www.springer.com)

Preface

This book is based on an in-depth research into the Colombian peace process under the Justice and Peace Law (Law 975 of 2005), with a view to the obligations set forth under the complementarity principle of the ICC Statute. The research was commissioned by GTZ-ProFis, a project funded by the German government with the goal of assisting Colombia's Unit of Justice and Peace (*Unidad de Justicia y Paz*) of the Office of the Prosecutor General (*Fiscalía General de la Nación*) which is the most important institution to make this process work. The research was conducted in 2008 and 2009 involving various missions to Colombia (see Annex I). The original Spanish language study was presented in October 2009 in Bogotá and was published by GTZ-ProFis and the Colombian publishing house Temis (www.editorialtemis.com) in February 2010; it is also available online at www.department-ambos.uni-goettingen.de/index.php/en/Forschung/friedensprozess-in-kolumbien-aufgrund-des-gesetzes-975-v-2272005.html.

The study pursues an inductive, situation-based approach with regard to the interpretation of the complementarity principle governing the relationship between the jurisdiction of the International Criminal Court and national criminal justice systems (Art. 17 ICC Statute). The situation it starts from is the Colombian peace process under the said Law 975. The question with regard to Article 17 is whether Colombia – as a party to the ICC Statute which has been monitored for years by the Office of the Prosecutor – has complied with its obligations under Art. 17 ICC Statute. The study is structured as follows: the *first part* contains a critical analysis of the process under Law 975, taking into account not only the relevant norms but especially the practical implementation of the law. With this part a gap is filled since there is thus far no systematic and chronological analysis of this process in English. In the *second part,* the complementarity test of Art. 17 ICC Statute is systematically analyzed and applied to the Colombian situation. First, the object of reference of this test, in particular the distinction between situation and case, is looked at. Then, the actual complementarity test, distinguishing between the (additional) gravity threshold of Art. 17 and complementarity *stricto sensu*, is examined. Some recommendations for the further application of Law 975 conclude this part.

At the end of the book, the reader is provided with various annexes containing additional sources with material for further research, including all the relevant norms and case law (Annex I), an English translation of Law 975 (II) and a schematic overview of this Law (III), in addition to the usual bibliography.

The publication of this study would not have been possible without the commitment and constant support of the GTZ-ProFis project and the Justice and Peace Unit of the *Fiscalía* with all its prosecutors and investigators who received and accompanied the author while he was in Colombia. I am also indebted to all the institutions and individuals who I was able to visit and interview in Colombia. They are all mentioned in Annex I, Section 5. I finally thank my research assistants and LLM/doctoral students Florian Huber (Göttingen) and John Zuluaga (Göttingen/ Medellín, Colombia) for their assistance in the English version of this study. Their assistance was also invaluable in the preparation of the original Spanish version of the study which was also supported by Rodrigo Andrés González-Fuente-Rubilar (Göttingen/Concepción, Chile). Last but not least, I thank my doctoral student Ousman Njikam, currently working at the ICTY in The Hague, for a final language revision. The English publication of this study would not have been possible without the generous financial support of the German Foreign Ministry (*Auswärtiges Amt*).

March 2010 Kai Ambos, Göttingen

Contents

Abbreviation xi

Part I Law 975 and its process

Chapter 1 Preliminary Remarks 3

Chapter 2 The Process Under Law 975 11
2.1 Demobilization, disarmament and reintegration 12
2.2 Preliminary investigation and "versión libre" 14
2.3 Formulation of "imputation" and charges 17
2.4 Reparation 21
2.5 Determination of the sentence 23

Chapter 3 Intermediate Conclusions 25

Part II The complementarity test (Art. 17) and its application to the Colombian situation

Chapter 4 Preliminary Considerations: The Object of Reference of the Complementarity Test (Situation–Case–Conduct) 37

Chapter 5 Gravity and Complementarity *Stricto Sensu* 43
5.1 Sufficient gravity (Art. 17 (1) (d)) 44
5.1.1 The standard in current practice 44
5.1.2 The own approach 48
5.1.3 Application to the situation in Colombia 51
5.2 Complementarity *stricto sensu* 54
5.2.1 Admissibility due to total State inaction 55
5.2.1.1 General considerations 55

5.2.1.2 Application to the situation in Colombia 57
5.2.2 Inadmissibility due to State action (Art. 17 (1) (a)–(c) and 20 (3)) 59
5.2.2.1 General considerations 59
5.2.2.2 Application to the situation in Colombia 63
5.2.3 Admissibility due to unwillingness or inability (Art. 17 (2) and (3)) 63
5.2.3.1 Preliminary remarks 63
5.2.3.2 Unwillingness 66
a) General considerations 66
b) Application to the situation in Colombia 72
aa) Purpose of shielding 72
bb) Unjustified delay 73
cc) Independent and impartial proceedings 75
dd) General and paradigmatic aspects 76
5.2.3.3 Inability 80
a) General considerations 80
b) Application to the situation in Colombia 83

Chapter 6 Conclusion: Classifying the Colombian Case with a View to Different Transitional Justice Scenarios 89

Chapter 7 Some Recommendations for the Further Application of Law 975 91

Documents and Materials

1. Bibliography 97

2. Additional Sources 107
2.1 NORMATIVE FRAMEWORK 107
2.1.1 Legislation 107
2.1.2 Executive Decrees 108
2.1.3 Resolutions, agreements, memoranda and others 108
2.2 JURISPRUDENCE 111
2.2.1 International Jurisprudence 111
2.2.2 Colombian Jurisprudence 113
2.3 DOCUMENTS 116
2.3.1 Governmental documents 116
2.3.2 International and non-governmental organizations 119
2.3.3 Press reports 124

2.4 (Further) BIBLIOGRAPHY 126
2.4.1 Monographs/Books 126
2.4.2 Articles in journals/books 131
2.5 FIELD WORK: INTERVIEWS AND MEETINGS 134
2.5.1 Interviews 134
2.5.2 Meetings 135

3. LAW NO. 975, 25 JULY 2005 (English translation) 139
CHAPTER I 139
Principles and definitions 139
CHAPTER II 142
Preliminary aspects 142
CHAPTER III 143
Procedural principles 143
CHAPTER IV 144
Investigation and prosecution 144
CHAPTER V 149
Alternative Sentence 149
CHAPTER VI 149
Regime for the deprivation of liberty 149
CHAPTER VII 150
Institutions for the execution of this law 150
CHAPTER VIII 151
Rights of victims with respect to the Administration of Justice 151
CHAPTER IX 153
Right to reparation for the victims 153
CHAPTER X 156
Conservation of archives 156
CHAPTER XI 157
Humanitarian Accords 157
CHAPTER XII 157
Entry into force and complementary provisions 157

4. Schematic Overview of the Procedure Under Law 975 161

Abbreviations

AFRC	Armed Forces Revolutionary Council
AI	Amnesty International
Ariz. J. Int'l & Comp. L	Arizona Journal of International and Comparative Law
art., arts.	Article, articles
ASIL	American Society of International Law
AUC	Autodefensas Unidas de Colombia (GAOML -Colombia-)
AVR	Archiv des Völkerrechts
BICC	Bonn International Centre for Conversion
CADH	Convención Americana de Derechos Humanos
CC	Corte Constitucional -Colombia-, i.e. Constitutional Court
CCJ	Comisión Colombiana de Juristas (NGO)
CCP	(Colombian) Code of Criminal Procedure
cf.	Compare, consult
CitPax	Centro Internacional de Toledo para la Paz (NGO)
CLF	Criminal Law Forum
CMH	Comisión de Memoria Historica (Commission on Historical Memory)
CNRR	Comisión Nacional de Reparación y Reconciliación, i.e. National Commission of Reparation and Reconciliation
CODA	Cómite Operativo de Dejación de Armas (Committee for Laying Down Arms)
CornJIntL	Cornell Journal of International Law
CP	Código Penal (Penal/Criminal Code)
CPP	Código de Procedimiento Penal (Criminal Procedure Code)
CUP	Cambridge University Press
DDR	Disarmament, Demobilization and Reintegration

DRC	Democratic Republic of Congo
e.g.	For example
ECtHR	European Court of Human Rights
EIUC	European Inter-University Centre for Human Rights and Democratisation
EJIL	European Journal of International Law
FARC	Fuerzas Armadas Revolucionarias de Colombia (Revolutionary Armed Forces of Colombia)
FGN	Fiscalía General de la Nación (Office of the Prosecutor General - Colombia)
FICHL	Forum for International Criminal and Humanitarian Law
FIDH	Fédération International de Droits de L'Homme
Fla. J. Int'l. L.	Florida Journal of International Law
fn.	Footnote(s)
FPLC	Foreign Policy Leaderchip Council
GAOML	Grupo(s) Armado(s) Organizado(s) al Margen de la Ley, i.e. groups operating outside the law
GMH	Grupo de Memoria Histórica, i.e. Group of Historical Memory
HarvIntLJ	Harvard International Law Journal
HRW	Human Rigths Watch
i.e.	Id est, latin for that is
IACHR	Inter-American Commission on Human Rights
IACtHR	Inter-American Court of Human Rights
ICC	International Criminal Court
ICL	International Criminal Law
ICLQ	*International and Comparative Law Quarterly*
ICLR	International Criminal Law Review
ICTJ	International Center for Transitional Justice
ICTR	International Criminal Tribunal for Rwanda
ICTY	International Criminal Tribunal for Yugoslavia
id.	Idem
IHL	International Humanitarian Law
ILC	International Law Commission UN
ILM	International Legal Materials
JCCD	Jurisdiction, Complementarity and Cooperation Division
JICJ	Justicia y Paz
JURA	Juristische Ausbildung (German law journal)
JyP	Journal of International Criminal Justice
LJIL	Leiden Journal of International Law
LRA	Lord's Resistance Army
MelbJIntL	Melbourne Journal of International Law

MichJIntL	Michigan Journal of International Law
MP	Magistrado Ponente -Colombia- (Reporting Judge/ Judge Rapporteur)
MPYBUN	Max Planck Yearbook of United Nations Law
OTP	Office of The Prosecutor
p.	Page
PAHD	Programa de Atención Humanitaria al Desmovilizado, i.e. Program of Humanitarian Attention for Demobilized Persons
para.	Paragraph(s)
PRIO	International Peace Research Institute, Oslo
PTC	Pre-Trial Chamber
rad.	Radicado-Colombia (case number)
RPE	Rules of Procedure and Evidence
SCSL	Special Court for Sierra Leone
TRC	Truth and Reconciliation Commission
UJP	Unidad de Justicia y Paz (Unit for Justice and Peace), Office of the Prosecutor General (FGN)
UNSC	United Nations Security Council
WCRO	War Crimes Research Office (American University, Washington D.C.)
ZaöRV	Zeitschrift für ausländisches öffentliches Recht und Völkerrecht

Part I
Law 975 and its process

Chapter 1
Preliminary Remarks

The so-called "Justice and Peace Law" (*Ley de Justicia y Paz*) of 25 July 2005 (hereinafter: "Law 975"), which entered into force on the same date (Art. 72), continues a policy of restorative justice which goes back to the 1980s[1] and pursues the objective to disarm, demobilize and reintegrate irregular armed groups ("Grupos Armados Organizados al Margen de la Ley", i.e. "groups operating outside the law", hereinafter: "GAOML"). While the earlier peace processes only referred to "left-wing" insurgents, the Law 975 also or even predominantly covers "right-wing" paramilitary groups.[2] The overall objective of the Colombian policy of restorative justice is, at least from an official perspective, to achieve a sustainable peace on the basis of concessions offered to irregular armed groups with a view to their definitive demobilization, disarmement and reintegration into society. Thus, this policy fits well into the general methodological framework of post-conflict Disarmament, Demobilization and Reintegration ("DDR") programs, at least in their narrow sense of "dismantling the machinery of war".[3] Yet, the problem with these programs has often been that they do not link the DDR process to transitional justice, in particular to the receiving communities and the victims. As a consequence they fall short of bringing about a real reintegration of the former

---

[1]It started in March 1981 with a conditional amnesty for political and related crimes for guerrilla groups (Ley 37 de 1981, Text: http://www.ideaspaz.org/secciones/publicaciones/download_boletines/boletinespaz_docs/05_ley_37_1981.doc last visited 18 November 2009); for a good summary in English *see* Inter-American Commission on Human Rights (IACHR), *Report demobilization* (2004), at 53 et seq.; Laplante/Theidon (2006) 28 *MichJIntL* 49, at 59 et seq.; for a good summary of the complex roots and causes of the long lasting Colombian armed conflict *see* Saffon/Uprimny, in Bergsmo/Kalmanovitz (eds.) 2009, at 217, 218 et seq.; *see* also Saffon, in Bergsmo (ed.) 2009, 93, at 94 et seq.; Burbidge (2008) 8 *ICLR* 557, at 559 et seq.

[2]Art. 1 Law 975 defines GAOML as guerrilla or self-defense (paramilitary) groups ("grupo de guerrilla o de autodefensas"). Interestingly however, Gómez Pardo, an official from the Colombian Foreign Ministry, writes that the Law "was born from the necessity to have a juridical frame to make the peace process with the AUC", i.e. with the paramilitary "Autodefensas Unidas de Colombia", *see* Gómez Pardo (2009) *Revista Debate Interamericano* 123, at 142.

[3]*See* Faltas, in BICC (ed.) 2005, at 2.

K. Ambos, *The Colombian Peace Process and the Principle of Complementarity of the International Criminal Court*,
DOI 10.1007/978-3-642-11273-7_1, © Springer-Verlag Berlin Heidelberg 2010

combatants and a sustainable peace based on reconciliation and justice.[4] This very problem may also arise in the Colombian case.

Be that as it may, Law 975 provides, as the central concession to the irregular groups, for a conversion of the "normal" punishment imposed by the competent court into a so-called "alternative sentence" (*pena alternativa*) of minimum five and maximum eight years for the crimes committed during membership in the irregular group (Art. 3, 29[5]). Thus, while Law 975 does not offer a full exemption of punishment, its mitigation is considerable compared to the normal punishment for this kind of crimes under Colombian criminal law since that would amount to 50–60 years (Art. 31 (2), 37 (1) Penal Code).[6] Clearly, this considerable mitigation being offered by the Colombian authorities cannot be conceded without further ado on the part of the potential beneficiary but calls for a serious service in return by the latter: He must contribute to "truth, justice and reparation" (Art. 1), in particular by providing full information about the crimes committed by him and/or his group.[7] The Constitutional Court has reinforced this obligation.[8] Thus, in sum, Law 975 can be called a law of a conditionally reduced penalty.[9] We will come back to the exact requirements for receiving this reduced penalty.

As to its *subject matter*, Law 975 applies to the international core crimes, i.e. genocide, crimes against humanity and war crimes, except – a concession to U.S. national interests – if the irregular group or the individual beneficiary was (primarily) involved in drug trafficking (Art. 10 no. 5 and Art. 11 no. 6).[10] According to traditional Colombian practice international core crimes must not be subject to an

---

[4]*See* for a good discussion de Greiff, in Ambos/Large/Wierda (eds.) 2009, 321, at 322 et seq., 348 et seq.; with regard to Colombia *see* also Laplante/Theidon (2006) 28 *MichJIntL* 49, at 57 et seq.; Espinal et al., *Desmovilización, desarme, reinserción* (2007). For a practical guide *see* Douglas et al., *Gender and disarmament* (2004).

[5]Art. without reference refer to Law 975. For the full text in English *see* Part III, 3.

[6]The relevant provisions read as follows: Art. 37 (1) Penal Code: "La pena de prisión para los tipos penales tendrá una duración máxima de cincuenta (50) años, excepto en los casos de concurso"; Art. 31 (2) Penal Code: "En ningún caso, en los eventos de concurso, la pena privativa de la libertad podrá exceder de sesenta (60) años".

[7]*Cf.* Art. 3 Law 975: "contribución del beneficiario a la consecución de la paz nacional, la colaboración con la justicia, la reparación a las víctimas y su adecuada resocialización." (*see* for English translation Part III, 3).

[8]Constitutional Court of Colombia (Corte Constitutional, hereinafter: "Constitutional Court") [18 May 2006] Judgment C 370 of 2006, Judge Rapporteur (*Magistrado Ponente,* hereinafter "MP") Manuel José Cepeda Espinoza et al., section 6.2.2.1.7.26. requiring that the confession ("versión libre", article 17) must be "completa y veraz" (complete and truthful) and declaring unconstitutional (sect. 6.2.2.1.) the part of article 25 which allowed for the benefit of the "alternative sentence" despite the suspect's omission to confess all crimes. For a good discussion of the improvements of Law 975 by this judgment *see* Uprimny/Saffon, in Uprimny (ed.) 2006, at 201 et seq. (215 et seq.).

[9]*Cf.* Kalmanovitz, in Bergsmo/Kalmanovitz (eds.) 2009, 7, at 15 ("law of conditional reduced penalties"). *See* also *infra* n 68 in Chap. 2.

[10]According to Art. 10 no. 5 a condition of the collective demobilization is that "the group was not organized for the purposes [*no se haya organizado para*] of drug trafficking or illicit enrichment",

amnesty, pardon or any other exemption of punishment.[11] For this very reason, a complete exemption from punishment, albeit on the table in the negotiations leading to Law 975,[12] would have meant a radical departure from this previous practice and thus could not be seriously considered.

The situation is however considerably complicated by an earlier law, *Law 782 of 2002*,[13] which is complementary to Law 975 and allows for amnesties, pardons and other exemptions with regard to offences which traditionally have been qualified as "*political offences*" in Colombia, i.e., rebellion and sedition, and for related crimes.[14] Traditionally, the privilege implicit in the qualifier "political" was limited to *left-wing insurgents* since it was considered – admittedly quite idealistic – that these groups want to change the society for the better and therefore deserve a more lenient treatment than right-wing paramilitaries.[15] Indeed, the Supreme Court confirmed this view in July 2007 arguing that membership in a *paramilitary group* does not qualify for a "political offence" since these groups act for selfish

---

according to Art. 11 no. 6 the individual demobilised' activity must "not have had as its purpose [*como finalidad*] narcotics trafficking or illicit enrichment."

[11]The first conditional amnesty mentioned above (n 1) already excluded ordinary crimes such as kidnapping, extortion and killings *hors de combat* (*see* IACHR, *Report demobilization*, 2004, para. 54). The forerunner of Law 975, Law 782 (*infra* n 13), also excluded "atrocious acts of ferocity or barbarism, terrorism, kidnapping, genocide, murder committed outside combat o put the victim in a state of defenslessness" from its benefits (Art. 19 last para.: "actos atroces de ferocidad o barbarie, terrorismo, secuestro, genocidio, homicidio cometido fuera de combate o colocando a la víctima en estado de indefensión").

[12]For the first "impunity" proposal of the Uribe government *see* Uprimny/Saffon, in Uprimny (ed.) 2006, 201, at 203; Laplante/Theidon (2006) 28 *MichJIntL* 49, at 77; Kalmanovitz, in Bergsmo/ Kalmanovitz (eds.) 2009, at 9. *See* also the Draft Law presented by the MPs Jesús Ignacio García, Barlahán Henao, Clara Pinillos, Carlos Arturo Piedrahita and Zamir Silva, reprinted in Fundación Social, *Trámite de la ley de justicia y paz* (2006), at 114–15.

[13]Official source: Ley 782 de 2002 (diciembre 23), "por medio de la cual se prorroga la vigencia de la Ley 418 de 1997, prorrogada y modificada por la Ley 548 de 1999 y se modifican algunas de sus disposiciones." Diario oficial (Law Gazette), year CXXXVIII, N. 45043, 23 December 2002, p. 1.

[14]Art. 19 of Law 782 provides for the possibility of a pardon for political offences but does not define these offences. In any case, the concept has a constitutional underpinning and the Constitution itself allows for amnesty, pardon and other forms of exemption of prosecution and punishment (*see* Arts. 35, 150 (17), 179 (1), 201 (2), 232 and 299 of the Constitution). In practice, the concept has always been understood – despite the absence of a precise legal definition – as encompassing the offence of rebellion ("rebelión, sedición y asonada") and related conduct (*see* for a good account Fundación Social/Asesoría de Derechos Humanos, *Sobre la noción del delito político*, available at: http://74.125.77.132/search?q=cache:5LMSfCdFt3YJ:www.derechoshumanosypaz.org/MATERIAL_DDHH/ANALISIS_COYUNTURAL/ALTERNATIVIDAD_PENAL/OBSERVATORIOS_2005/DELITOPOLTICOABRIL10.DOC+delito+politico+ley+782+de+2002&cd=3&hl=de&ct=clnk&gl=de, last visited 7 October 2009). On the other hand, Law 782 excludes core crimes from the exemption, *see supra* n 11.

[15]*See* the fundamental work of Pérez, *Tratado de Derecho Penal, vol. III* (1978), at 111 et seq., in particular 135 et seq. referring to insurgent rebels.

motives and count with the support of important institutional actors.[16] This is, unsurprisingly, not the view of the current Colombian government of President Alvaro Uribe who personally made more than once clear that he does not see a difference between membership in left-wing or right-wing irregular armed groups on the basis of their political ideology but considers them all as equally criminal.[17]

Be that as it may, with the recently confirmed position of the Supreme Court it is impossible to apply Law 782 directly to paramilitary groups for the simple reason that these groups are not considered – in the sense of the Colombian concept of political offence – as political actors. Thus, their members can only be treated as ordinary criminals falling under the jurisdiction of the ordinary criminal justice system or, as recognized members of an irregular armed group,[18] under Law 975. While Law 782 is theoretically applicable to the offence of *simple* conspiracy ("*concierto para delinquir simple*") and some minor (related) offences (by way of the *renvoi* in Art. 69 of Law 975),[19] it is not applicable to simple *membership* ("*pertenencia*") in a paramilitary group since this is qualified by the Supreme Court as an *aggravated* form of conspiracy with a view to the paramilitaries' further or

[16]Supreme Court of Justice – Criminal Chamber (Corte Suprema de Justicia – Sala de Casación Penal, hereinafter: "Supreme Court") [11 July 2007] Rad. 26945, MP Yesid Ramirez Bastidas and Julio Enrique Socha Salamanca. *See* for an earlier discussion Ambos, *Justicia de transición* (2008), 195 et seq.; *see* also Burbidge (2008) 8 *ICLR* 557, at 564.

[17]*See* e.g. the statement of President Uribe on 18 Oct. 2007 ("Palabras del Presidente Uribe en el encuentro de la Jurisdicción Ordinaria", 18.10.2007, available at: http://web.presidencia.gov.co/sp/2007/octubre/18/15182007.html, last visited 18 November 2009): "Y he dicho, desde el punto de vista sociológico ¿qué diferencia hay entre el campesino que pertenece al grupo paramilitar, y el campesino que pertenece al grupo guerrillero? Y he insistido en una tesis: desde el punto de vista del padecimiento de la víctima, ¿qué diferencia hay entre el delito del uno y el delito del otro? Y desde el punto de vista rigurosamente jurídico -y permítanme asomar esta reiteración ante ustedes, lo hago con todo respeto- creo que violan por igual el ordenamiento jurídico, que es el Estado, quienes quieren suplantarlo, para establecer un gobierno guerrillero, o quienes lo desconocen, so pretexto de atacar a la guerrilla y de defender el orden socioeconómico. Los dos, finalmente, están por fuera y en contra de ese ordenamiento jurídico y del Estado. Yo no participo de la tesis de que los paramilitares están a favor del Estado. Su accionar viola el ordenamiento jurídico, lo desafía, que es finalmente el Estado". – On this difficult and polemical issue *see* also Gutiérrez, in Bergsmo/Kalmanovitz (eds.) 2009, 99, at 116 acknowledging on the one hand that "the moral identification of insurgents and counterinsurgents is a given of the Colombian public opinión" but on the other referring to the "type of conflict", i.e., the fact that the insurgents fought against the state while the paramilitaries fought to defend it which ultimately turns the peace process with them into a "bargain between *amigos*" (at 118).

[18]On the so called "postulation" in the administrative phase of the Justice and Peace procedure *see infra* Sect. 2.1.

[19]Art. 69 of Law 975 refers to Law 782 and declares it applicable for the mentioned simple conspiracy (Art. 340(1) Criminal Code, Law 599 of 2000, hereinafter "CC") as well as for the illegal use of uniforms and insignia, the instigation to commit crimes in the sense of Art. 348 CC and manufacturing, trafficking and wearing arms and munitions.

ulterior purpose to promote (their) illegal armed groups.[20] As a consequence, about 19,000 paramilitaries who invoked Law 782 after their demobilization and whose applications had not been granted before the Supreme Court's veto of July 2007[21] found themselves in a kind of judicial limbo, on the one hand unable to benefit from Law 782 and on the other unsure if they would be prosecuted for aggravated conspiracy by the ordinary criminal courts on the basis of their membership in a GAOML. Ultimately, a reform of the Code of Criminal Procedure ("CCP", Law 906 of 2004) was approved,[22] extending the prosecutorial discretion to suspend, interrupt or abstain from proceedings (opportunity principle, Art. 323 CCP) to demobilised members of irregular armed groups for simple membership in the group (Art. 324 no. 17 CCP).[23] The Prosecutor may request the application of the opportunity principle on an individual or collective basis and the beneficiary shall sign a sworn statement affirming that he did not commit any other offence than simple membership in a GAOML;[24] he will lose the benefit, i.e. the procedure may be reopened, if his statement later turns out to be wrong.[25] In addition, the application of the principle is explicitly ruled out with regard to the grave breaches of IHL, crimes against humanity, (other) war crimes and genocide.[26]

The situation is much simpler for the left-wing *insurgent groups*, in particular the FARC. In their case, Law 782 remains applicable for acts which do not constitute international core crimes in the sense of Law 975, i.e., in this case a

[20]This qualification (Supreme Court, n 16) is based on Art. 340(2) second alternative CP, i.e., (aggravated) conspiracy to promote armed groups (concierto "para organizer, promover, armar o financiar grupos armados al margen de la ley") which must be distinguished from the first alternative, i.e., (aggravated) conspiracy to commit grave crimes (concierto "para cometer delitos de genocidio, desaparición forzada de personas, tortura, desplazamiento forzado, homicidio, terrorismo, narcotráfico, secuestro extorsivo, extorsión").

[21]Supreme Court (n 16).

[22]Law 1312 of 2009 (9 July) Diario Oficial No. 47.405.

[23]According to Art. 324 no. 17 CCP, as introduced by Art. 2 of Law 1312 (n 22), the opportunity principle is applied (and the investigation/prosecution terminated, Art. 323 CCP) if the respective group member "haya manifestado con actos inequívocos su propósito de reintegrarse a la sociedad, siempre que no haya sido postulado por el Gobierno Nacional al procedimiento y beneficios establecidos en la LJP y no cursen en su contra investigaciones por delitos cometidos antes o después de su desmovilización con excepción de la pertenencia a la organización criminal, que para efectos de esta Ley incluye la utilización ilegal de uniformes e insignias y el porte ilegal de armas y municiones".

[24]Art. 324 no. 17 inc. 4 CCP requires the beneficiary to declare "no haber cometido un delito diferente a los establecidos en esta causal" and inc. 1 refers – as the offence covered – to "pertenencia a la organización criminal, que para efectos de esta ley incluye la utilización ilegal de uniformes e insignias y el porte ilegal de armas y municiones.", i.e., to the offences covered by Art. 69 of Law 975 (n 14 at the end).

[25]Art. 324 no. 17 inc. 4 CCP: "... so pena de perder el beneficio ...".

[26]Art. 324 no. 17 para. 3 CCP ("No se podrá aplicar el principio de oportunidad en investigaciones o acusaciones por hechos constitutivos de graves infracciones al Derecho Internacional Humanitario, delitos de lesa humanidad, crímenes de guerra o genocidio, ni cuando tratándose de conductas dolosas la víctima sea un menor de dieciocho (18) años").

parallel application of both legal regimes is possible. As a result, members of these groups could benefit from a full exemption as far as political (non-international) offences are concerned (Law 782) but would be treated like members of paramilitary groups as far as international crimes are concerned (Law 975); insofar, i.e. as to these international crimes, Law 975 complements Law 782.[27]

As to *pending investigations or trials* against members of irregular groups in general, Art. 20 of Law 975 provides for their "joinder" and the "accumulation of sentences" if the respective offences have been committed "during or on occasion of membership" in the respective group;[28] crimes committed before membership are excluded from Law 975, i.e., they must be dealt with exclusively by the ordinary criminal justice system. Thus, in case of conflict between the ordinary procedure and the Justice and Peace procedure with regard to the same crimes committed "during and on occasion of membership" one must distinguish as follows: The ordinary criminal proceedings are *temporarily suspended* when these same crimes are the object of a (successive or partial) imputation under Law 975; they are *definitely joined* ("*accumulated*") with the Law 975 proceedings if the charges are confirmed ("legalized") by the Higher Tribunal's Justice and Peace Chamber.[29] In the case of a prior sentence for crimes committed "during and on occasion of membership", this sentence shall be "accumulated" with the sentence to be imposed under Law 975 according to the normal rules of cumulative sentencing (*concours*) under the Criminal Code.[30] In any case, while the "accumulated" sentence can be

[27]Laplante/Theidon (2006) 28 *MichJIntL* 49, at 79.

[28]". . . por hechos delictivos cometidos durante y con ocasión de la pertenencia del desmovilizado a un grupo armado organizado al margen de la ley." *See* also Supreme Court [27 August 2007] Rad. 27873, MP Julio Enrique Socha Salamanca, section 2.1. ("Naturaleza jurídica y estructura del trámite previsto por la ley 975 de 2005"): "De adelantarse el trámite, las *investigaciones* cursadas por las conductas punibles realizadas por el postulado durante y con ocasión de su pertenencia al grupo armado ilegal, o por la organización delincuencial que puedan comprometer su responsabilidad deberán ser *acumuladas* a la investigación, así mismo, se *adicionarán* jurídicamente las *penas* impuestas en otros procesos por esa misma clase de delitos a la que se le llegue a imponer, sin que la pena alternativa pueda superar el término legal, de ser ella impuesta." (emphasis added).

[29]*See* Supreme Court [25 September 2007] Rad. 28250, MP María del Rosario González de Lemos, Consideraciones de la Corte.

[30]According to Art. 31 CP, in case of various offences, the gravest sentence will be increased but must not exceed 60 years. *See* for the applicability of these rules Art. 460 of Law 906 of 2004 (current CCP), Art. 470 of Law 600 of 2000 (former CCP). *See* also on the requirements of an "accumulation of sentences" Supreme Court [19 November 2002] Rad. 7026, MP Yesid Ramírez Bastidas, Sobre la acumulación de penas.: ". . . la acumulación jurídica de penas procede cuando se cumplan las siguientes exigencias: a) Que contra una misma persona se hayan proferido sentencias condenatorias en diferentes procesos y las mismas estén ejecutoriadas. b) Que las penas a acumular sean de igual naturaleza. c) Que los delitos no se hayan cometido con posterioridad al proferimiento de sentencia de primera o única instancia en cualquiera de los procesos. d) Que las penas no hayan sido impuestas por razón de delitos cometidos por la persona cuando se encontraba privada de la libertad. e) Que las penas no estén ejecutadas y no se encuentren suspendidas."

higher than the alternative sentence,[31] the finally executed sentence will never go beyond the range of 5–8 years fixed by the alternative sentence.[32]

As to the *temporal scope of application* Law 975 does not apply to crimes committed after its entry into force, i.e., 25 July 2005 (Art. 72).[33] The Supreme Court recently confirmed this by stating that the clear letter of the law does not allow for an extension of its application beyond its entry into force.[34] As a consequence, the government issued a draft law by which the scope of application should be extended to all crimes committed before the demobilization of the irregular group, i.e., the temporal reference should no longer be the entry into force of the law but rather the demobilization of the group.[35] This is problematic since it undermines the original rationale of the temporal application, i.e., to require the respective group to stick to the negotiated agreement and, in any case, abstain from committing further crimes after the entry into force of Law 975 *independent of its demobilisation*.[36] While it may be argued that many groups and commanders did not trust the government until the entry into force of the law and only then started their demobilization,[37] the demobilization must not be confused with the ongoing commission of crimes. In fact, the deadline for demobilization is set for 21 December 2010[38] but it would be quite awkward to link the temporal application

[31]The Constitutional Court (n 8), section 6.2.1.6.4 has declared the last part of para. 2 of art. 20 ("... but in no case may the alternative sentence be greater than that provided for in this law") unconstitutional; *see* also the following fn.

[32]Constitutional Court (n 8), section 6.2.1.6.4.: "... si el desmovilizado condenado con anterioridad, por hechos delictivos cometidos durante y con ocasión de su pertenencia al grupo armado organizado al margen de la ley, se acoge a la Ley 975 de 2005, y cumple los requisitos correspondientes, dicha condena previa se acumulará jurídicamente a la nueva condena que se llegare a imponer como resultado de su versión libre y de las investigaciones adelantadas por la Fiscalía. Después de efectuada dicha acumulación jurídica, el juez fijará la condena ordinaria (pena principal y accesorias), cuya ejecución se suspenderá y se concederá el beneficio de la pena alternativa." *See* for the first concrete application Tribunal Superior de Bogotá [19 March 2009], Sala de Justicia y Paz, MP Eduardo Castellanos Roso, Aprobada Acta No. 08, Rad. 110016002532006 80526, Wilson Salazar Carrascal ("El Loro"), para. 164–166.

[33]According to Executive Decree 4760 of 2005, Art. 26, this temporal limitation also applies to continuous or permanent offences, e.g., the forced disappearance of persons, i.e., Law 975 only applies to these offences if their execution commenced before its entry into force, the violation of the legal interest protected ceased to exist at the moment of demobilization and the beneficiary actively cooperates in order to ascertain the victims' rights.

[34]Supreme Court [24 February 2009] Rad. 30999, MP Gomez Quintero, para. 7.

[35]Available at: www.altocomisionadoparalapaz.gov.co/web/noticias/2009/marzo/documentos/PROYECTO% 20DE%20LEY-VIGENCIA.pdf (last visited 7 October 2009).

[36]*See* also Supreme Court (n 30) para. 5, 7.

[37]While only 12 paramilitary groups demobilized between November 2003 and June 2005, 22 groups demobilized within one year after the entry into force of Law 975 in July 2005, *see* Oficina del Alto Comisionado para la Paz, *Proceso de Paz* (without date). Two groups (the Cacique Pipinta block and the Autodefensas Campesinas del Casanare block) refrained from demobilizing.

[38]According to Law 1106 of 2006, *see* Supreme Court (n 34) Consideraciones de la Sala.

of the Law to that date, thereby de facto facilitating the continued commission of crimes.

While a lot has been written about the Colombian peace process in general and the Law 975 in particular, mostly in Spanish[39] and only rarely in English[40] or German,[41] and while most analysts agree that the procedure under Law 975 is the backbone of the current Colombian peace process, a systematic and chronological overview of this procedure in English is still missing.[42] This gap shall be filled by the following chapter.

[39]*See* for example: CCJ, *Ley de Justicia y Paz* (2007); Fundacíon Social, *Ley de alternatividad penal* (2007) 68; Fundacíon Social, *Observatorio* (2003); Gaitán, *Esclarecimiento de la verdad* (2006); Huber, *Ley de justicia y paz* (2007), at 463; Mora Sarasti (2005) *Revista Colombiana de Derecho Internacional* 119–157; Procuraduría General, *Desmovilización y reinserción* (2008), 2 Vol.; Zuluaga Lopéz (2007) *Divergencia*, at 10–13; from the perspective of the judiciary Gómez Quintero, in Almqvist/Espósito (eds.) 2009, at 157 et seq.

[40]Burbidge (2008) 8 *ICLR* 557, at 589 et seq.; Díaz, in Ambos/Large/Wierda (eds.) 2009, 469–501; Easterday (2009) 26 *Ariz. J. Int'l & Comp. L.* 49; Laplante/Theidon (2006) 28 *MichJIntL* 49; Saffon, in Bergsmo (ed.) 2009, 93 et seq.; Uprimny/Saffon, *Transitional Justice* (2005); Saffon/Uprimny, in Bergsmo/Kalmanovitz (eds.) 2009, 217 et seq.; Kalmanovitz, in Bergsmo/Kalmanovitz (eds.) 2009, 7 et seq.; (too short) Valiñas, in Stahn/van den Herik (eds.) 2010, at 278–79.

[41]Bastidas, in FDCL e.V. & Kolumbienkampagne Berlin (ed.) 2007, at 22–29; Beck, *Demobilisierungsprozess* (2008); Figari Layus/Kintzel (2008) 13(2) *MenschenRechtsMagazin*, 39 et seq.

[42]There are brief overviews though in some of the papers quoted in n 40, e.g. Kalmanovitz, in Bergsmo/Kalmanovitz (eds.) 2009, at 15.

Chapter 2
The Process Under Law 975

Following the Colombian Supreme Court one may distinguish between an administrative and a judicial phase under Law 975.[1] The latter can be divided, in line with traditional Colombian doctrine,[2] in a "pre-procedural" phase, directed by the General Prosecutor's Office (*Fiscalía General de la Nación*), and a "procedural" one, directed by the special Justice and Peace Chambers of the Higher Tribunals (*Salas de Justicia y Paz de los Tribunales Superiores de Distrito Judicial*).[3] The whole procedure has been summarized in a schematic way in Part III, document 4.[4]

[1]Supreme Court (n 28 in Chap. 1) section 2.1. ("Naturaleza jurídica y estructura del trámite previsto por la ley 975 de 2005"); *id.* [23 August 2007] Rad. 28040, MP María del Rosario González de Lemus ("Consideraciones de la Corte, cuestion previa, section 2"); *id.* [25 September of 2007] Rad. 28040, MP María del Rosario González de Lemus ("Consideraciones de la Corte, Estructura del proceso de justicia y paz").

[2]The distinction between a "pre-procedural" and a procedural phase *stricto sensu* is a particular feature of Colombian law and doctrine, *see* the quote in the following footnote. In contrast, in most other Latin American procedural systems it is understood – as in modern criminal procedure – that the criminal process starts with the *notitia criminis,* i.e. the knowledge of the prosecutorial authorities (police and/or prosecutor) that a crime has been committed.

[3]For an overview *see* Supreme Court (n 1) section 2.1. (Naturaleza jurídica y estructura del trámite previsto por la ley 975 de 2005): "Este procedimiento está integrado por *dos etapas*, una administrativa y otra judicial, esta última compuesta por los ciclos preprocesal y procesal (...). El *trámite judicial*, está integrado por dos etapas, una *pre-procesal* a cargo de la Fiscalía General de la Nación y otra *procesal* de competencia de las Salas de Justicia y Paz de los Tribunales de Distrito Judicial. La primera, está constituida por un ciclo preliminar y otro de investigación. El *preliminar* discurre desde el arribo de la lista de postulados a la fiscalía hasta la recepción de la versión libre, pasando por la formulación de la imputación, hasta la formulación de cargos. El de *investigación* se extiende desde la versión libre, pasando por la imputación y hasta la formulación de cargos ante el magistrado de control de garantías. La etapa de juzgamiento a partir de que quede en firme el control de legalidad de la formulación de cargos ante la Sala de Justicia y Paz del Tribunal de Distrito Judicial de conocimiento, hasta el fallo." (emphasis added).

[4]*Infra* p. 161.

K. Ambos, *The Colombian Peace Process and the Principle of Complementarity of the International Criminal Court*,
DOI 10.1007/978-3-642-11273-7_2, © Springer-Verlag Berlin Heidelberg 2010

2.1 Demobilization, disarmament and reintegration

The demobilization is the first step in the *administrative phase* and consists of the "individual or collective act of disarming and abandoning the irregular group".[5] While in the latter case the group as such demobilizes and, in a way, takes its members with it, in the case of the individual demobilization a single member of an irregular group decides to surrender (Art. 10, 11). In the case of a collective demobilization the group's commander or representative must prepare a list with the group's members to be received and checked by the Presidency's High Commissioner for Peace (*Alto Comisionado para la Paz*); in the case of the individual demobilization the responsibility lies with the "Committee for Laying Down Arms" (*Cómite Operativo de Dejación de Armas*, CODA) and the "Program of Humanitarian Attention for Demobilized" (*Programa de Atención Humanitaria al Desmovilizado*, PAHD) of the Ministry of Defense.[6] In fact, the rationale of this form of demobilization is to motivate members of an irregular group to leave it (to "desert") and thus ultimately to destabilize and break up the group. The subsequent facilitation of the demobilization of imprisoned group members pursues the same rationale.[7] In another turn, the government even went a step further and promised the suspension of arrest warrants for those members of GAOML which release kidnapped persons.[8] This last measure shows how quickly an instrument of transitional justice can be converted into an instrument of ordinary criminal justice policy, *in casu* to tackle the widespread kidnapping practice in Colombia.

Apart from not being involved in drug trafficking (Art. 10 no. 5, 11 no. 6), the respective member must fulfill certain *conditions*, i.e., disarm, give up any criminal activity, surrender any goods from criminal activity and cooperate with the investigating authorities (Art. 10, 11). Once the respective member of a group is recognized as such the final list of "postulated" members is sent to the General Prosecutor by the Ministry of the Interior and Justice.[9]

While the sending of the list normally implies the completion by the respective group members of the disarmament and demobilization phase, their *reintegration* into society will require more time and additional measures. The demobilized members shall receive certain economic assistance to facilitate their reintegration. Yet, the reintegration does not only depend on their conduct but also on the attitude

---

[5]*See* Art. 9 Law 975: "el acto individual o colectivo de dejar las armas y abandonar el grupo armado organizado al margen de la ley ..." (free translation by the author). *See* also Supreme Court (n 1).

[6]*See* Executive Decrees 128/2003, available at: http://www.alcaldiabogota.gov.co/sisjur/normas/Norma1.jsp?i=7143 (last visited 29 October 2009), and 423/2007, available at: http://www.alcaldiabogota.gov.co/sisjur/normas/Norma1.jsp?i=22993 (last visited 29 October 2009).

[7]Executive Decree 1059/2008 (with regard to imprisoned members of left-wing guerilla groups) and 4719/2008 (with regard to imprisoned members of demobilized groups which have not been listed).

[8]Executive Decree 614/2009.

[9]*See* Executive Decrees 3360/2003, 423/2008 and 1364/2008.

of the communities where they should be received. For this very reason it is highly important that these become actively involved in the process. In this regard the link between DDR and transitional justice, already mentioned above, becomes apparent.

Clearly, the recognition of a person as a member of an irregular group and his postulation is the *first filter* in the process of Law 975. Thus, the question arises whether this decision as well as the *exclusion* of a person from the list is of administrative-political (executive) or judicial nature. The answer depends on the moment this decision is taken: As long as we are in the administrative phase of selecting the persons who may benefit from Law 975, the process is completely controlled by the government; once the judicial process is initiated, i.e. with the passing of the list of the demobilized members to the Prosecutor General,[10] the Prosecutor and the competent Courts take over the process, i.e., it ceases to be purely executive and becomes strictly judicial.[11]

While a voluntary and explicit renunciation of the postulated person leads to the automatic and irrevocable *exclusion* from Law 975, the exclusion for other reasons, i.e. due to the non-fulfillment of the eligibility requirements, must be decided – at the request of the Prosecutor – by the Justice and Peace Chamber (*Sala de Justicia y Paz*), composed of three judges.[12] Concretely speaking, the person may be excluded due to his or her unjustified non attendance of the free version hearings, the commission of crimes after demobilization or the incomplete or false confession of crimes. As to the non attendance of a free version hearing, the decision if this was justified or not, entails a difficult normative judgment by the Chamber.[13] The commission of a crime must be demonstrated by a conviction to be issued by an ordinary criminal tribunal.[14] The same applies with regard to the completeness of the confession: the allegedly omitted crime or crimes must be real and proven accordingly.[15]

[10]The case law puts the reception of this list on an equal footing with the *notitia criminis* in the ordinary procedure, *see* Supreme Court [27 August de 2007] Rad. 27873, MP Julio Enrique Socha Salamanca, section 2.1. ("Naturaleza jurídica y estructura del trámite previsto por la ley 975 de 2005"); *id.* [23 August de 2007] Rad. 28040, MP María del Rosario González de Lemus; *id.* [25 September 2007] Rad. 28040, MP María del Rosario González de Lemus ("Consideraciones de la Corte, Estructura del proceso de justicia y paz").

[11]Supreme Court [10 April 2008] Rad. 29472, MP. Yesid Ramírez Bastidas, para. 11 ("... el trámite deja de ser político-gubernativo para convertirse en estrictamente judicial.").

[12]*See* for more details Ambos et al., *Justicia y Paz* (2010), para. 118 et seq.

[13]Supreme Court [11 March 2009] Rad. 31162, MP Julio Enrique Socha Salamanca, Consideraciones, 5.2.: " ... que la Sala de Justicia y Paz del Tribunal verifique si procesal y objetivamente se representa el comportamiento omisivo e injustificado del postulado ... "; in the same vein, Supreme Court [15 April 2009] Rad. 31181, MP Maria del Rosario González de Lemos (Consideraciones de la Corte, 1.).

[14]Supreme Court [10 April 2008] Rad. 29472, MP Yesid Ramírez Bastidas, Consideraciones de la Corte, 17.: "... solamente se podrá señalar a una persona como responsable de un delito cuando en contra de la misma se haya proferido una sentencia que alcanza ejecutoria formal y materia ... ".

[15]Constitutional Court (n 8 in Chap. 1) section 6.2.2.1.7.27: "El delito ocultado debe ser real, no fruto de la imaginación o la sospecha, lo cual exige que exista una sentencia judicial que otorgue certeza durante el periodo de libertad a prueba sobre la comisión del delito ocultado."

2.2 Preliminary investigation and "versión libre"

Once the administrative phase with the listing of the possible beneficiaries is completed, the Prosecutor's "Unit for Justice and Peace" (*Unidad Nacional de Fiscalía para Justicia y Paz,* UJP) starts its investigation in order to determine, in a reasonable time,[16] the facts and circumstances necessary to establish criminal responsibility and the reparation for the victims.[17] In this so-called "preliminary investigations before the free version" (*actuaciones previas a la versión libre*) phase it is also possible to hold preliminary hearings in order to, for example, secure important evidence or adopt measures regarding victims' protection.[18]

The competent Prosecutor then proceeds to receive the so-called "free version" (*versión libre*)[19] of the postulated GAOML member which is preceded by his confirmation (*ratificación*) to submit to the procedure of the Law 975. In fact, this confirmation is to be given at the beginning of the free version.[20] In the free version itself the respective members of the irregular group must give a complete and true account (*confesión completa y veraz*) regarding "time, manner and place" of all the criminal acts committed "on occasion of their membership" in an irregular group.[21] There is certain confusion on the (sequential) structure of the *versión.* According to the *Fiscalía's Informe de Gestión* there are three phases:[22] in the first phase the beneficiary must inform about his relationship with the respective irregular group,

[16]*See* Art. 1 Decree 2898 of 2006 and Art. 1 (2) Decree 4417 of 2006.

[17]*See* Art. 15, 16 Law 975 and Art. 4 Decree 4760 of 2005. From that moment on, the prosecutors of the Justice and Peace Unit initiate their investigations designing the so called "methodological program" ("*programa metodológico*", art. 207 CPP = Law 906 of 2004, *see* also *infra* n 36) and recollect all relevant information about the paramilitary group (origin, structure, assets, areas of influence, etc.), the postulated person (identity, criminal record, etc.) and the crimes reported or confessed in the so called *dossier*. This *programa metodológico* is updated in accordance with the dynamics of the proceedings (FGN-UJP, *Oficio 012896* (2009), at 2).

[18]*See* Legislative Act 03 of 2002 and Law 906 of 2004. *See* also Supreme Court [3 October 2008] Rad. 30442, MP Alfredo Gómez Quintero ("Consideraciones de la Sala, problema jurídico); for a different view *see id.* [8 September 2008] Rad. 30360, MP Yesid Ramírez Bastidas, para. 6.

[19]The concrete development of this act has been described in various norms: cfr. Art. 17 Law 975, Art. 5 Decree 4760 of 2005 and Art. 9 Decree 3391 of 2006; Decree 315 of 2007 of the Ministry of the Interior; Resolutions No. 3998 of 2006, 387 of 2007, 2296 of 2007 and 4773 of 2007 of the Prosecutor General. There are also various instructions from the Prosecutor General to the Special Unit of Justice and Peace, to be found in the following memoranda: 034/2006, 02/2007, 026/2007, 031/2007, 035/2007, 053/2007, 72/2007, 079/2007, 086/2007, 31/2008, 41/2008, 64/2008, 67/2008.

[20]*See* Art. 1 of Decree 4417 of 2006.

[21]Art. 17 (2) Law 975 ("tiempo, modo y lugar en que hayan participado en los hechos delictivos cometidos con ocasión de su pertenencia a estos grupos . . .") and Art. 9 Decree 3391 of 2006. *See* also Constitutional Court, *supra n* 8 in Chap. 1, section 6.2.2.1.5. ("Análisis conjunto de los artículos 17 parcial, 25 parcial y 29 parcial de la Ley 975 de 2005").

[22]FGN, *Informe de Gestión* (2008), at 59–60.

provide all available information about this group and indicate which crimes he will confess. In the second phase, he must inform in detail about these crimes. In the third phase, the beneficiary is interrogated about other crimes in which he was allegedly involved. However, the report uses indiscriminately the terms "phase" (*fase*) and "session" (*sesión*) and contradicts the *Fiscalía's* own regulation according to which the version consists of two sessions.[23] In fact, what is called the third phase in the *Informe de Gestión* constitutes, according to the Regulation, the final phase of the second session of the *versión*.[24] In any case, for all practical purposes, it is clear that the sessions consist of various sub-sessions or hearings which may take weeks or months.[25] In case of giving incomplete or even false information the suspect will lose the right to the benefit of the "pena alternativa".[26] Further, he must list the objects and goods which will be provided for the reparation of the victims.

While the hearing of the versión libre is not open to the general public the *victims* have a right to full participation, *inter alia*, by being present and participating in the hearings.[27] The victims may have a legal representative and – indirectly (via the competent prosecutor) – ask questions and request clarifications from the suspect.[28] They are also entitled to receive copies of documents produced in the hearing, present evidence and make any declaration they consider pertinent.[29] In practice, however, victims face a series of problems in the realization of their rights.[30]

---

[23]Resolución 3998 of 2006 of the Prosecutor General, Art. 4.

[24]*Ibid.*, Art. 4 para. 3 (b).

[25]*See* also the Prosecutor General's Resolución No. 3998, by which guidelines for the reception of the "free version" ("directrices para el procedemiento de recepción de version libre") are established and whose article 4 distinguishes between two sessions ("sesiones") of the version which in turn may be developed in various hearings ("jornadas"). In the same vein, Resolución No. 2296 of 3 July 2007, article 2 (2).

[26]Constitutional Court (n 8 in Chap. 1) section 6.2.1.4.2.

[27]In this sense Constitutional Court [24 January 2008] Judgment T-049 of 2008, MP Marco Gerardo Monroy Cabra; Council of the State (*Consejo del Estado*), Administrative Chamber (*Sala de lo Contencioso Administrativo*), Fourth Section, Counciller Rapporteur (*Consejera Ponente*) Ligia López Díaz [26 July 2007] Rad. 2500023240002007-00290-01; Supreme Court [8 June 2008] Rad. 27484, MP Alvaro Orlando Perez Pinzón. Generally on the rights and protection of victims *see* Art. 37, 38 Law 975 and Ambos et al., *Justicia y Paz* (2010), para. 258 et seq. On the specific measures mentioned in the text *see* Fiscalía (n 22) at 62 et seq. From the perspective of transitional justice and international law *see* Ambos, in Ambos/Large/Wierda (eds.) 2009, para. 10 et seq; for the practical difficulties of a victim-centered approach (with regard to the "Khmer Rouge Tribunal") *see* Mohan (2009) 9 *ICLR* 733 et seq.

[28]FGN-UJP, *Oficio 012896* (2009), at 22 et seq.

[29]Constitutional Court, *supra* n 8 in Chap. 1. According to the Supreme Court [23 May 2007] Rad. 27052, MP Álvaro Orlando Pérez Pinzón) the rights of the victims must be protected already during the preliminary investigation and the "Judges of Control of Individual Rights" ("Magistrados de Control de Garantías") may already intervene during the "versión libre".

[30]*Cf.* Ambos et al., *Justicia y Paz* (2010), para. 97, 290 and passim.

As most victims live in the countryside far away from the major Colombian cities where the hearings take place,[31] they are not able to attend them easily. In fact, most victims only have the possibility to follow the hearings if these are transmitted, via video link, to places and halls near their homes.[32] Apart from this logistical problem victims must be recognized as such and identified correspondingly in order to get access to the hearing or its transmission. Thus, pursuant to the definition of Law 975, the respective person must have suffered "direct harm", e.g. physical injury or emotional suffering, by criminal acts carried out by the irregular groups; or indirect 'harm by having lost a family member or permanent partner.[33] In addition, the legal representation of victims is highly deficient, their potential legal representatives of the *Defensoría del Pueblo* are understaffed, underpaid and sometimes lack the necessary commitment; some victims do not even know their assigned lawyers.[34] Finally, victims may not participate because they still live in fear and are intimidaded by the very paramilitaries (or their comrades) whose confessions they should observe.[35]

Once the versión libre is finished the prosecutor with the assistance of the investigators of the judicial police (*policía judicial*) evaluates the information received by the potential beneficiary and determines the further investigatory

---

[31]The hearings are taking place in particular in Bogotá, Medellín, Barranquilla, Cali, Cartagena, Cúcuta, Bucaramanga, Ibagué, Pereira, Montería and Santa Marta, *see* http://fgn.fiscalia.gov.co:8080/Fiscalia/contenido/controlador/controlador?opc=23&accion=10 (last visited 18 November 2009).

[32]In this sense the German GTZ-ProFis project has done a great job in setting up the infrastructure to make these transmissions possible. Thus, between July 2008 and September 2009, the (re) transmissions of 117 free version hearings were attended by 8,100 victims. The positive results of the project have also been recognized by the 13th Report of the Observer Mission (Missión de Apoyo al Proceso de Paz en Colombia, MAPP) of the Organization of American States (OAS): "Por su parte, la GTZ, a través del Programa de Apoyo a la Fiscalía 'PROFIS', continúa apoyando las transmisiones satelitales en la región Caribe, que han sido acompañadas por la MAPP/OEA. Se valora la puesta en marcha de un programa que haga efectiva la réplica en diferido de diligencias relevantes en lugares específicos. Dichas réplicas pueden servir para que tanto la Fiscalía como otras instituciones puedan llevar a cabo jornadas integrales de atención.", at 6, available at: www.mapp-oea.org/documentos/informes/XIII%20INFORME%20MAPP09.pdf (last visited 29 October 2009).

[33]*See* Art. 5 Law 975: "(...) daños directos tales como lesiones transitorias o permanentes que ocasionen algún tipo de discapacidad física, psíquica y/o sensorial (visual y/o auditiva), sufrimiento emocional, pérdida financiera o menoscabo de sus derechos fundamentales. Los daños deberán ser consecuencia de acciones que hayan transgredido la legislación penal, realizadas por grupos armados organizados al margen de la ley.
También se tendrá por víctima al cónyuge, compañero o compañera permanente, y familiar en primer grado de consanguinidad, primero civil de la víctima directa, cuando a esta se le hubiere dado muerte o estuviere desaparecida." In addition, Resolution 4773 of 2007 of the Prosecutor General, article 1 refers to a "real, concrete and specific harm" ("daño real, concreto y específico").

[34]*Cf.* Ambos et al., *Justicia y Paz* (2010), para. 77, 281. According to the Comité Interinstitucional de Justicia y Paz, *Matriz* (2009) 121 lawyers of the Defensoría represent 46.726 victims.

[35]*Cf.* Ambos et al., *Justicia y Paz* (2010), para. 287.

steps to be taken. The objective of this so called "*programa metodológico*"[36] is to verify the confession of the beneficiary and to possibly find out further relevant facts as to his responsibility and the criminal activities of his group. The program must be carried out in a reasonable time[37] and it is a prerequisite for the following phase of the "formulation of the imputation" (*formulación de imputación*).[38]

2.3 Formulation of "imputation" and charges

If the process of verification of the "free version" leads to the conclusion that no crime has been committed, the investigation will immediately be ceased and the proceedings terminated (Art. 27). It is, however, much more probable that the subsequent verification procedure confirms the confessed crimes or even indicates additional ones; in the latter case the beneficiary must be confronted with these additional (alleged) crimes to give him a chance to complement and/or modify his first confession. While this possibility of a (first) follow-up interrogation is provided for in a resolution of the Prosecutor General,[39] it is not regulated how many chances the beneficiary should have to get his confession right. Clearly, if the obligation of a "full and true confession" in return for the mitigation of punishment is to be taken seriously, a restrictive interpretation is called for; indeed, the repeated failure to confess serious offences may entail the exclusion from the procedure of Law 975.[40]

As soon as all possible crimes are established the "imputation" will be formulated (Art. 18: *formulación de imputación*). It constitutes a procedural act by which the demobilized person becomes formally a defendant (*imputado*)[41] and the statute of limitation (*prescripción*) is interrupted. It takes place in a hearing before the judge of control of individual rights (*magistrado de control de garantías*) who must examine its formal and material legality. As to the former, the judge must make sure that the defendant belonged to an irregular group, that he demobilized with a view to contribute to national reconciliation and that the imputed criminal acts have been

---

[36]This "program" is explicitly provided for in Art. 207 of the Colombian Code of Criminal Procedure (Law 906 of 2004, hereinafter CCP) and serves to organize and structure the investigation in a systematic way. In particular the following aspects must be taken into account: "la determinación de los objetivos en relación con la naturaleza de la hipótesis delictiva, los criterios para evaluar la información, la delimitación funcional de las tareas que se deban adelantar en vista de de los objetivos trazados, los procedimientos de control en el desarrollo de las labores y, los recursos de mejoramiento de los resultados obtenidos."

[37]Constitutional Court (n 8 in Chap. 1) section 6.2.3.1.6.5.

[38]*See* Supreme Court [28 May 2008] Rad. 29560, MP Augusto José Ibáñez Guzmán.

[39]Resolución No. 3998 (n 19) article 4 b) para. 3 provides for the interrogation of the beneficiary regarding acts that he has not confessed "spontaneously"; para. 5 allows for the repetition of the session as often as necessary to guarantee that the version be "complete and true".

[40]On the exclusion *see* already *supra* n 12 with main text.

[41]*Cf.* Art. 286 CCP.

committed during membership in the group.[42] As to the material legality the judge must examine the motives from which the commission of the imputed acts by the defendant may reasonably be inferred.[43]

A controversial issue is the prosecutorial practice to present partial, i.e. successive, instead of complete or full "imputations" at once (*imputaciones parciales*), i.e., to attribute ("impute") a part of the confessed crimes in order to advance and terminate the process more rapidly at least with this part of the crimes linked to a certain suspect, notwithstanding the continuation of the free version and the confession of further crimes in separate proceedings. The recourse to successive imputations has been a consequence of the tension between, on the one hand, the requirement of a complete truth by a full confession and a context related investigation and, on the other, the (public) expectation of a speedy procedure with quick results. While the Supreme Court originally authorized the use of successive imputations arguing that they neither violate procedural rules nor negatively affect the victims' rights to justice, truth and reparation, but rather contribute to the acceleration of the proceedings,[44] the fear of an inadequate or even excessive use of this technique which may hamper or impede a comprehensive investigation of the pattern of violence caused the Court to reconsider its initial position. In a recent appeals decision it stresses the exceptional character of successive imputations.[45] In the Court's new view, the prosecutorial indictment ("escrito de acusación") must not only refer to the individual crimes committed by the demobilized person, but

[42]Supreme Court [8 June 2007] Rad. 27848, MP Alvaro Orlando Pérez Pinzón.

[43]*Ibid.*

[44]Supreme Court [23 July 2008] Rad. 30120, MP Gómez Quintero, Consideraciones de la Sala, Problema Jurídico Planteado: "... la imputación parcial no lesiona los derechos de las víctimas (...) se avanza más rápidamente en el trámite y solución de fondo del asunto."; *id.* [9 February 2009] Rad. 30955, MP José Leonidas Bustos Martínez, Consideraciones, La imputación parcial: "El sentido de la imputación parcial está vinculado con imprimir al proceso agilidad y la seguirdad progresiva a la judicialización . . ."; *id.* [18 February 2009] Rad. 30775, MP Jorge Luis Quintero Milanés, Consideraciones de la Corte: ". . . la imputación parcial constituye un instrumento del trámite de la Ley 975, en la medida en que con él también se garantizarían los derechos de las víctimas, dándole a la actividad procesal la celeridad y eficacia requerida."; *id.* [16 April 2009] Rad. 31115, MP José Leonidas Bustos Martínez, Consideraciones: ". . . la imputación parcial no genera como consecuencia la imposibilidad jurídica de que el desmovilizado continúe su versión . . ."; *id.* [11 May 2009] Rad. 31290, MP Augusto J. Ibáñez Guzmán, Consideraciones: ". . . la figura de la imputación parcial se ajusta a los parámetros legales y se justifica (. . .) porque (i) imprime agilidad al proceso, (ii) otorga seguridad progresiva (. . .) y (iii) garantiza a las víctimas sus derechos a la verdad, justicia y reparación."; *id.* (n 38) Rad. 29560, Consideraciones, 3. Decisión Modulada: "... la sentencia que surja de esta formulación parcial de cargos, deberá suspender la aplicación de la pena alternativa, la cual queda supeditada a la prosperidad de la actuación paralela que se ordena por las imputaciones omitidas. (. . .) se condicionará la pena alternativa a la prosperidad de la actuación paralela que deberá promoverse (. . .) por las otras imputaciones . . .".

[45]*See* Supreme Court [31 July 2009] Rad. 31539, MP Augusto Ibánez Guzmán, Consideraciones, 1.3.: "... las imputaciones parciales no pueden convertirse en una herramienta usual por parte de la fiscalía, sino extraordinaria."

also to the harm collectively caused by the activities of the illegal armed group;[46] moreover, the collective right of society to historical truth, which encompasses, *inter alia*, the clarification of the motivation, structure, chains of command, criminal plans and activities of the illegal armed groups,[47] calls for an investigation which goes beyond the narration of individual cases reaching out to the historical and political context of the criminality, the patterns of violence and the responsible masterminds.[48] Therefore, all procedural acts and all facts to be imputed must be joined together at latest when the charges are being formulated such that thereafter a unified case and procedure exists.[49] In other words, a successive imputation may only stand alone until the formulation of charges, at that moment it should be turned into a complete formulation of charges.[50] While this new position of the Court is driven by an ideal model of the investigation and prosecution of macrocriminality, there are good reasons to doubt whether its strict requirements can be fulfilled in practice given the complexe structure and *modi operandi* of the paramilitary groups as the main actors of violence. Thus, it is to be welcomed that the Court clarified in a subsequent decision that successive imputations remain admissible in complex cases involving a multiplicity of charges.[50a] Similarly, the Higher Tribunal's Justice and Peace Chamber also accepted recently successive imputations against commanders of paramilitary groups who have confessed numerous crimes.[50b]

[46] Supreme Court (n 38) Rad. 29560: "... el escrito [de acusación] debe contener: (...) los hechos jurídicamente relevantes que se imputan directamente al desmoviliazado (. . .), los daños que la organización armada al margen de la ley colectivamente haya causado . . . ".

[47] Supreme Court (n 45) Rad. 31539, Consideraciones, 1.1.: "... la construcción de la verdad histórica debe tener como punto de partida el esclarecimiemnto de los motivos por los cuales se conformó la organización ilegal, las candenas de mando, el modelo delictivo del grupo, la estructura de poder, las órdenas impartidas, los planes criminales trazados, las acciones delictivas (. . .), las razones de la victimización y la constatación de los daños individual y colectivamente causados . . . ".

[48] *Ibid.*, Consideraciones, 1.1.: ". . . el funcionario judicial debe no solo analizar el caso concreto sino contextualizarlo dentro del conflicto, identificando los patrones de violencia y los demás actores seguramente de rango superior que también son responsables . . . ".

[49] *Ibid.*, Consideraciones, 1.4.: "... las actuaciones (. . .) deberán unirse antes de proferirse fallo de primera instancia y, específicamente en el momento de la formulación de cargos, para que este acto se realice como una unidad . . . ").

[50] *Ibid.*, Consideraciones, 1.6.: ". . . las actuaciones adelantadas en forma paralela y separada, deben fusionarse en el acto de formulación de cargos."

[50a] *See* Supreme Court [14 December 2009] Rad. 32575, MP María del Rosario González de Lemos, Consideraciones de la Sala.

[50b] *See* Tribunal Superior de Bogotá [7 December 2009], Sala de Justicia y Paz, MP Uldi Teresa Jiménez López, Aprobada Acta No. 13, Rad. 110016000253200680281, Jorge Iván Laverde Zapata ("El Iguano"), Competencia, 1.1.; Tribunal Superior de Bogotá [25 January 2010], Sala de Justicia y Paz, MP Uldi Teresa Jiménez López, Rad. 110016000253200680077, Uber Enrique Banquez Martínez and Edwar Cobos Téllez ("Juancho Dique" and "Diego Vecino"), Competencia, para. 4–11.

It remains to be seen if the judicial authorities will be able to develop precise requirements with regard to the admissibility of successive imputations.

Another hearing for the formulation and admission of the charges (*"formulación y aceptación de cargos"*, Art. 19), is to be held before the judge of control not later than 120 days after the verification of the acts imputed to the beneficiary.[51] In this hearing the acts (allegedly) committed by the beneficiary are, on the basis of an exact factual and substantive assessment,[52] finally determined and presented to him. He then shall decide, in a "free, voluntary and spontaneous" way, assisted by his lawyer, which ones he (finally) admits (Art. 19). The charges which he does not admit will be excluded from the justice and peace procedure and passed to the ordinary criminal justice system. The admitted charges will be sent by the respective judge to the Justice and Peace Chamber, composed of three judges.[53] This Chamber shall hold a hearing within max. 10 days in order to examine the formal and material legality of the admission of charges. Concretely speaking, it must examine whether the confession was complete and truthful, the criminal acts have been indicted adequately and the defendant fulfills the eligibility criteria set out in Art. 10, 11 of Law 975.[54]

It is important to note in this context that the Colombian jurisprudence has stressed on different occasions that the investigation of the acts confessed by the beneficiary and possibly further acts not (yet) confessed is a continuous task of the Prosecutor. It starts with the first verification after the free version and only finishes with the formulation of charges, i.e., runs through the whole judicial phase of the process from the start until the end.[55] In particular, it was held that the investigation

---

[51]Art. 18 Law 975 allows for 60 days to request this hearing but Art. 6 Decree 4760 of 2005 extends this period to max. 120 days; in addition, the Judge has a period of max. 10 days to hold the hearing after having received the request by the Prosecutor.

[52]For the importance of the substantive control of the legality *see* Supreme Court (n 38) and Constitutional Court (n 8 in Chap. 1) section 6.2.3.2.2.9.: "Para la Corte reviste particular importancia este control que se asigna al juez de conocimiento, el cual debe entenderse como control material de legalidad de la imputación penal que surge a partir de la aceptación de los cargos . . . ".

[53]Currently there exists only one such Chamber in Bogotá.

[54]*See* for the first decisión Tribunal Superior de Bogotá (n 32 in Chap. 1) para. 66 et seq. (examining the requirements of article 10).

[55]Supreme Court (n 38): "surge imperioso recordar que el artículo 15 de la ley ordena que *los servidores públicos-aplicadores de la ley-dispondrán lo necesario para que se asegure el esclarecimiento de la verdad* y determina que a la fiscalía le corresponde investigar las circunstancias de tiempo, modo y lugar en que se realizaron las conductas punibles; las condiciones de vida, sociales, familiares e individuales del imputado o acusado y su conducta anterior; los antecedentes judiciales y de policía, y los daños que individual y colectivamente haya causado de manera directa a las víctimas, tales como lesiones físicas o psicológicas, sufrimiento emocional, pérdida financiera o menoscabo sustancial de derechos fundamentales. Por manera que, de cara a ese deber ser de la ley, resulta *insuficiente limitar la instrucción* a los hechos confesados y a los daños individualmente causados por el procesado, tal como lo revela la actuación examinada." (emphasis added). *See* also Tribunal Superior (n 32 in Chap. 1), para. 77 demanding "a major activity" by the Prosecutor.

does not terminate with the formulation of the imputation but must be continued until the formulation of charges.[56]

2.4 Reparation

Immediately after having affirmed the legality of the charges the Chamber may, at the request of a party, set, within 5 days, a date for a reparation hearing (*incidente de reparación integral*, Art. 23).[57] In this hearing the victim and his legal representative may ask for reparation and present the respective evidence. The Chamber will dismiss the request if the petitioner cannot be considered a victim[58] or his harm was already compensated. If, in contrast, the request is well founded the Chamber will either try to find a conciliatory agreement between the defendant and the victim or decide contentiously the matter. As to the definition of the damage to be compensated the Chamber shall take into account the special vulnerability of the victim and his right to effective and real reparation.[59] The respective reparation decision forms part of the final sentence.

The primary responsibility to grant reparations lies on the members of the illegal armed groups.[60] Thus, in principle, the demobilized group and/or its members are obliged to indicate during the free version hearing all assets in order to make their

[56]*Ibid.*: "Y si bien la Corte no desconoce las dificultades que entrañan estas actuaciones, a esa complejidad operativa se adicionan malentendidos de orden procedimental, como el de concebir agotado el plan metodológico antes de la formulación de *imputación* y luego de este acto procesal conformarse con el transcurso del tiempo para llegar a la formulación de *cargos*, con lo que resulta inane la etapa probatoria concebida para la elaboración argumentativa de la atribución de daños colectivos y el ejercicio de la vocación probatoria de las víctimas con miras a la formulación de cargos adicionales." (emphasis added).

[57]*See* for more detail Ambos et al., *Justicia y Paz* (2010), para. 215 et seq.

[58]For the definition *see* already n 33 and main text.

[59]*Cf.* Huber, *Ley de justicia y paz* (2007), at 280.

[60]*See* Art. 37 (3) of Law 975: ". . . las víctimas tendrán derecho: a una pronto e integral reparación de los daños sufridos, a cargo del autor o partícipe del delito."; Art 42 (1): "Deber general de reparar. Los miembros de los grupos armadas que resulten beneficiados con las disposiciones previstas en esta ley tienen el deber de reparar a las víctimas de aquellas conductas punibles por las que fueren condenados mediante sentencia judicial." *See* also Constitutional Court (n 8 in Chap. 1) section 6.2.4.4.11.: ". . . los primeros obligados a reparar son los perpetradores de los delitos, en subsidio y en virtud del principio de solidaridad, el grupo específico al que pertenezcan los perpetradores. Antes de acudir a recursos del Estado para la reparación de las víctimas, debe exigirse a los perpetradores de los delitos, o al bloque o frente al que pertenecieron, que respondan con su propio patrimonio por los daños ocasionados a las víctimas de los delitos."; also section 6.2.4.4.13.: ". . . todos y cada uno de los miembros del grupo armado organizado al margen de la ley, responden con su propio patrimonio para indemnizar a cada una de las víctimas de los actos violatorios de la ley penal por los que fueren condenados; y también responderán solidariamente por los daños ocasionados a las victimas por otros miembros del grupo armado específico al cual pertenecieron." *See* finally also Art. 15 Decree 3391 of 2006 (De la responsabilidad de reparar a las víctimas).

confiscation possible and to secure the payment of reparations in the case of a conviction; they are obliged to hand over all illegally obtained assets.[61] In contrast, the State's role is subsidiary since it only may offer reparation if the assets of the demobilized members are insufficient to cover the reparation as determined by the Higher Tribunal's Special Chamber of Justice and Peace or if the perpetrators have not been identified through the Law 975 proceedings.[62]

On the other hand, the victim's renunciation of its right to reparation or the failure to exercise this right does not affect the beneficiary's right to obtain an alternative sentence (Art. 23 para. 2). Similarly, the impossibility of compensation, as such, cannot be a reason to exclude the demobilized person from the justice and peace procedure; rather, the lack of monetary reparation may be compensated by a greater collaboration with the prosecution or alternative means of reparation, e.g., asking publicly for forgiveness.[63] Yet, the flexibility of the reparation regime is problematic in that it gives the perpetrator the possibility to put pressure on the victim not to exercise his right and to get away with it without further consequences.[64] Indeed, a victim who renounces his right under such circumstances would rarely dare to come forward and inform the authorities of the pressure exercised by the defendant.[65] This flexibility also shows that, ultimately, the

---

[61]*See* Art. 10 (2) 11 (5) of Law 975, *see* also Constitutional Court (n 8 in Chap. 1) section 6.2.4.1.18.: "... los bienes de procedencia ilícita no le pertenecen [a la persona] y, por lo tanto, la entrega no supone un traslado de propiedad sino una devolución a su verdadero propietario – mediante la restitución del bien – o al Estado. Sin embargo, su patrimonio lícito le pertenecerá hasta tanto no exista una condena judicial que le ordene la entrega."

[62]Constitutional Court (n 8 in Chap. 1) section 6.2.4.4.11.: "... el Estado ingresa en esta secuencia sólo en un papel residual para dar una cobertura a los derechos de las víctimas, en especial a aquellas que no cuentan con una decisión judicial que fije el monto de la indemnización al que tienen derecho (inciso segundo del artículo 42 de la Ley 975 de 2005) y ante la eventualidad de que los recursos de los perpetradores sean insuficientes." *See* also Art. 42 (2) of Law 975 and its interpretation by the Supreme Court of Justice [11 December 2007] Rad. 28769, MP María del Rosario González de Lemos; *id.* [21 April 2008] Rad. 29240 MP Javier Zapata Ortíz; *id.* [23 May 2008] Rad. 29642, MP Yesid Ramírez Bastidas; *id.* [12 March 2009] Rad. 31320, MP Sigifredo Espinoza Pérez.

[63]*Cf.* Tribunal Superior (n 32 in Chap. 1) para. 83.

[64]An inquiry into the assets received by *Acción Social* as the trustee of the Victims Reparations Fund reveals that very few postulated persons have effectively handed over assets, *see* http://www.accionsocial.gov.co/contenido/contenido.aspx?catID=455&conID=1667 (last visited 6 November 2009). In several cases, Acción Social has rejected the administration of assets offered by demobilized persons arguing that the assets are not free of mortgages or debts and therefore useless for the reparation of victims. The Victims Reparations Fund currently has a value of 28.174.806.936 Colombian Pesos (aprox. 9.400.000 Euros) and consists of movable property (valued at $ 195.144.000 Colombian Pesos; aprox. 65.000 Euros), immovable property (valued at $ 18.632.018.092 Colombian Pesos; aprox. 6.210.000 Euros), and money (valued at $ 9.347.635.851 Colombian Pesos; aprox. 3.120.000 Euros); figures taken from Comité Interinstitucional de Justicia y Paz Matriz (2009) and http://www.cnrr.org.co/bcnrr/numero10/CNRR_boletin10justiciaypaz.pdf (last visited 10 November 2009).

[65]Crit. also Kalmanovitz, in Bergsmo/Kalmanovitz (eds.) 2009, 17, at 18–19.

disarmament and demobilization of the paramilitaries prevails over victims' rights and leaves them in the role of spoilers of the peace process.[66]

2.5 Determination of the sentence

Once the Chamber confirmed the legality of the charges, a sentencing hearing shall be held within 10 days. The sentencing decision contains the main and accessory (ordinary) sentence (*pena principal y accesoria*) and the "alternative" sentence;[67] it may also contain certain rules of conduct, reparation obligations and the confiscation of goods to make the reparation effective. It is important to note that the alternative sentence suspends the whole ordinary sentence, i.e., not only its main part consisting of the term of imprisonment but also the accessory part which may for example impose an inhibition of exercise of public rights and functions.[68]

Thus, in the first sentence in the case of Wilson Salazar Carrascal, aka "El Loro" ("the parrot"), the defendant was sentenced to 460 months of imprisonment (main sentence) and 20 years of inhibition of exercise of public rights and functions (accessory sentence). This whole ordinary sentence was suspended and replaced by an alternative sentence of 70 months.[69] Further, the defendant had to commit himself in writing to contribute to his resocialization and promote activities to further "the demobilization of the irregular group".[70] While the latter requirement is explicitly mentioned in Art. 29 (3),[71] it creates some confusion since the defendant already contributed to his demobilization at the beginning of the process (when he decides to demobilize), i.e., his group should already be demobilized when he receives the final (alternative) sentence. Individual and collective demobilization is an "access" requirement, i.e. a prerequisite to be included in the regime of Law 975 in the first place (Art. 10 (1) and 11 (1)). Such "access" requirements must be distinguished from "keeping" requirements,[72] i.e., conditions to be fulfilled to

---

[66]*See* also Gutiérrez, in Bergsmo/Kalmanovitz (eds.) 2009, 99, at 119; similarly Saffon/Uprimny, in Bergsmo/Kalmanovitz (eds.) 2009, 217, at 232.

[67]Art. 29 Law 975 and Art. 8 Decree 4760 of 2005. About the main features of the "pena alternativa" *see* also Constitutional Court (n 8 in Chap. 1) section 6.2.1.4.2.

[68]According to Art. 10 of Decree 3391 of 2006 the "ordinary sentence", consisting of the main and accessory sentence, will be suspended by the "alternative sentence" (in the same vein Constitutional Court (n 8 in Chap. 1) section 6.2.1.4.2.). The alternative sentence may therefore be interpreted as a "penal surrogate" ("subrogado penal"), *see* Uprimny/Saffon, in Uprimny (ed.) 2006, 201, at 211. The main sentence, in turn, encompasses the inhibition of the exercise of political rights (article 35 CC in connection with Art. 43 No. 1 CC).

[69]Tribunal Superior (n 32 in Chap. 1) para. 153, 159.

[70]Tribunal Superior (n 32 in Chap. 1) para. 160: "desmovilización del grupo armado al margen de la ley".

[71]"... promover actividades orientadas a la desmovilización del grupo armado al margen de la ley ..."

[72]The distinction between "access" and "keeping" requirements stems from Kalmanovitz, in Bergsmo/Kalmanovitz (eds.) 2009, 17, at 16.

maintain the status of a demobilized beneficiary, which are contained in Art. 29 (3).[73] Indeed, it does not make sense to demand from a demobilized member that he continues to contribute to the demobilization of the group which should already have been demobilized when he is sentenced. Contrary to the Chamber's suggestion such an effect "pro future" does not follow from Art. 8 of Decree 4760 of 2005 since this provision presupposes that the eligibility criteria, including the contribution to the group's demobilization, have already been fulfilled.

Once the alternative sentence has been served (in an ordinary penitentiary!)[74] the convicted beneficiary will be on parole for a period of half of the alternative sentence. If he does not comply with the conditions imposed, the parole must be revoked and the convict must serve the ordinary sentence imposed. Ultimately, it is the Justice and Peace Chamber which grants and revokes the benefits of Law 975, in particular excludes a demobilized from the legal regime of Law 975, e.g. if he commits crimes after his demobilization (Art. 25).[75]

---

[73]It reads in the relevant part: "Para tener derecho a la pena alternativa . . .".

[74]The Constitutional Court (n 8 in Chap. 1) section 6.2.3.3. correctly declared unconstitutional article 31 which reduced the alternative sentence by the time (max 18 months) the members of irregular groups stayed in the so called "concentration zone" (*zona de concentración, zona de ubicación*), i.e., an area provided by the government for their retreat without any State control. Yet, the Government tried to reintroduce the benefit of art. 31 (which was part of the informal agreements with the AUC during the peace negotiations) through the backdoor by invoking the prohibition of retroactive application of the Constitutional Court´s ruling (*see* Art. 20 of Decree 3391 of 2006). In the Salazar Carrascal judgment the Higher Tribunal's Chamber for Justice and Peace did not decide on the issue, *see* Tribunal Superior de Bogotá (n 32 in Chap. 1), para. 277 ("Como quiera que este tema toca esencialmente con la ejecución de la pena, que de conformidad con el artículo 32 de la ley 975 de 2005, corresponderá a esta Sala vigilar, la solicitud será estudiada en su oportunidad previo el aporte de los requisitos para ello."). *See* on this issue also Uprimny/Saffon, in Uprimny (ed.) 2006, 201, at 213–14.

[75]On the exclusion of demobilized members from the regime of Law 975 *see* Supreme Court (n 10) Rad. 27873; *id.* [26 October 2007] Rad. 28492, MP Yesid Ramírez Bastidas; *id.* (n 11) Rad. 29472. *See* also n 12 with main text.

Chapter 3
Intermediate Conclusions

A thorough analysis of Law 975 and its implementation reveals a number of difficulties which hamper the effectiveness of the transitional justice process.

(i) The application of Law 975 is complicated by a highly sophisticated and sometimes contradictory *normative and jurisprudential framework*. Thus, Law 975 is, on the one hand, governed by a series of executive decrees and administrative regulations and, on the other, by a highly sophisticated case law trying to set standards and clarify the procedural and substantive arising from a sometimes not sufficiently precise Law 975. A good example of the confusion produced by Law 975 is its lack of clarity with regard to other legal regimes, on the one hand, to Law 782 already discussed above[1] and, on the other, to the two Procedural Codes applicable to the Justice and Peace Process to be discussed in the next point.

(ii) There exists a *tension between the special procedure under Law 975 and the ordinary criminal justice system*. First of all, Art. 62 provides that the CCP, i.e., the rules for ordinary criminal proceedings, shall complement Law 975 "[F]or all matters not provided for in this law". Yet, it does not determine which of the two procedural laws applicable at the time of commission of the crimes (Law 600 of 2000 or Law 906 of 2004) shall be applicable for the Law 975 proceedings. The Supreme Court of Justice has pursued a flexible approach indicating that the criminal proceedings under Law 975 must be interpreted in the context of a *transitional and restorative justice* process[2] which seeks to

---

[1] *See* n 13 in Chap. 1 et seq. and main text.

[2] Supreme Court [31 March 2009] Rad. 31391, MP Alfredo Gómez Quintero, Consideraciones: ". . . Evidentemente la Ley de Justicia y paz no regula un proceso de partes (. . .), sino un proceso especial, particular y transicional . . ."; *id.* [25 Septiembre de 2007] Rad. 28250, MP María del Rosario González de Lemos, Consideraciones de la Corte, Aspectos generales: ". . . a efectos de interpretar los diversos postulados de la Ley 975 de 2005, es preciso considerar su naturaleza especial, inspirada en un modelo de *Justicia Restaurativa* . . ." (emphasis added).

K. Ambos, *The Colombian Peace Process and the Principle of Complementarity of the International Criminal Court*,
DOI 10.1007/978-3-642-11273-7_3, © Springer-Verlag Berlin Heidelberg 2010

grant reparation to the victims and contribute to reconciliation and peace.[3] For the Court, Law 975 incorporates elements of the former inquisitorial (Law 600 of 2000)[4] and the new (Law 906 of 2004) criminal procedure, sometimes characterized as "accusatory"[5] or "adversarial".[6] Therefore, the recourse to Law 600 or Law 906 must be decided on a case by case basis taking into account that, on the one hand, most of the crimes subject to Law 975 were committed during the validity of the old Code (Law 600), i.e. before the gradual entry into force of the new Code (Law 906) since 1 January 2005,[7] and, on the other, that Law 975 shows certain parallels with the new Code as to procedural principles,[8] structure,[9] institutions[10] and the victims' role during

[3]Supreme Court (n 2) Rad. 31391, Consideraciones: ". . . con ella [la ley 975 de 2005] se busca la solución pacífica al conflicto a través del relativo perdón, la reconciliación y la reparación del daño, involucrando a la víctima, al victimario y a la sociedad."

[4]*See* Supreme Court [12 May 2009] Rad. 31159, MP Augusto J. Ibáñez Guzmán, Consideraciones, 7.3.: ". . . el Magistrado de control de garantías tiene vocación probatoria y (. . .) su rol es diferente al del Juez de garantías de la Ley 906 de 2004, en la medida que también le compete la construcción de la verdad . . ."

[5]*See* Supreme Court [27 August 2008] Rad. 27873, MP Julio Enrique Socha Salamanca, Consideraciones de la Sala, 2.1. Naturaleza jurídica y estructura del trámite previsto por la ley 975 de 2005: ". . . la ley 975 de 2005 y sus decretos reglametarios diseñaron un proceso armónico con los principios del sistema penal acusatorio. . .".

[6]*See* Supreme Court [31 March 2009] Rad. 31491, MP Alfredo Gómez Quintero, Consideraciones: ". . . Ley 906 de 2004 regula un procedimiento dispositivo regido por el principio adversarial. . ."; *id.* [2 April 2009] Rad. 31492, MP María del Rosario González de Lemos, Consideraciones de la Sala: ". . . el modelo al cual se adscribe la ley 906 de 2004 tiene por eje el principio adversarial. . .". – The use of the term "adversarial" in this context is misleading though, since the new Procedural Code does not provide for a common law like party procedure but leaves the fundamental responsibility for investigation, prosecution and trial in the hands of strong State institutions, especially the Fiscalía General de la Nación. In this sense, it may rather be compared to the reformed inquisitorial ("accusatorial") procedure of French and German systems (for a historical account *see* Ambos (2008) *JURA* 30, at 586 et seq.; for a Spanish version of this paper *see* bibliography in Part III, 1).

[7]Supreme Court [26 October 2007] Rad. 28492, MP Yesid Ramírez Bastidas, Consideraciones de la Corte, 7.: "si se trata de un asunto ocurrido en época anterior al 1° de enero de 2005, la regla general para efectos de la remisón normativa será la de acudir a la Ley 600 de 2000, salvo que se trate de instituciones que solamente pueden tener identidad con las sagradas en la Ley 906 de 2004, caso en el cual la integración se debe hacer con el estatuto de estirpe acusatoria."

[8]Supreme Court (n 5) Rad. 27873. Characteristic principles of the new criminal procedure are the orality of the procedure (*principio de oralidad*, Art. 12 of Law 975 and Art. 9 of Law 906) and a speedy process (*principio de celeridad*, Art. 13 of Law 975), *see id.* [23 May 2007] Rad. 27052, MP Álvaro Orlando Pérez Pinzon, Consideraciones.

[9]The criminal procedure of Law 975 – like under Law 906 of 2004 – provides for the possibility of a preliminary (Art. 13 of Law 975) and an imputation hearing (Art 18 of Law 975) before a Judge of Control (similar to a Pre-Trial Chamber).

[10]Supreme Court (n 7), Consideraciones de la Corte, 5.: ". . . inicialmente la remisión se debe hacer al estatuto procesal de 2000, pero por (. . .) la similitud de algunas instituciones de la nueva codificación procesal de 2004 con las consagradas en la ley de transición, también resulta imperativo examinar las nuevas instituciones."

the proceedings.[11] Unfortunately, this position of the Court did not contribute much to overcome the uncertainty as to recourse to Laws 600 or 906 as far as the correct filling of legal gaps and the solution of procedural disputes is concerned.

Secondly, the application of the *opportunity principle*, introduced by the CCP of 2004, to the so called "foot soldiers" of the irregular groups creates problems with regard to the substantive concept of "aggravated conspiracy".[12] While the Supreme Court requires prosecutors to impute the crime of aggravated conspiracy as a so-called "basic offence" (*delito base*),[13] Law 1312 extended the application of the opportunity principle to this very offence for the prosecution of the footsoldiers under the ordinary criminal justice system. In any case, given the exclusion of pure members of paramilitary groups from the benefits of Law 782 by the Colombian Supreme Court,[14] there was no other remedy than to take recourse to the opportunity principle to resolve the legal impasse as to these persons. Also, from the perspective of international criminal law, the mere membership in an armed group does not imply criminal responsibility for international crimes, nor does it lead to an international duty of States to prosecute and punish such conduct.[15] Indeed, the offence of conspiracy to commit war crimes or crimes against humanity has neither been incorporated in the Statutes of the ICTY or ICTR nor in the Rome Statute of the ICC (the later only foresees a form of collective participation in subpara. (d) of Art. 25 (3)).[16] On the other hand, conspiracy and membership in an illegal armed group must not be confused with the concept of "joint criminal enterprise" for this form of participation presupposes the actual commission of a crime or crimes, not just the discussion or plan to commit crimes. However, despite all these good reasons to solve this problem procedurally, it remains to be seen if the actual application of the opportunity principle in these cases does not create additional or different problems which may turn this "solution" only in an apparent one.

Third, the practice of prosecutors belonging to the ordinary criminal justice branch (e.g. the units of human rights or drug trafficking of the *Fiscalía*) to *use* the "*informations*" coming out of the confessions of the demobilized during

[11]Cfr. Art. 11 of Law 906 of 2004 and Art 37 of Law 975 of 2005 regarding victims' participation.

[12]*See* n 19 in Chap. 1 et seq. and main text (especially n 20 in Chap. 1 on the distinction between the two forms of aggravated conspiracy).

[13]Supreme Court (n 38 in Chap. 2) Rad. 29560; *id.* (n 45 in Chap. 2) Rad. 31539, Consideraciones, 1.5.:". . . ante la ausencia de pronunciamiento respecto del delito base en la Ley de Justicia y Paz -concierto para delinquir- no es posible aplicar la pena alternativa y, obviamente, es utópico proferir una sentencia que no evidencie el nexo de causalidad entre los hechos imputados (. . .) y su ejecución y consumación al interior de la organización armada ilegal."

[14]Supreme Court (n 16 in Chap. 1).

[15]*See* Olásolo, '*Criminal responsibility*' (2009), at 28.

[16]*Cf.* Ambos, in Triffterer (ed.), 2008, Art. 25 mn. 24 et seq.

the free version in ordinary criminal proceedings against *these same* persons[17] is highly questionable from the perspective of legal certainty and fairness. As to the former, the ordinary criminal procedure should be suspended by the special procedure of justice and peace as long as this procedure goes on and the respective persons are not excluded.[18] As to the fairness it is quite clear that the persons under the Justice and Peace procedure have only renounced their right of non self-incrimination (*nemo tenetur se ipsum accusare)* on the condition that their confessions would only be used in this same procedure. These persons would most probably not have confessed under the ordinary criminal procedure (if they were not promised a considerable mitigation of punishment under the guilty plea like *sentencia anticipada* procedure); in fact, they would not have surrendered under other conditions than the ones promised under Law 975 in the first place and they could certainly never have been arrested under the old system.

(ii) The *administrative phase* (*supra* Sect. 2.1.) is decisive for the determination of the personal jurisdiction of Law 975 and the subsequent judicial process. The government selects those persons or members of irregular groups which it considers eligible for the justice and peace process. However, this phase has been fraud with irregularities as to the selection of the right persons and a lack of independent (judicial) control. Thus, it is of common knowledge that pure drug traffickers who are not eligible under Law 975 in the first place[19] have "bought" complete paramilitary blocks or fronts[20] to surrender as paramilitary fighters and thereby benefit from the alternative sentence.[21] Also, the demobilisation process did not succeed in dismantling the paramilitary structures often lacking efficient mechanisms of reintegration of the demobilized and failing to cut off their links with the illegal economic structures which finance their activities. We have to come back to these problems when evaluating the unwillingness standard of Art. 17 ICC Statute.[22]

(iv) The importance of a proper *participation of the victims* in the justice and peace process cannot be overestimated. Indeed, it is one of its core elements which decides about the success or failure of the process. Although the existing legal

[17]*See* for example, the case of Ever Veloza García, aka HH, Press Release of the Office of the Prosecutor General, 'Condenado alias HH por crimen de concejal', available at: http://www.fiscalia.gov.co/PAG/DIVULGA/noticias2009/secantioquia/SaAliasHHJul21.htm (last visited 8 October 2009). On the use of these informations with regard to investigations of third parties *see infra* n 252 in Chap. 5 with main text.

[18]*See* on joinder and accumulation already *supra* n 28–29 in Chap. 1 with main text.

[19]*See* on Art. 10 no. 5 and Art. 11 no. 6 Law 975 already *supra* n 10 in Chap. 1.

[20]The so called "United Self-Defence Forces of Colombia" (*Autodefensas Unidad de Colombia*, AUC) was the umbrella organization of 34 paramilitary groups called "blocks" (*bloques*); every block consists of several "fronts" (*frentes*).

[21]This is especially the case of aka "Gordo Lindo" (of the Pacifico Block) and aka "El Tuso" (of the Héroes de Granada Block).

[22]*See infra* n 247 in Chap. 5 et seq.

obligations are fully recognized by Colombia,[23] the practice does not live up to these obligations. In fact, victims' participation is limited due to mainly practical difficulties concerning access to the hearings, legal representation and personal security of the victims.[24] The national institutions mainly responsible for victims' assistance (*Acción Social*, *Defensoría del Pueblo*, Procuraduría, Comisión Nacional de Reparación y Reconciliación)[25] do not comply fully with their obligations, especially *Acción Social* is fiercely criticized by the victims themselves.[26] As a consequence the UJP is often approached by the victims and asked for assistance thereby assuming functions which do not correspond to a prosecutorial body.

(v) The lack of adequate victims' participation also affects the *truth seeking function* of the Justice and Peace procedure (*see* e.g. Art. 1, 4 Law 975). The Colombian jurisprudence does not only require the establishment of the *individual truth*, i.e., the clarification of the individual defendant's acts and role in the crimes, but also and in particular the *collective side* of it, i.e., the organizational and structural context of the criminality.[27] Yet, this truth seeking process is predicated on the cooperation of the demobilized. In fact, the prosecutors and their investigators depend almost exclusively on the confessions of the demobilized, they may even give the investigation a certain direction and they certainly determine the traces to be pursued by the investigators in the verification procedure following the confessions. Only the victims are able to provide additional information which may confirm or

[23] *See supra* n 27 in Chap. 2 with further references.

[24] *See supra* n 30 in Chap. 2 et seq. and main text.

[25] *Acción Social*, the Presidential Agency for Social Policy, operates as the trustee of the Victims Reparations Fund (*Fondo de Reparación*) and manages the implementation of the administrative program for individual reparations established by Decree No. 1290 of 2008. The *Defensoría del Pueblo* (Office of the Human Rights Ombudsman, *see* Art. 282 of the Colombian Constitution) has, *inter alia*, the duty to offer free legal assistance and representation for victims under the Law 975 proceedings. The *Procuraduría General de la Nación* whose main task is to defend the public interests and supervise the conduct of public officials (*see* Art. 277 of the Colombian Constitution) participates in the criminal proceedings in order to guarantee the fundamental rights and freedoms of the intervening persons. The *Comisión Nacional de Reparación y Reconciliación* (CNRR, National Commission for Reparation and Reconciliation) was created by Art. 50 of Law 975; its main functions are set out in Art. 51 of Law 975. For a detailed analysis of all these institutions *see* Ambos et al., *Justicia y Paz* (2010), para. 73 et seq.

[26] *Cf.* Ambos et al., *Justicia y Paz* (2010), para. 97.

[27] *See* Supreme Court (n 38 in Chap. 2) Rad. 29560, stressing that the investigation refers to the organizational structure of the criminality: "(...) se perfila como primer supuesto fáctico que el procesado por esta jurisdicción es un confeso infractor del delito, por lo menos, de concierto para delinquir agravado; (...) conforme a esa premisa (...), los crímenes a confesar, imputar y por los que se habrá de acusar se ejecutaron y consumaron para y dentro de la organización delictiva. El examen judicial no está referido a un acontecer delictivo individual, sino a los *fenómenos propios de la criminalidad organizada* (...)." (emphasis added). *See* also Tribunal Superior (n 32 in Chap. 1) para. 44 et seq. examining in detail the structure of the paramilitary group "Héctor Julio Peinado Becerra".

disprove the paramilitaries' account. Indeed, this information is vital given the limited manpower and other rescources of the Fiscalía. Thus, if the victims are not effectively integrated into the process the most important source of information, apart from the demobilized themselves, is lost.

(vi) The limited investigative capacity of the *Fiscalía* and its dependence on the confessions of the demobilized hamper in particular the discovery of the *collective truth*. In some cases the prosecutors do not find those demobilized who posses the relevant information about the functioning of a block or front of the illegal armed groups, in other cases they may receive this information but lack the means to verify it. On the other hand, it is expected, by the international and national public opinion, that the process produces *quick and visible results* without, however, compromising the search for the (collective) truth. While it is difficult to reconcile these apparently contradictory demands – in fact the Prosecutor's practice of *successive imputations*[28] has stirred considerable controversy –, it is not impossible. With regard to the in principle useful technique of successive imputations it is necessary to assess this practice in light of a comprehensive investigative strategy. If such a strategy exists successive imputations can be used as an important instrument to advance the proceedings without compromising the truth. This presupposes that such imputations reflect representative patterns of violence and criminality encompassing historical events interrelated by historical, temporal, territorial or functional links, e.g. massacres, systematic attacks against civilians, crimes committed in the context of the invasion or occupation of certain territories, sexual violence used as an instrument of war or expression of social control. In any case, notwithstanding particular selection or charging techniques, it is too much to expect from a national criminal justice system, especially if it is confronted with a peace process of this magnitude, to establish much more than the individual truth. In fact, the sheer number of crimes and persons responsible to be dealt with in such a process stretches even the most efficient and developed criminal justice system to its limits and may make it impossible to even treat all individual cases adequately. Thus, the *collective truth* may only be established by an effective truth commission.[29]

Such a commission is however lacking in Colombia. The "*Group of Historical Memory*" (*Grupo de Memoria Histórica*, GMH), set up by the National Commission of Reparation and Reconciliation (*Comisión Nacional de*

[28]*Supra* n 44 in Chap. 2 et seq. and main text.

[29]This was also recognized by the Supreme Court of Justice in a recent decision concerning an appeal against the decision taken by the High Court for Justice and Peace to declare the legality of the charges during the hearing of verification of acceptance of charges (Supreme Court [21 September 2009] Rad. 32022, Consideraciones de la Corte, 3. La construcción de la verdad en el proceso de justicia y paz). For the criteria of an "effective" Truth Commission *see* Ambos, in Ambos/Large/Wierda (eds.) 2009, para. 16.

Reparación y Reconciliación, CNRR)[30] in order to comply with its task to present a "public report about the reasons for the emergence and evolution of the irregular armed groups",[31] has essentially an academic function and methodology.[32] It intends to explain the history and dynamics of the armed conflict, to achieve an "authentic social memory of the violence".[33] At the end of its mandate it should, apart from the mentioned report, propose public policies with a view to avoid the repetition of the crimes, conserve the public memory and, "most importantly, lay the foundations of a truth commission."[34] From this it is clear that the CMH is not itself a truth commission.[35] In fact, it does not possess any coercive authority, i.e., it must not carry out investigations with a view to bring persons to justice, recommend such investigations or even sanctions or determine reparations. The CNRR itself acknowledges these self-imposed limits of the CMH,[36] albeit partly stressing too much the temporal aspect, i.e., that it has not been

---

[30]*See* crit. Laplante/Theidon (2006) 28 *MichJIntL* 49, at 91 et seq.; Uprimny/Saffon, in Uprimny (2006) 173, at 183–84.

[31]Art. 51 (2): "presentar un informe público sobre las razones para el surgimiento y evolución de los grupos armados ilegales". *See* also Art. 7 (right to truth), 56 (duty of memory) 57 (means to preserve archives), 58 (means to facilitate access to archives) and Art. 21 of decree 4760 of 2005 (about the functions of the CNRR).

[32]*See* www.memoriahistorica-cnrr.org.co (last visited 7 October 2009). – The GMH pursues 11 lines of action (CNRR, *Plan*, 2007, at 5, 17 et seq. listing the following lines of action: I. Historia y memoria de los actores armados ilegales; II. La Economía del conflicto; III. Marco normativo de los procesos de memoria histórica; IV. Prácticas forenses de búsqueda de la verdad; V. Dimensiones psicosociales del conflicto: lógicas de la guerra, vínculo social y reconciliación; VI. Iniciativas sociales e institucionales de verdad y memoria; VII. Roles de género en la vivencia y la resistencia al conflicto; VIII. Las dimensiones internacionales del conflicto. Procesos, actores e intervenciones; IX. Historia, memoria y promoción de las expresiones culturales del conflicto; X. Marco cuantitativo de análisis sobre la violencia en Colombia; XI. Iniciativas de archivo y seguridad de la información). The lines of action are to be developed in three phases ((i) fase de implementación o lanzamiento, (ii) fase de desarrollo, (iii) preparación de productos) within 3 years (i.e. until February 2010). For a more detailed analysis Ambos et al., *Justicia y Paz* (2010), para. 313 et seq.

[33]CNRR, *Plan* (2007), at 7: "autentica memoria social de la violencia". *See* also *ibid.*, at 6: "coadyuvar con la verdad judicial y la reconciliación nacional desentrañando la naturaleza de los actores, de los procesos y de los escenarios socio-políticos en los cuales se ha desenvuelto el conflicto armado interno, para poder comprenderlo en perspectiva histórica y contribuir a su superación."

[34]CNRR, *Plan* (2007), at 28: "lo más importante, sentar las bases para una eventual comisión de verdad."

[35]That was also recognized by the director of the GMH, *see* El Espectador, "No somos comisión de la verdad", http://www.elespectador.com/impreso/nacional/articuloimpreso163545-no-somos-comision-de-verdad (last visited 7 October 2009).

[36]*Cf.* CNRR, *Plan* (2007), at 28: "no tiene funciones ejecutoras, ya que no es de reparación; no tiene funciones judiciales, porque así no lo previó la ley, ni tendría instrumentos para llevarlos a cabo. Tampoco es de reconciliación o unidad nacional, ya que no se crea al final sino en el curso del conflicto."

established at the end of an armed conflict as other TRCs.[37] In any case, at most, the work of the CMH may establish "collective and institutional, but not individual responsibilities"[38]

(vii) The *extradition* of nine high level paramilitary commanders in 2008 and 2009 to the US for drug-related crimes[39] has generated doubts as to the government's willingness to fully investigate these commanders and as to its commitment to the full truth.[40] Along the same lines extradition requests of high and mid level paramilitary commanders were not authorized by the Supreme Court arguing that it would violate the spirit of Law 975 as well as the victims' rights to truth, justice and reparation, hinder the Colombian administration of justice and ignore the priority of prosecuting serious international crimes like war crimes and crimes against humanity instead of drug-related crimes.[41]

While the extradition as such does not exclude the extradited persons from Law 975,[42] its legally required cause, i.e., that the extradited persons were

---

[37]The GMH "no había sido concebida propiamente como una Comisión de la Verdad, fundamentalmente debido a la persistencia del conflicto armado interno. Las Comisiones de la Verdad que se han creado en el mundo en las últimas tres décadas han tenido como objeto explicar qué pasó, cómo pasó, quién fue responsable y cómo evitar que se repitan estos episodios dolorosos en el futuro. Es decir, se crearon al final de las dictaduras militares (Cono Sur), de las guerras civiles (Centroamérica) o del sistema de discriminación racial (Sudáfrica)." (http://www.cnrr.org.co/memoria_historica.htm [last visited 7 October 2009]).

[38]CNRR, *Plan* (2007), at 6: "responsabilidades colectivas e institucionales, pero no individuales . . .".

[39]The following commanders (and at the same time official representatives) have been extradited: Salvatore Mancuso (commander of the Catatumbo and Córdoba blocks), Rodrigo Tovar Pupo (aka "Jorge 40"; commander of the North block), Diego Fernando Murillo (aka "Don Berna"; commander of the Cacique Nutibara, Héroes de Granada and Héroes de Tolová blocks), Ever Veloza García (aka "HH"; commander of the Bananero and Calima blocks), Hernan Giraldo (aka "El Patrón"; commander of the Tayrona block), Ramiro Vanoy (aka "Cuco Vanoy"; commander of the Mineros block), Carlos Mario Jiménez Naranjo (aka "Macaco"; commander of the Central Bolívar Block), Muguel Angel Mejía Múnera (aka "El Mellizo"; commander of the Vencedores de Arauca block) and Guillermo Pérez Alzate (aka "Pablo Sevillano"; commander of the Libertadores del Sur block). Apart from them, further paramilitaries of lower ranks or drug traffickes linked to paramilitary groups have been extradited (e.g. Nodier Giraldo Giraldo, Edwin Mauricio Gómez Luna, Martín Peñaranda Osorio, Francisco Javier Zuluaga Lindo, Juan Carlos Sierra Ramírez, Eduardo Enrique Vengoechea, Diego Alberto Ruiz Arroyave).

[40]*See* IACHR, Press Release N°. 21/08, IACHR expresses concern about extradition of Colombian paramilitaries. Washington, D.C., May 14, 2008, http://www.cidh.oas.org/Comunicados/English/2008/21.08eng.htm (last visited 7 October 2009); IACtHR, Case of the Mapiripán Massacre v. Colombia. Monitoring Compliance with Judgment. Order of the Inter-American Court of Human Rights of July 08, 2009, para. 40, 41. For a more detailed analysis *see* Ambos et al., *Justicia y Paz* (2010), para. 319 et seq.

[41]Supreme Court [19 September 2009] Rad. 30451, MP Yesid Ramírez Bastidas (Concepto de la Corte, 10. Fundamentos para emitir concepto desfavorable a la solicitud de extradición); Supreme Court [17 February 2010] Rad. 32568, MP José Leonidas Bustos Martínez (6.- Improcedencia de la extradición del ciudadano Edwar Cobos Téllez).

[42]Ambos et al., *Justicia y Paz* (2010), para. 124.

involved in drug trafficking,[43] would have been a reason not to apply Law 975 to them in the first place, at least if they were *primarily* dedicated to drug trafficking.[44] From a practical perspective the extraditions clearly have a negative impact on the truth-seeking function of the process since it is much more difficult, albeit not impossible, to continue with free versions and judicial hearings within the framework of Law 975 with beneficiaries who are outside the country; for most victims the access to these persons is clearly imposible. We will return to this matter in the context of the complementarity analysis.[45]

[43]The extradition of Colombian nationals to the US is based on Art. 35 of the Colombian Constitution with Art. 490 et seq. CCP. It requires, *inter alia*, that the offence for which extradition is sought is punishable with a sentence of more than 4 years (Art. 493 (1) CCP); this is the case for drug trafficking (Art. 376 CC).

[44]*See* on Art. 10 no. 5 and Art. 11 no. 6 Law 975 already *supra* n 10 in Chap. 1.

[45]*See infra* Sect. 5.2.1.2 with n 94 et seq. in Chap. 5.

Part II
The complementarity test (Art. 17) and its application to the Colombian situation

The complementarity test is an *on-going process* and may be revisited several times before the commencement of the trial.[1] The *Kony* Pre-Trial Chamber ("PTC") made the continuing nature of the test clear stressing the possibility of "multiple determinations" of and "multiple challenges" to admissibility in a given case.[2] It concluded:

> Considered as a whole, the corpus of these provisions delineates a system whereby the determination of admissibility is meant to be an ongoing process throughout the pre-trial phase, the outcome of which is subject to review depending on the evolution of the relevant factual scenario. Otherwise stated, the Statute as a whole enshrines the idea that a change in circumstances allows (or even, in some scenarios, compels) the Court to determine admissibility anew.[3]

It also follows from this that complementarity, being part of the admissibility of a situation, is to be examined at a very *early stage* during pre-trial proceedings, or, more exactly, during *preliminary inquiries* or the pre-investigation stage of the proceedings. In fact, once the OTP's "Jurisdiction, Complementarity and Cooperation Division" (JCCD) has affirmed the ICC's jurisdiction in all its aspects (*ratione temporis, personae and materiae*), it has to analyze the complementarity issue. Only if a situation is considered admissible, the Prosecutor is in a position to analyze more closely whether a formal investigation in the sense of Art. 53 may be opened.[4] In fact, Art. 53 itself requires a positive decision with regard to

---

[1] *See* also Stigen, *Relationship* (2008), at 245. On the double effect of this dynamic character of complementarity (*vis-à-vis* States but also *vis-à-vis* the ICC) see Olásolo, in Almqvist/Espósito (eds.) 2009, at 279.

[2] ICC-PTC II, *Prosecutor v. Kony et al.* [10 March 2009], Decision on the admissibility of the case under article 19 (1) of the Statute (ICC-02/04-01/05) para. 25, 26.

[3] *Ibid.*, paras. 25 et seq. (28), 52. - On the possibility of a retroactive abolishment of the basis of admissibility by a State's activity after the Prosecutor's start of an investigation, Pichon (2008) 8 *ICLR* 185, at 199–200.

[4] *See* on the structure of the pre-trial phase before the ICC Ambos, *Internationales Strafrecht* (2008), § 8 mn. 20a et seq.; Ambos, in Bohlander (ed.) 2007, 429, at 433 et seq.

jurisdiction and admissibility before coming to the more policy-based and discretional criteria of subparas. (c) of paras. 1 and 2. The Art. 53 decision is at least as complex as the decision under Art. 17 and the criteria to be applied, especially the "interests of justice" test (Art. 53 (1) (c), (2) (c)), may even be considered more relevant with regard to the specific challenges posed by transitional justice processes.[5] This is especially true for the Colombian situation where it may well be possible that a situation or even a case may be considered admissible but, still, an investigation will not (formally) be opened for the reasons spelt out in Art. 53 (1) and/or (2). In any case, this last procedural step in the pre-trial phase of the ICC proceedings is not the object of this study but we must limit ourselves to a detailed analysis of the complementarity test. This analysis will first discuss, as necessary preliminary considerations, the object of reference of this test, examining in particular the distinction between situation and case (*infra* Chap. 4). Then, the actual complementarity test will be analysed distinguishing between complementarity *stricto sensu* on the one hand, and an *additional gravity threshold* on the other (Chap. 5).

---

[5] *See* for an analysis of the interests of justice clause Ambos, in Ambos/Large/Wierda (eds.) 2009, at 82 et seq.; for a recent call for a broad prosecutorial discretion and the taking into account of the political context Rodman (2009) *22 LJIL* 99; for criteria with regard to amnesties Olásolo, in Almqvist/Espósito (eds.) 2009, at 286 et seq.

Chapter 4
Preliminary Considerations: The Object of Reference of the Complementarity Test (Situation–Case–Conduct)

While Art. 17 and 53 explicitly only refer to (individual) "*cases*"[1] – i.e. "specific incidents during which one or more crimes (...) seems to have been committed by one or more identified suspects"[2] – it is clear that not cases but (general) "*situations*" – "generally defined in terms of temporal, territorial and in some cases personal parameters"[3] – are referred to the Prosecutor under the triggering procedure (Art. 13). This also follows from PTC I's *situation–case demarcation* focusing on the issuance of a warrant of arrest or a summons to appear, i.e., considering that a case only starts with Art. 58 proceedings.[4] Accordingly, the *procedural development* from a situation to a case goes as follows:

1. The OTP obtains *notitia criminis*
2. Starts pre-investigating
3. Identifies a situation
4. Checks the criteria enshrined in Art. 53 (1), 15 (3), rule 48 with regard to the situation as a whole
5. Starts a formal investigation (in the case of a referral), or asks for authorization of a formal investigation (in the case of information under Art. 15) in the sense of Art. 54
6. Investigates all-embracing and ideally identifies individual suspects

---

[1] *See* also Benzing (2003) 7 *MPUNYB* 591, at 603.

[2] ICC-PTC I, Prosecutor v. Lubanga [17 January 2006], Decision on the applications for participation in the proceedings of VPRS-1, VPRS-2, VPRS-3, VPRS-4, VPRS-5, VPRS-6 (ICC-01/04-101-tEN-Corr) para. 65.

[3] *Ibid.*; *see* also Olásolo (2003) 3 *ICLR* 87, at 99–100; Kleffner, *Complementarity* (2008), 199; WCRO, *Relevance of a situation* (2009), 21–22.

[4] Prosecutor v. Lubanga (n 2) para. 65; *see* also *Situation in DRC* [9 November 2005] Decision following the consultation held on 11 October 2005 and the Prosecution's submission on Jurisdiction and admissibility filed on 31 October 2005 (ICC-01/04-93) 4; Olásolo (2007) 20 *LJIL* 193, at 194; Rastan (2008) 19 *CLF* 435, at 442–3.

K. Ambos, *The Colombian Peace Process and the Principle of Complementarity of the International Criminal Court*,
DOI 10.1007/978-3-642-11273-7_4, © Springer-Verlag Berlin Heidelberg 2010

7. Ultimately applies for a warrant of arrest or summons to appear if the reasonable grounds standard of Art. 58 (1), (7) is met; and
8. The PTC issues a warrant of arrest or summons to appear

Only with this last step does a formal or legal case exist in the PTC's view. Within a situation, the OTP applies a *sequential approach*,[5] i.e., it investigates specific cases within a situation one after another rather than all at once, whereby cases inside the situation are selected according to gravity.[6] Upon completion of each case the Office examines whether other cases in the situation warrant investigation – bearing in mind the gravity and admissibility thresholds of the ICC Statute – or whether to select a new situation.[7]

In practice, however, the stages mentioned above are blurry since the OTP will most likely focus on individuals before a legal case in the sense of Art. 58 exists. In fact, a case could begin at three potential stages: (1) during pre-investigation and investigation stages; (2) at the moment the Prosecutor makes an application for an arrest warrant or summons to appear; or (3) when the PTC issues a decision to issue a warrant of arrest or summons to appear.[8] Therefore, one may distinguish between cases in a *broad and narrow sense*. The later refer to the (strict) legal cases that only come into being once a warrant of arrest or summons to appear is issued. Cases in a broad sense evolve very early during investigations and even during pre-investigations. As soon as the OTP bundles allegations against one or more specific individuals, and possibly even generates a "case file" with their names, a case in the broader sense arises. Such a broad case which may exist at an early stage of the (preliminary) investigation constitutes, in fact, a "*case hypothesis*", i.e., a likely set of cases that arises from the investigation of a situation.[9] The design of a solid case hypothesis is fundamental for the subsequent process, and it must cover: (1) the status of authority or role of the suspect; (2) the structure of the organization instrumental to the crime and subordinated or associated to the suspect; (3) the pattern and *modus operandi* of the criminal events; and (4) a conclusion on the

---

[5]ICC-OTP, *Criteria for selection* (2006), para. 31 (on this paper *see* also Seils, in Bergsmo (ed.) 2009, 55, at 56–7); ICC-OTP, *Update on communications* (2006), 1, 5; ICC-OTP, *Report on activities* (2006), at 8; *see* also Swaak-Goldman, 'Outlining the Three-Year Report', in ICC-OTP, *Second public hearing* (2006), session 1: interested States; Guariglia, in Stahn/Sluiter (eds.) 2009, 209, at 215. Sceptical Mattioli, in ICC-OTP, *Second public hearing* (2006), session 2: NGOs and other experts, who fears "delays in the investigations and consequences for the preservation of evidence or serious problems of perception for the Office;" similarly, Bernard, in *ibid.*; Dicker, in *ibid.*, session 4: NGOs and other experts ("selective justice"); Schiff, *Building the ICC* (2008), 118–9.

[6]ICC-OTP, *Report on activities* (2006), 2, 8; ICC-OTP, *Third Report Security Council* (2006), at 2; ICC-OTP, *Prosecutorial Strategy* (2010), para. 20. In favour of this approach to gravity Mattioli, *supra* n 5.

[7]ICC-OTP, *Update on communications* (2006), 1, 5.

[8]Rastan (2008) 19 *CLF*, 435 at 440.

[9]Rastan (2008) 19 *CLF*, 435, at 441. *See* also Burke-White/Kaplan, in Stahn/Sluiter (eds.) 2009, 79, at 88: "investigative hypothesis" (also in (2009) 7 *JICJ* 257, at 260).

mode of responsibility.[10] In any case, it is clear that cases – understood broadly or narrowly – may only result from a long and thorough investigation.[11]

From all this follows that the Prosecutor has, at the pre-investigation stage, i.e. when he has not yet decided whether he will formally initiate an investigation in the sense of Art. 53, to examine the admissibility with regard to the *situation* referred.[12] The Prosecutor operates on the basis of the said case hypothesis, and checks admissibility only in a "generalized manner",[13] albeit taking into account its general selection criteria, in particular the importance of the suspect and his role in the crimes.[14] Only if the Prosecutor has identified concrete cases, potential criminal conduct and/or suspects, i.e. within the course of the Art. 53 decision,[15] the admissibility test shifts to the *case*. This shift from situation to case also follows from Art. 18 and 19: While the former refers to "a situation" referred (Art. 18 (1)) and "criminal acts which may constitute crimes" (Art. 18 (2)), the latter provides for challenges as to the admissibility of "a case". Thus, it has correctly been argued that the specificity increases from a comparatively general standard (Art. 53 (1)) – via Art. 18 – to selecting individual cases (Art. 53 (2)), until it reaches the highest level of cases in the strict sense (Art. 19).[16] As a consequence, admissibility must be assessed both at the situation and case stage.[17]

With the shifting of the investigation from the general situation to a more concrete case the question of the *object of reference* of the national proceedings vis-à-vis the ICC proceedings arises. The case law tends towards an identity requiring that the national proceedings must refer specifically ("*specificity" test*)[18] to the OTP's case encompassing "both the *person* and the *conduct* which is the subject of the case before the Court".[19] The Prosecutor requires an

---

[10]Agirre A., in Bergsmo (ed.) 2009, 147, at 148–9.

[11]*See* also Stigen, *Relationship* (2008), at 91; Kleffner, *Complementarity* (2008), at 195 et seq.; Razesberger, *Complementarity* (2006), 32–3; Stahn, in Stahn/Sluiter (eds.) 2009, 247, at 268. In addition, in the case of "inability" (Art. 17 (3)), the effect of a collapse of the national justice system may go well beyond the specific case and extend to the situation as a whole (*cf.* Bergsmo (1998) 6 *Eur.J.Cr., Cr. L. & Cr. J.* 29, at 43; Cárdenas, *Zulässigkeitsprüfung* (2005), 130–1).

[12]*See* also Kleffner, *Complementarity* (2008), at 195 et seq.

[13]Stahn, in Stahn/Sluiter (eds.) 2009, 247, at 268–9; for the criteria to be considered *see* Olásolo, *Triggering procedure* (2005), at 164 et seq.

[14]For this *ratione personae* limitation *see* also Olásolo, in Almqvist/Espósito (eds.), 2009, at 267–68. For a critique in the the context of the gravity test *see infra* n 30 in Chap. 5 with main text.

[15]*See* para. 1 (b): "case is or would be admissible"; para. 2 (b): "case is admissible".

[16]Kleffner, *Complementarity* (2008), at 197–98. *See* also his preceding analysis of articles 18, 19 at 168 et seq., 181 et seq.; for a detailed analysis *see* also El Zeidy, *Complementarity* (2008), at 239 et seq.; Razesberger, *Complementarity* (2006), 32–3, at 72 et seq., 123 et seq.

[17]Stahn (2008) 19 *CLF* 87, at 106; Olásolo, in Almqvist/Espósito (eds.) 2009, at 266–67.

[18]Rastan (2008) 19 *CLF* 435, at 436.

[19]ICC-PTC I, *Prosecutor v. Lubanga and Ntaganda* [10 Feb. 2006] Annex II, Decision on the Prosecutor's application for warrants of arrest, article 58 (ICC-01/04-01/07), para. 31 (emphasis added); ICC-PTC I, *Prosecutor v. Harun and Kushayb* [27 April 2007], Decision on the Prosecution application under article 58 (7) of the Statute (ICC-02/05-01/07), para. 24; ICC-PTC I,

investigation as to "the *same incidents or conduct* that are the subject of the case now before the Court".[20] The significance of "conduct" also follows from the interplay of Art. 17 (1)(c) and 20 (3).[21] "Conduct" in this sense, i.e., in the sense of the "idem" (the same) of the *ne bis in idem* principle enshrined in Art. 20, is to be understood strictly as *incident-specific*.[22] This follows from the wording of the relevant ICC provisions[23] and the general understanding of the *ne bis in idem* principle referring to the specific factual or procedural conduct of the respective case.[24] Indeed, the Pre-Trial Chambers correctly examine whether the concerned suspect is being prosecuted at the national level for the *same* crimes referred to in the Prosecutor's Application.[25] Thus, in *Lubanga* and *Ntaganda* the PTC held that the DRC's arrest warrants issued against the suspects did not encompass the same (factual) conduct of the Prosecutor's application,[26] namely the specific incidents relating to the "alleged UPC/FPLC's policy/practice of enlisting into the FPLC, conscripting into the FPLC and using to participate actively in hostilities children under the age of fifteen between July 2002 and December 2003".[27] In *Katanga* and *Chui* the admissibility test did not even reach this level of conduct-comparison and the Chamber did not decide on the "same conduct test" as such, because the State in question – the DRC – clearly expressed unwillingness to prosecute the case, i.e. the

---

Prosecutor v. Chui [6 July 2007] Decision on the evidence and information provided by the Prosecution for the issuance of a warrant of arrest (ICC-01/04-02/07), para. 21. *See* also El Zeidy, *Complementarity* (2008), at 161; Rastan (2008) 19 *CLF* 435, at 436–37; Stigen, *Relationship* (2008), at 261.

[20]ICC Prosecutor Presents Evidence on Darfur Crimes, The Hague, 27 February 2007, ICC-OTP-20070227-206-En (emphasis added); on the same conduct test *see* also the controversy before Trial Chamber II in *Prosecutor v. Katanga and Chui* [16 June 2009] Motifs de la décision orale relative à l'exception d'irrecevabilité de l'affaire (article 19 du Statut) (ICC-01/04-01/07-1213) paras.11 et seq., 17 et seq., 95; *Prosecutor v. Katanga and Chui* [11 March 2007], Motion challenging the admissibility of the case by the Defence of Germain Katanga, pursuant to article 19 (2) (a) of the Statute (ICC-01/04-01/07-949) paras. 39 et seq.; *Prosecutor v. Katanga and Chui* [30.3.2009], Public redacted version of the 19th March 2009 Prosecution response to motion challenging the admissibility of the case by the Defence of Germain Katanga, pursuant to article 19 (2) (ICC-01/04-01/07-1007) paras. 50 et seq.

[21]Rastan (2008) 19 *CLF* 435, at 437; *see* also conc. Sedman, in Stahn/van den Herik (eds.) 2010, at 262 et seq.

[22]*Cf.* Rastan (2008) 19 *CLF* 435, at 438 et seq.; *see* also Stigen, *Relationship* (2008), at 199 ("case specific"); Pichon (2008) 8 *ICLR* 185, at 225–26 with regard to Ali Kushayb (Sudan).

[23]Article 20 (3) refers to the "same conduct" and article 17 (1) (c) to conduct "subject of the complaint"; article 17 (1) (a) and (b) refer to the more specific "case" instead of "situation". *See* also articles 89 (4), 94 referring to a "different" crime or case with regard to domestic prosecutions.

[24]*See* for example for the discussion of the "European" ne bis in idem rule of article 54 Schengen Agreement Ambos, *Internationales Strafrecht* (2008) § 12 mn. 38 et seq. (49 et seq.).

[25]*Prosecutor v. Bemba* [10 June 2008] Mandat d'arrêt à l'encontre de Jean-Pierre Bemba Gombo remplaçant le mandat d'arrêt décerné le 23 mai 2008 (ICC-01/05-01/08-15) para. 21.

[26]*Prosecutor v. Lubanga and Ntaganda* (n 19) para. 38.

[27]*Ibid.*, para. 39, 40.

DRC did not challenge admissibility and remained totally inactive, which rendered the *Katanga* case admissible without further ado.[28]

In sum, for a case to be declared inadmissible, national proceedings must refer to the *same concrete conduct and suspect*(s) as the investigation before the ICC unless the State remains totally inactive anyway. Clearly, there is a certain risk that this relatively strict requirement may too strongly limit a State's legitimate choice in selecting conduct and crimes. One must not overlook that the complementarity regime should encourage domestic proceedings[29] and that States should therefore have a certain margin of appreciation as to their prosecutorial policies.[30] In addition, specificity also must be construed dynamically and with certain flexibility with regard to the different criteria of admissibility to be analyzed in the following section.[31]

[28] *Prosecutor v. Katanga and Chui*, Motifs (n 20) para. 95.

[29] For a thorough discussion *see* Kleffner, *Complementarity* (2008), at 309 et seq.; *see* also El Zeidy, *Complementarity* (2008), at 298 et seq. discussing positive vs. traditional complementarity; on an effective positive complementarity prosecution strategy Hall, in Stahn/Sluiter (eds.) 2009, at 219 et seq.; most recently also ICC-OTP, *Prosecutorial Strategy* (2010), para. 17.

[30] *See* convincingly Kleffner, *Complementarity* (2008), at 201.

[31] Kleffner, *Complementarity* (2008), at 202–03.

Chapter 5
Gravity and Complementarity *Stricto Sensu*

According to the Lubanga PTC, Art. 17 provides for a twofold test distinguishing between complementarity *stricto sensu* pursuant to Art. 17 (1) (a)–(c), (2) and (3) on the one hand, and an *additional gravity threshold* pursuant to Art. 17 (1) (d) on the other.[1] Thus, complementarity *stricto sensu* only becomes relevant if the respective case is of sufficient gravity in the first place.[2] It seems therefore logical to examine gravity first and only then, if the gravity standard is satisfied, complementarity *stricto sensu.*[3]

[1]*Prosecutor v. Lubanga and Ntaganda* (n 19 in Chap. 4) para. 29: "The Chamber considers that the admissibility test of a case arising from the investigation of a situation has two parts. The first part of the test relates to national investigations, prosecutions and trials concerning the case at hand insofar as such a case would be admissible only if those States with jurisdiction over it have remained inactive in relation to that case or are unwilling or unable, within the meaning of article 17 (1) (a) to (c), 2 and 3 of the Statute. The second part of the test refers to the gravity threshold which any case must meet to be admissible before the Court. Accordingly, the Chamber will treat them separately". (footnotes omitted).

[2]Apart from *Prosecutor v. Lubanga and Ntaganda* (n 1) *see* also PTC I, Situation in the DRC in the case of *Prosecutor v. Thomas Lubanga Dyilo* [24 February 2006], Decision concerning PTC I's Decision of 10 February 2006 and the Incorporation of Documents into the Record of the case against Mr. Thomas Lubanga Dyilo (ICC-01/04–01/06), para. 41 (" ... this gravity threshold is in addition to (...) the crimes included in articles 6 to 8 of the Statute ..."). *See* also ICC-OTP, *Report on activities* (2006), at 6: "Although any crime falling within the jurisdiction of the Court is a serious matter, the Rome Statute (...) clearly foresees and requires an additional consideration of 'gravity' ...". *See* also Guariglia, in Stahn/Sluiter (eds.) 2009, 209, at 213 ("overarching consideration ... analyzed before any decision to investigate ..."). For further references *see* Ambos et al., *Justicia y Paz* (2010), para. 38 with fn. 352.

[3]This is also the approach taken by the OTP. Thus, in the Iraq situation the Prosecutor reached a negative conclusion on "gravity", and therefore found it unnecessary to elaborate on complementarity (Iraq response, Annex to the ICC-OTP, *Update on communications* (2006), at 9; available at http://www.iccnow.org/documents/OTP_letter_to_senders_re_Iraq_9_February_2006.pdf (last visited 23 November 2009)). For a similar solution Meißner, *Zusammenarbeit* (2003), at 79.

K. Ambos, *The Colombian Peace Process and the Principle of Complementarity of the International Criminal Court*,
DOI 10.1007/978-3-642-11273-7_5,

5.1 Sufficient gravity (Art. 17 (1) (d))

5.1.1 The standard in current practice

Gravity in the sense of Art. 17 (1) (d) is relevant at *two different stages* of the proceedings, i.e., with a view to the initiation of the investigation of a *situation* and of the *case*(s) arising from this situation.[4] Indeed, the OTP has so far[5] applied gravity in this twofold way regarding situations and cases.[6] One may in this sense distinguish between situation- and case-related gravity. Yet, the OTP has not systematically elaborated the gravity criteria or even proposed a more sophisticated gravity theory. In fact, the Office affirmed gravity in the situations of the Democratic Republic of Congo, Uganda and Sudan without further reasoning[7] and only made public some more profound deliberations regarding the Iraq situation.[8] Here it rejected gravity in the sense of Art. 53 (1) (b) comparing the relatively low number of victims (four to twelve) of alleged crimes by British troops with the large-scale violence in the situations of DRC, Uganda and Sudan. While this has been criticized as "comparing apples and oranges"[9] there was not much choice for the OTP given that it had only jurisdiction over British troops by way of the active personality (nationality) principle (Art. 12 (2) (b)). In any case, the OTP could have avoided criticism by taking a more systematic and consistent approach to gravity in the first place, especially by clarifying the concrete factors it takes into consideration and by

---

[4]PTC I (n 2) para. 44. *See* also WCRO, *Gravity threshold* (2008), at 21 et seq., 25 et seq.; El Zeidy (2008) 19 *CLF* 35, at 39; crit. now regarding situational gravity WCRO, *Relevance of a situation* (2009), 28 et seq.

[5]Between mid 2003 and 2005 gravity played no role, *see* Schabas, in Stahn/Sluiter (eds.) 2009, 229, at 229 et seq. Interestingly, it attracted either much attention in the negotiation history of the ICC Statute (Stahn, in Stahn/Sluiter (eds.) 2009, 247, at 267).

[6]ICC-OTP, *Report on activities* (2006), at 8. *See* also Ambos, in Ambos/Large/Wierda (eds.) 2009, at 73–4, para. 38; El Zeidy (2008) 19 *CLF* 35, at 39; WCRO, *Gravity threshold* (2008), at 21 et seq.; Stegmiller (2009) 9 *ICLR* 547, at 557.

[7]ICC-OTP, *Report on activities* (2006), at 10: "The Office selected the DRC and Northern Uganda as the first situations because they were the gravest admissible situations under the Statute's jurisdiction, and, after the referral, the Office confirmed that the Darfur situation clearly met the gravity standard. The Office will continue to adhere to the rigorous standard of gravity established in the Statute".

[8]Iraq response (n 3), at 8–9; Stegmiller (2009) 9 *ICLR* 547, at 558–9; Schüller (2008) 21 *HuV-I* 73, at 77; Murphy (2006) 17 *CLF* 281, at 309 et seq.; *see* also Ambos, in Bohlander (ed.) 2007, 429, at 438–39.

[9]Schabas, *Introduction* (2007), at 190; *id.* (2008) 6 *JICJ* 731, at 741; *id.*, in Stahn/Sluiter (eds.) 2009, 229, at 240. Schabas further criticizes that the Prosecutor did not compare the total number of deaths in Iraq with the total in the DRC or Uganda nor did he compare the total number of deaths resulting from the crimes attributed to specific perpetrators with those blamed on the British troops in Iraq (*ibid.*, at 747 and 240). Crit. also El Zeidy (2008) 19 *CLF* 35, at 40–1; Heller, in Stahn/van den Herik (eds.) 2010, at 234 and passim.

distinguishing between the more legal and more policy (discretional) side of the complementarity test.[10]

Regulation 29 No. 2 of the OTP Regulations refers for the assessment of the gravity of "situations" to "various factors, including their scale, nature, manner of commission, and impact."[11] This provision is a result of an ongoing process of external and internal consultation of the OTP and it has seen many changes. As to the specific factors mentioned – equally applicable to situations and cases[12] – the OTP has offered definitions in declarations, papers and submissions. As to the "*scale*" the Office referred, as in the Iraq case mentioned above,[13] to the number of victims[14] and also took the geographic and temporal scope of the crimes into account.[15] This approach has been criticized because of the difficulty to establish exact victim numbers,[16] the lack of qualitative criteria[17] and a proper methodology as to what to compare.[18] Yet, the reference to "both qualitative and quantitative factors" in the last version of the Draft Regulations[19] was replaced by "various factors" in the finally adopted version. With respect to the *nature* of the crimes, the OTP considers that all ICC crimes "are crimes of concern to the international community and, as such, grave in themselves";[20] still, assuming that there is an

[10]*See* already Ambos, in Bohlander (ed.) 2007, 429, at 439; in a similar vein also crit. Schüller (2008) 21 *HuV-I* 73, at 78; McAuliffe deGuzman, *Gravity* (2008), at 30, 32; Stegmiller (2009) 9 *ICLR* 547, at 562.

[11]Regulations of the Office of the Prosecutor, ICC-BD/05-01-09, entry into force 23 April 2009. *See* also ICC-OTP, *Prosecutorial Strategy* (2010), para. 20; ICC-OTP, *Report on activities* (2006), at 6 and ICC-OTP, *Report prosecutorial strategy* (2006), at 5, referring to the scale and nature of the crimes, the manner of commission and the impact of the crimes. *See* also Seils, in Bergsmo (ed.) 55, at 57.

[12]El Zeidy (2008) 19 *CLF* 35, at 43.

[13]Iraq response (n 3), at 8.

[14]Statement by Luis Moreno-Ocampo: Informal meeting of Legal Advisors of Ministries of Foreign Affairs, 24.10.2005, at 6; "Five minutes with Luis Moreno-Ocampo: An interview with the ICC Prosecutor", Adele Waugaman (2006) XV *International Affairs Review* 2.

[15]McAuliffe deGuzman, *Gravity* (2008), at 35; Guariglia, in Stahn/Sluiter (eds.) 2009, 209, at 214.

[16]*See* on this issue Brunborg, in ICC-OTP, *First public hearing* (2003), 2.

[17]See for the prioritization of qualitative criteria, i.e., the systematicity of the crimes, the social alarm caused and State involvement Heller, in Stahn/van den Herik (eds.) 2010, at 229 et seq. arguing, essentially, that his qualitative approach would lend greater legitimacy to the Court and produce a greater impact in terms of deterrence and general prevention ("greater expressive value", at 236). Yet, Heller's approach, albeit certainly thought-provoking and allegedly principled, is from a theoretical perspective, apart from its practical implications, full of consequentalist assumptions and thus "more like a prudent concession to practical *realpolitik*, ... than a strong, independent argument for what the ICC is really about, what it is truly for." (Osiel, in Stahn/van den Herik (eds.) 2010, at 258).

[18]Schabas, *Introduction* (2007), at 190; *id.* (2008) 6 *JICJ* 731, at 741, 747–48; *id.*, in Stahn/Sluiter (eds.) 2009, 229, at 245–46; *see* also Ambos, in Bohlander (ed.) 2007, 429, at 439.

[19]Draft OTP Regulations 9 Oct. 2007, Regulation 24 no. 2.

[20]ICC-OTP, *Criteria for selection* (2006), para. 16.

inherent hierarchy of crimes,[21] killing, rape and child conscription are considered crimes of particular concern.[22] It is worth noting in this regard that the Special Court for Sierra Leone ("SCSL") took the same view with regard to crimes against UN personnel and child soldiers qualifying these as "inherently grave".[23] Regarding the *manner of the commission*, the OTP refers to aspects of particular cruelty, crimes against particularly vulnerable victims and involving discrimination, abuse of *de jure* or *de facto* power, and, under certain circumstances, a so-called "added factor", for example, if the crimes were apparently committed with the aim or consequence of increasing the vulnerability of the civilian population at large (through attacks on peacekeepers).[24] Last but not least, the *impact* criterion, albeit finally adopted by the Regulations, still seems to be controversial within the OTP, very much favored by the Chief Prosecutor[25] but not by (all) his staff members.[26] More importantly, it is not at all clear how impact is to be understood. In a June 2006 draft document the Prosecutor stated that he "will consider the broader impact of crimes on the community and on regional peace and security, including longer term social, economic and environmental damage".[27] This very much sounds of "social alarm" as employed by PTC I (see next para.) and in any case smacks more of a policy (*cf.* Art. 53 (1) (c) and (2) (c)) than of a strictly legal criterion. We will return to this point.

As to *judicial pronouncements* on gravity the issue remains largely unsettled at the ICC level. Although the Lubanga Pre-Trial Chamber[28] proposed at least some abstract criteria regarding a case – the nature and social impact ("social alarm") of the crimes (systematic or large-scale?), the manner of commission (e.g. particular

[21]*Cf.* Seils, in Bergsmo (ed.), 2009, 55, at 57; Heller, in Stahn/van den Herik (eds.) 2010, at 230 et seq.

[22]Guariglia, in Stahn/Sluiter (eds.) 2009, 209, at 214. *See* also McAuliffe deGuzman, *Gravity* (2008), at 35 referring to crimes resulting in death and rape.

[23]SCSL, T.Ch. I, Prosecutor v. Issa Hassan Sesay, Morris Kallon and Augustine Gbao [8 April 2009] Sentencing Judgement (SCSL-04-15-T), paras. 179 et seq., 188 et seq., 204.

[24]ICC-OTP, *Criteria for selection* (2006), para.17. *See* also McAuliffe deGuzman, *Gravity* (2008), at 35; Guariglia, in Stahn/Sluiter (eds.) 2009, at 214.

[25]Moreno Ocampo mentioned impact on various occasions (Statement by Luis Moreno-Ocampo: Informal meeting, *supra* n 14, at 6; ICC-OTP, *Third Report Security Council* (2006), at 2). The OTP also referred to the "nature, manner and impact" regarding the Haskanita attack in the Darfur situation (ICC-OTP, *Eight Report Security Council* (2008), para. 56).

[26]A senior member of OTP, Senior App. Counsel Fabricio Guariglia, did not include impact in a recent paper (in Stahn/Sluiter (eds.) 2009, at 212 et seq.); crit. also Seils, in Bergsmo (ed.) 2009, 55, at 59, former Head of the Situation Analysis Section of OTP (August 2004 to October 2008) and mainly responsible, *inter alia*, for the OTP selection paper which does not contain this criterion (ICC-OTP, *Criteria for selection* (2006), para. 12).

[27]Schabas, *Introduction* (2007), at 742; also Hall, *Suggestions concerning ICC prosecutorial policy and strategy* (2003), 21; Stegmiller (2009) 9 *ICLR* 547, at 560–1; Meißner, *Zusammenarbeit* (2003), at 79; McAuliffe deGuzman, *Gravity* (2008), at 35; Osiel, (2009) *The Hague Justice Portal*, at 2.

[28]PTC I (n 2), para. 42 et seq. (46, 50–4, 63).

brutality or cruelty) and the status and role of the suspected perpetrators (are they the most responsible?) – these criteria have been widely criticized[29] and rejected by the Appeals Chamber. It reversed the PTC's decision holding that its gravity test is flawed and thus constitutes an error of law in the sense of Art. 81 (a)-(iii).[30] In particular, as to the status and role of the suspect – a criterion used by the OTP only with regard to its policy[31] – the Chamber correctly pointed out that the "predictable exclusion of many perpetrators" on these grounds "could severely hamper the preventive, or deterrent role of the Court ...".[32] However, the Chamber did not propose an alternative interpretation; only Judge Pikis, in his separate and partly dissenting opinion, tried to determine gravity,[33] without, however, proposing a concrete testing mechanism.

---

[29]*See* Schüller (2008) 21 *HuV-I* 73, at 80; Schabas (2008) 6 *JICJ* 731, at 743; Schabas, *Introduction* (2007), 190, at 241 ("gravity in a vacuum", "comparing apples with nothing"); WCRO, *Gravity threshold* (2008), at 36 et seq. recommending a "sufficiently flexible" analysis (at 42) and taking into account exceptional circumstances as "the impact of victims, the manner in which the crimes were carried out, and the vulnerability of the victim population"; crit. in particular on the "social alarm" criterion Schüller (2008) 21 *HuV-I* 73, at 80–1; McAuliffe deGuzman, *Gravity* (2008), at 36; Osiel, (2009) *The Hague Justice Portal*, at 6; WCRO, *Gravity threshold* (2008), at 5, 39; El Zeidy (2008) 19 *CLF* 35, at 45 ("weird novelty"), who additionally points out (at 44) that these factors are illustrative and not exclusive; Murphy (2006) 17 *CLF* 281, at 288 et seq. (289); Smith (2008) 8 *ICLR* 331, at 340 et seq.; Stegmiller (2009) 9 *ICLR* 547, at 551–2; crit. also Judge Pikis (*infra* n 32) para. 34; contrary Heller, in Stahn/van den Herik (eds.) 2010, at 233 et seq. invoking this criterion as part of his qualitiative approach (*supra* n 17); against him Osiel, in Stahn/van den Herik (eds.) 2010, at 257. Crit. as to the quantitative approach Schabas (2008) 19 *CLF* 5, at 28 et seq.; Williams/Schabas, in Triffterer (ed.) 2008, Art. 17 mn. 28; Heller, in Stahn/van den Herik (eds.) 2010, at 227 et seq. *See* also El Zeidy (2002) 32 *MichJIntL* 869, at 905; Cárdenas, *Zulässigkeitsprüfung* (2005), at 93 et seq. focusing on the international concern ("internationaler Belang", at 98, 100) of the matter. Crit. on the gravity standard also Ohlin, in Stahn/Sluiter (eds.) 2009, at 185, 200 ("unclear what kind of legal threshold is established"). - On the difficult relation between OTP and Chambers in this matter *see* El Zeidy (2008) 19 *CLF* 35, at 51 et seq.

[30]*Situation in DRC* [13 July 2006], Judgment on the Prosecutor's appeal against the decision of Pre-Trial Chamber I entitled "Decision on the Prosecutor's application for warrants of arrest, article 58" (ICC-01-04-169) [reclassified as public on 23.9.2008 pursuant to *Situation in DRC*, Decision on the unsealing of judgment of the Appeals Chamber issued on 13 July 2006, 22.9.2008 (ICC-01-04-538-PUB-Exp), paras.1–3], paras. 54 et seq. (68 et seq.); in the same vein, *Prosecutor v. Al Bashir*, [4 March 2009] Decision on the Prosecutor's application for a warrant of arrest against Omar Hassan Ahmad Al Bashir (ICC-02/05-01/09-3) para. 48 with fn. 51

[31]*Cf.* Guariglia, in Stahn/Sluiter (eds.) 2009, 209, at 214–5; Schabas, in Stahn/Sluiter (eds.) 2009, 229, at 243; calling for flexibility if using this criterion at all WCRO, *Gravity threshold* (2008), at 43 et seq. (50–1); in a similar vein Seils, in Bergsmo (ed.) 2009, 55, at 56.

[32]*Situation in DRC* (n 30) para. 73 et seq. (75). *See* also Seils, in Bergsmo (ed.) 55, at 56.

[33]*Situation in DRC*, Judgment on the Prosecutor's appeal against the decision of Pre-Trial Chamber I (n 30), Separate and partly dissenting opinion of Judge Georghios M. Pikis, para. 38 et seq. He focused on the ordinary meaning of the term and understands it as "weightiness" (para. 39) excluding cases "unworthy of consideration" by the Court, i.e. cases that are "insignificant in themselves" ; where the criminality on the part of the culprit is wholly marginal; borderline cases" (para. 40) and holds a crime to be insignificant if "the acts constituting the crime are wholly peripheral to the objects of the law in criminalising the conduct" (*ibid.*).

Interestingly enough, gravity of an offense has been a primary consideration ("litmus test") at the ICTY, ICTR and SCSL with regard to *sentencing*.[34] While the considerations of the Ad Hoc Tribunals are not binding for the ICC and also refer to a different stage of the proceedings (the sentencing instead of pre-investigative stage), they may nevertheless provide important elements of a general gravity concept. According to a recent empirical study the most frequent factors taken into account by the ICTY with regard to gravity and aggravating circumstances were (1) abuse of superior position/position of authority or trust (accepted in 35 cases); (2) special vulnerability of victims (accepted in 31 cases); (3) extreme suffering or harm inflicted on victims (accepted in 25 cases); (4) large number of victims (accepted in 15 cases); and (5) cruelty of the attack (accepted in 14 cases).[35] The SCSL has largely followed the ICTY criteria.[36] In sum, the *ad hoc* tribunals took a *case-specific approach* and did consider *quantitative* and *qualitative* factors equally, referring, on the one hand, to the gravity of the crime (taking into account factors such as scale, systematic character, continuing nature, genocide and rape, discriminatory nature, vulnerability of victims, manner of commission, and effects on victims), and, on the other, to the individual circumstances of the accused (taking into account, *inter alia*, planning, form of participation, motive, position and role).

5.1.2 The own approach

In order to understand gravity in its full meaning and to develop a consistent gravity concept one has to start from a distinction between the two forms of gravity referred to in Art. 53, i.e. *legal* (non-discretionary) gravity pursuant to Art. 53 (1) (b), 17 (1) (d) and *relative* (discretionary) gravity pursuant to Art. 53 (1) (c).[37] Gravity applies, in principle, to all situations equally, independent of the trigger mechanism (Art. 13) used to bring the situation before the Court.[38] Legal and relative gravity differ in

---

[34] *Prosecutor v. Milutinović et al.*, Trial judgement, Volume 3 of 4, 26.2.2009 (IT-05-87-T) para. 1147; *Prosecutor v. Simić*, Trial judgement, Sentence, 17.10.2002 (IT-95-9/2-S) para. 37; *Prosecutor v. Deronjić*, Trial judgement, Sentence, 30.3.2004 (IT-02-61-S) para. 184.

[35] Holá/Smeulers/Bijlevled (2009) 22 *LJIL* 79, at 86. *See* also Murphy (2006) 17 *CLF* 281, at 296 et seq.; WCRO, *Gravity threshold* (2008), at 39 et seq.

[36] *Prosecutor v. Brima, Kamara and Kanu (AFRC trial),* Sentencing judgement, 19.7.2007 (SCSL-04-16-T) para. 11, 19; *Prosecutor v. Fofana and Kondawa (CDF trial),* Judgement on the sentencing of Moinina Fofana and Allieu Kondawa, 9.10.2007 (SCSL-04-14-T) para. 33.

[37] This part is based on the proposal developed by my doctoral student Ignaz Stegmiller (2009) 9 *ICLR* 547, at 561 et seq. For a dual use gravity *see* also McAuliffe deGuzman, 'Gravity and the legitimacy of the ICC', 2008, at 5–6; WCRO, *Gravity threshold* (2008), at 7–8, 51 et seq. For an autonomous gravity concept in the sense of article 17 (1)(d) Judge Pikis (n 32) para. 29.

[38] Apparently contrary to this view McAuliffe deGuzman, *Gravity* (2008), at 32–33 argues that in case of a (Security Council or State) referral "the Prosecutor *must* initiate an investigation of any admissible case" and "is not free to decline to investigate" on the basis of a lack of (comparative)

that the former conditions – as an admissibility criterion – the Court's exercise of jurisdiction and for that reason is to be understood strictly in a legal sense while the latter constitutes – like "the interests of victims" (Art. 53 (1) (c)) – a sub-criterion of the interests of justice clause thereby leaving the Prosecutor a broad discretion.[39] The above listed gravity related factors, following from the Ad Hoc Tribunals' case law, encompass the ICC OTP's first three sub-criteria of gravity (*scale*, *nature*, *manner of commission*) and constitute elements of legal gravity; in contrast, the *individual circumstances* refer to the concrete perpetrator and its role in the crime, i.e. they involve subjective considerations to be taken into account when analyzing the relative gravity of a concrete case (*cf.* Art. 53 (2) (c) explicitly referring to the "alleged perpetrator"). The legal-relative gravity dichotomy also determines the application of *quantitative and qualitative factors* in assessing gravity.[40] As the value and weight of qualitative factors, being vague and highly normative, are per se controversial,[41] they should primarily be applied to relative gravity and only exceptionally to legal gravity; in contrast, quantitative factors can be applied to both legal and relative gravity. The exceptional application of qualitative factors to legal gravity may be reasonable in cases where the quantitative factors alone would not overcome the admissibility threshold despite the qualitative importance of the crime, e.g., in the case of a quantitatively little, but qualitatively highly relevant commission of genocide as an inherently grave crime.[42] Last but not least, the *impact* criterion, finally adopted by the OTP Regulations,[43] also belongs to relative gravity in that it refers – like impact on victims – to the "interests of victims"

---

gravity while in case of acting *proprio motu* "he has complete discretion (. . .) as long as he abides by the requirements of jurisdiction and admissibility", i.e. the legal gravity threshold only plays a role in the latter case. Yet, this would mean that even less grave cases would have to be considered admissible if only they have been referred by a State or the Security Council. Art. 17 (1) (d) does not make this distinction. Apart from that, there is a general consensus that complementarity applies to all trigger mechanisms, including a Security Council referral (*cf.* Stigen, *Relationship* (2008), at 238 et seq.; Kleffner, *'Complementarity'* (2008), at 165–66, 213 et seq.; Pichon (2008) 8 *ICLR* 185, at 188 et seq.; Bothe (2008) 83 Friedenswarte 59, at 67).

[39]Crit. of such a broad discretion and thus of article 53 however Ohlin, in Stahn/Sluiter (eds.) 2009, 185, at 201 et seq. arguing, on the basis of a dualist individualist-retributive and collective-security theory of International Criminal Law (201 et seq.) that the ICC and its Prosecutor must only act with regard to the former leaving collective security and policy issues to the UN-Security Council (207, 209).

[40]For a both quantitative and qualitative interpretation of the term complementarity Stigen, *Relationship* (2008), at 188; for three visions of admissibility (complementarity) stressing correctly the respect for State sovereignty Burke-White/Kaplan, in Stahn/Sluiter (eds.) 2009, 17, at 91 et seq.

[41]*See* also Osiel, (2009) *The Hague Justice Portal*, at 4–5. This is the main criticism against Heller's approach (*supra* n 17), *see* Osiel, in Stahn/van den Herik (eds.) 2010, at 256 et seq. pointing, in addition, to the risk of political manipulation inherent in this approach.

[42]In this sense Heller's approach (*supra* n 17) is helpful since it elaborates the argument of quantitatively small, but qualitatively important (= grave) situations, *see* Heller, in Stahn/van den Herik (eds.) 2010, at 234–35, 243, 249.

[43]*See supra* n 11.

(Art. 53 (1) (c), 53 (2) (c)) and even broader – like impact on the community and on regional peace – to policy (interest of justice) considerations.

As to the general interpretation of legal vs. relative gravity it follows that the former should – to be understood strictly legal – be interpreted narrowly with regard to the admissibility threshold, i.e. the threshold should be low. It must be recalled that legal gravity was originally introduced with a broader subject matter jurisdiction of the Court (including, for example, treaty crimes) in mind.[44] Now, given the Court's limited jurisdiction over international core crimes, it may be argued with good reason that the "definitional" gravity of the ICC crimes entails a presumption in favor of legal gravity[45] and that the additional gravity threshold is practically only relevant with regard to war crimes.[46] Such a low legal gravity threshold would also reduce the risk that a lack of situational gravity hinders the investigation and prosecution of really grave cases.[47] In contrast, relative gravity gives the Prosecutor a broad discretion expressed by the "interests of justice" clause and thus enables him to take out comparably less grave cases. This means that the relative gravity threshold is rather high, in any case higher than the legal gravity threshold.

Taking into account the double twofold approach with regard to a case and a situation (see *supra* Chap. 4) on the one hand and legal and relative gravity on the other, the following four scenarios must be distinguished:

- *Legal* gravity with regard to *situations* pursuant to Art. 53 (1) (b), 17 (1) (d)
- *Relative* gravity with regard to *situations* under the "interests of justice" concept pursuant to Art. 53 (1) (c)
- *Legal* gravity with regard to *cases* pursuant to Art. 53 (2) (b), 17 (1) (d)
- *Relative* gravity with regard to *cases* under the "interests of justice" concept pursuant to Art. 53 (2) (c)

Both situation- and case-related *legal* gravity have a generally low threshold while situation- and case-related *relative* gravity require a high threshold.[48]

---

[44] *See* already the discussion in the Int. Law Commission ("ILC") in Yearbook of the ILC 1994, Volume I, Summary records of the meetings on the forty-sixth session, 2 May–22 July 1994 (A/CN.4/SER.A/1994) 25, para. 41, 27, para. 59; ILC Draft Statute 1994, at 32, 35–6. *See* also WCRO, *Gravity threshold* (2008), at 12 et seq.; McAuliffe deGuzman, *Gravity* (2008), at 14–5.

[45] For a general affirmation of gravity Cárdenas, 'The admissibility test before the ICC under special considerations of amnesties and truth commissions', in Kleffner/Kor (eds.) 2006, 115, at 120. For general gravity in case of genocide Cárdenas, *Zulässigkeitsprüfung* (2005), at 99; *id.*, in Werle (ed.) 2006, 239, at 244; *id.*, in Hankel (ed.) 2008, 127, at 138. For higher gravity of genocide and crimes against humanity vis-á-vis war crimes Schabas (2008) 19 *CLF* 5, at 25 et seq.

[46] McAuliffe deGuzman, *Gravity* (2008), at 45.

[47] Out of this concern WCRO, *Relevance of a situation* (2009), 28 et seq. (31, 35–36) wants to limit the application of the gravity threshold to cases (35: "... ICC should not forgo prosecuting the relevant cases solely on the ground that the situation does not involve a wider range of cases that could be prosecuted by the Court."). The same result can, however, be reached by a low threshold and/or the recourse to qualitative criteria in the sense of Heller's approach (as discussed in *supra* n 42).

[48] *See* also McAuliffe deGuzman, *Gravity* (2008), at 45.

The difference between situations and cases consists only of the scope of the factual information available to the Prosecutor when assessing gravity: in the former case it refers in a still quite abstract way to all possible crimes committed in a situation, while cases refer to more specific and individualized crimes. Examining relative gravity the Prosecutor may invoke non-legal, policy arguments for his decision not to initiate an investigation based on considerations of comparable gravity of situations or cases. At this stage, it is evident that a stricter selection must take place in light of the limited resources of the OTP and the Court as a whole. In any case, the Prosecutor must – finally setting aside his earlier practice of conflating legal and relative gravity – make clear when his decision is based on legal gravity as an admissibility threshold and when on relative gravity on the basis of the discretional prioritizing of situations or cases for policy ("interest of justice") reasons. In terms of the available criteria the difference is that in the latter case the Prosecutor may also take recourse to the already mentioned qualitative factors and, as to cases, individual circumstances (see Art. 53 (2) (b)) and the impact criterion. This allows him to make a comparable gravity analysis of all situations and cases before the Court. Thus, while the legal gravity test is limited to crime-related quantitative factors, the relative gravity analysis also embraces qualitative and subjective factors and thus enables the Prosecutor to concentrate the Court's resources on the most serious situations and, generally, on the most serious cases within each situation.[49]

5.1.3 Application to the situation in Colombia

As to Colombia the gravity standard must initially be evaluated on the basis of *quantitative criteria*, especially in light of the scale, nature and manner of the violence and crimes committed. While it is difficult to find hard and reliable data due to the complexity and intensity of the violence, the high number of undetected crimes and the lack of a nationwide information system, there still exist some quantitative indicators, especially with regard to the crimes covered by Law 975. Thus, it has been alleged that Colombia is a true *country of victims* since more than 10% of the population have been directly affected by the consequences of the armed conflict.[50] Although it is impossible to establish a consolidated and absolutely reliable number of victims, the former Chief Prosecutor himself spoke of 230,000 registered victims until 23 July 2009.[51] Clearly though, the magnitude of violence as expressed by the number of violent acts and the intensity of the conflict suggest

[49] *See* also McAuliffe deGuzman, *Gravity* (2008), at 47.

[50] Redepaz, *Víctimas* (2008), at 8.

[51] Mario Iguarán, former Prosecutor General of Colombia, during the inaugural speech of the international conference "Justicia Transicional en Colombia, 4 años en el contexto de la Ley de Justicia y Paz", Bogotá, 23 July 2009.

that the real number of victims, including the unreported ones, is much higher.[52] As to *homicides*, the National Forensic Institute has for example stated that:

> the common or simple homicide which explains 60% of violent deaths in the country has diminished. But the aggravated form of homicide, among which we find massacres or extrajudicial killings of Colombians as the result of the social conflict and the armed confrontation, the drug-trafficking and the activity of other violent actors of organized criminal structures, has increased.[53]

As to homicides constituting violations of human rights and IHL three forms have been distinguished: first, the ones of state agents or of private persons supported by the former; second, the ones resulting from the armed conflict and, third, the ones resulting from socio-political violence.[54] Between 1964 and 2007, 673,930 homicides have allegedly been perpetrated in Colombia; during the same period about 95,000 deaths as a result of armed conflict, 51,530 kidnappings, 24,579 terrorist acts and 4,499 massacres have been reported.[55]

With regard to the phenomenon of *internal displacement*, as of July 2009 the Colombian government speaks of almost 3 million displaced persons and NGOs speak of 4.6 million.[56] In any case, these are alarming figures which make Colombia probably the country with the second highest number of displaced persons after Sudan.[57] Not less worrying is the number of *forced disappearances*. According to the *Associación de familiares de detenidos desaparecidos* ("Association of family members of detained and disappeared persons", "ASFADDES") there were 7,132 disappearances between 1977 and 2004;[58] official figures report complaints of 30.710 disappereances received by family members until the end of 2009.[58a] There exist also alarming numbers of cases of *torture*[59] and of *indiscriminate attacks* due to the use of land mines and other explosive devices. According to the "International Campaign to Ban Landmines", in 2007, Colombia had the highest rate of victims caused by land mines in the world.[60]

---

[52]*See* Pizarro, http://www.verdadabierta.com/web3/reconciliacion/45-reparaciones-a-victimas/231-la-hora-de-las-victimas?format=pdf.

[53]Instituto Nacional de Medicina Legal y Ciencias Forenses, *Forensis* (2008), at 26 ("el homicidio común o simple que explica cerca del 60% del total de muertes violentas en el país ha disminuido. Pero el homicidio agravado entre el cual encontramos las masacres y ejecuciones extrajudiciales de colombianos como resultado del conflicto social y la confrontación armada, del narcotráfico y la acción de otros agentes violentos de estructuras delincuenciales organizadas, se incremento"., translation by the author).

[54]*Ibidem,* at 25.

[55]*See* Otero, *Cifras del conflicto* (2007).

[56]*See* internal Displacement Monitoring Centre (iDMC), http://www.internal-displacement.org/8025708F004CE90B/(httpCountries)/CB6FF99A94F70AED802570A7004CEC41?OpenDocument (last visited 28 December 2009).

[57]AI, *Leave us in peace* (2008), at 38.

[58]*See* Otero, *Cifras del conflicto* (2007), 109.

[58a]Figure provided by Comité Interinstitucional de Justicia y Paz, *Matriz* (2009).

[59]*See* AI, *Leave us in peace* (2008), at 40.

[60]*See* Landmine Monitor Report 2007.

Against this background it is little surprising that the Colombian (judicial) authorities themselves have recognized the gravity of the situation. On the one hand, the high courts (*Corte Constitucional* and *Corte Suprema de Justicia*) have characterized the crimes as "serious" or even "most serious".[61] The Constitutional Court has defined the *concept of gravity* as acts "which entail grave assaults on human rights and international humanitarian law and a grave threat for the peace and the collective conscience."[62] Crimes against humanity are considered paradigmatic examples of such grave acts since their commission "alters significantly the basic consensus of civilized nations and constitutes the negation of the basic principles of the prevailing social order."[63] On the other hand, the *Procuraduría General de la Nación* refers to the members of the demobilized illegal armed groups as the "authors of grave damages against the personal integrity, of massacres, selective executions" etc.[64] The IACHR has repeatedly expressed great concern by referring to the gravity of the crimes and to the grave breaches of IHL. It has emphasized the scale and repeated commission of the crimes and the terror caused to the civil population.[65] Last but not least, international human rights organizations have confirmed the nature, scale and systematic character of the crimes committed in Colombia.[66]

For all these reasons, there can be no doubt that the Colombian *situation* – seen from a general perspective – overcomes the threshold of gravity of Art. 17 (1) (d), understood as *legal (non discretionary)* gravity.[67] However, that does not necessarily mean that all *cases* covered by Law 975 reach this (legal) threshold. For the participation of the members of the illegal armed groups in human rights or IHL violations may differ in each concrete case and according to their position within the respective organization. Thus, some cases of low rank members of paramilitary groups – the so called "foot soldiers" (*miembros rasos*) – who only execute superior

---

[61]*See* Constitutional Court (n 8 in Chap. 1), sección 6.2.2.1.7.6. ("delitos más graves"), 6.2.2.1.7.11 ("delitos que la humanidad entera ha considerado de la mayor gravedad"), 6.2.2.1.7.20. ("múltiples y graves delitos", "terror"), 6.2.2.1.7.24. ("delitos, inclusive tan graves como masacres, secuestros masivos, asesinatos y desapariciones. . ."), 6.2.2.1.7.29, 6.2.2.2.5. and 6.2.3.1.5.4. ("delitos de suma gravedad"), 6.2.3.3.4.3. ("grave criminalidad"); Supreme Court, *supra* n 16, V 2.6. ("graves atentados a la humanidad"), V 3.5. ("graves violaciones a los derechos humanos").

[62]Constitutional Court [21 March 2003] judgment T-249, MP Eduardo Montealegre Lynett, at 16.3. ("Los hechos punibles que revisten dicha gravedad, serán aquellos que impliquen graves atentados contra los derechos humanos y el derecho internacional humanitario y una severa puesta en peligro de la paz colectiva".; translation by the author).

[63]*Ibid.*, at 17 ("altera significativamente el mínimo orden de la civilización y supone la ignorancia de los principios fundadores del orden social dominante"; translation by the author).

[64]Procuraduría General, *Desmovilización y reinserción* (2008), at 128 ("autores de graves daños a la integridad personal, las masacres, ejecuciones selectivas"; translation by the autor).

[65]IACHR, *Report demobilization* (2004), para. 59, 66, 11.

[66]HRW, *Breaking the Grip?* (2008), 131; AI, *Targeting Civilians* (2008), 25.

[67]To be distinguished from *relative (discretionary)* gravity only applicable in relation to article 53, *see supra* Sect. 5.1.2.

orders and are easily replaceable may not reach the gravity threshold. These persons may not even be investigated or tried under Law 975 since their cases may fall under the opportunity principle and thus be suspended or terminated.[68] For, in fact, with this principle it is suggested that the mere low-level-membership in an illegal armed group is not sufficiently grave to trigger a public interest for criminal proceedings. It must not be overlooked, however, that any conduct going beyond mere membership does not fall under the opportunity principle. While these low-level persons are, in principle, not of interest for the ICC since it aims at the most responsible,[69] on the national level it is still of relevance to establish the cases which are sufficiently grave so as to be investigated and tried. In this regard it may be decisive to determine the importance of the respective member's participation in the group with regard to its most serious offences. If the respective member's participation amounts to more than a simple conspiracy in the sense discussed above[70] the opportunity principle must not be applied. We have to come back to this matter with regard to the possible unwillingness or inability of the Colombian state to investigate or prosecute serious crimes.[71]

5.2 Complementarity *stricto sensu*

In the case of complementarity *stricto sensu* it follows from the wording of Art. 17 (1) ("... the Court shall determine that a case is inadmissible where ...") that admissibility is *presumed*[72] and that this presumption may be refuted by – apart from insufficient gravity (Art. 17 (1) (d)) – some action on the part of the respective State with regard to its investigation and prosecution obligations (Art. 17 (1) (a)–(c)). Clearly, this action must be examined more closely with a view to the requirements established in Art. 17 (1) (a), (b) and (c) in connection with Art. 20 (3). If the respective State action fulfills these requirements the case or situation are inadmissible. If, in contrast, the state action indicates or entails unwillingness or inability in the sense of Art. 17 (2) and (3) the situation or case must be declared admissible. If, on the other hand, such action is lacking at all, i.e. in the case of (total) inaction, admissibility may be presumed without extensive further reasoning. Thus, the complementarity test *stricto sensu* may be structured in a threefold way:[73]

---

[68] *See supra* n 22 et seq. in Chap. 1 and main text.

[69] *See* Ambos, in Ambos/Large/Wierda (eds.), 2009, at 51 (para. 21), 70–1 (para. 36).

[70] *Supra* n 19 in Chap. 1 and main text.

[71] *See infra* n 242 et seq. with main text.

[72] *Cf.* Cárdenas, *Zulässigkeitsprüfung* (2005), at 116; also Meißner, *Zusammenarbeit* (2003), at 70–1; Kleffner, *Complementarity* (2008), at 104 et seq. Contrary apparently Gómez Pardo (2009) *Revista Debate Interamericano* 123, at 141 without however analyzing article 17 properly.

[73] *See* also Stegmiller, Complementarity thoughts (2010) 21 *CLF* (forthcoming). For a twofold text merging the first two requirements into one El Zeidy, *Complementarity* (2008), at 161.

- First, situations and cases are admissible if the State remains inactive (*admissibility due to total State inaction, infra* Sect. 5.2.1)
- Second, if the State develops some activity, a case may be inadmissible pursuant to Art. 17 (1) (a)–(c) and 20 (3) (*inadmissibility due to State action, infra* Sect. 5.2.2)
- Third, as an exception to the inadmissibility mentioned before, despite or because of the State activity, unwillingness or inability on the part of the State is established pursuant to Art. 17 (2) and (3) (*admissibility due to unwillingness or inability, infra* Sect. 5.2.3)

5.2.1 Admissibility due to total State inaction

5.2.1.1 General considerations

International treaty and customary law provides for a general duty of States to investigate, prosecute and punish international core crimes.[74] While this duty already existed before the ICC Statute, at least regarding the State parties of the respective treaties and/or regarding the respective customary law norms, the ICC Statute has reinforced it with regard to the Statute crimes and with regard to its state parties.[75] Consequently, if a State party remains inactive in the face of genocide, crimes against humanity or war crimes within the meaning of Art. 5–8 of the ICC Statute it fails to comply with its duty flowing both from the Statute and from general international law. This inaction alone must then make the case admissible under Art. 17.[76] This also follows, as correctly held by the Lubanga PTC,[77] from an *e contrario* interpretation of Art. 17 (1) (a)–(c) for if this provision requires at least some action (initial investigative steps)[78] for a case to be declared inadmissible, no action whatsoever makes the case admissible without further ado.[79]

---

[74] *See* Ambos, in Ambos/Large/Wierda (eds.) 2009, at 29 et seq. (para. 8).

[75] Ambos, in Ambos/Large/Wierda (eds.) 2009, at 31 (para. 8).

[76] *Cf.* Benzing (2003) 7 *MPUNYB* 591, at 105 ("(. . .) effective prosecution, and the purpose of ending impunity, would clearly be significantly undermined if cases in which States remained completely inactive were inadmissible") and 115 ("complete inaction on the national level would thus allow the ICC to take up a case without having to enter into an assessment of the admissibility criteria in Article 17 (1) (a) to (c)").

[77] *Prosecutor v. Lubanga* (n 2) para. 29 with fn. 19.

[78] Kleffner, *Complementarity* (2008), at 105.

[79] *See* also ICC-OTP, *Complementarity in practice* (2003), paras. 17–8: "[. . .] First, the most straightforward scenario is where no State has initiated any investigation (the inaction scenario). In such a scenario, none of the alternatives of articles 17 (1) (a)–(c) are satisfied and there is no impediment to admissibility. Thus, there is no need to examine the factors of unwillingness or inability; the case is simply admissible under the clear terms of Article 17". *See* also Stigen, *Relationship* (2008), at 199 et seq. (201); Kleffner, *Complementarity* (2008), at 104–05, 342; El Zeidy, *Complementarity* (2008), at 106, 161, 230, 318; Schabas (2008) 19 *CLF* 5, at 7–8;

In practice, the OTP heavily relies on the dichotomy of inaction-some action[80] and alleges an "*uncontested admissibility*" in the former case.[81] Also, PTC I held in *Lubanga* that "in the absence of any acting State, the Chamber need not make any analysis of unwillingness or inability."[82] PTC II confirmed the admissibility of the case against Kony et al., invoking its *proprio motu* powers under Art. 19 (1),[83] because the scenario of "total inaction" has not substantially changed given that the February 2008 Agreement and its Annex providing for the establishment of a special division of the Ugandan High Court have still not been implemented.[84] Thus, it seems to be settled that if no State is acting in relation to a specific case a further analysis of unwillingness or inability is not warranted.[85] In *Katanga* and *Chui*, Trial Chamber II and the Appeal Chamber recently acknowledged this automatic admissibility in the case of inaction without analyzing in-depth unwillingness or inability and arguing that this does not affect an additional determination of *ne bis in idem* and gravity in accordance with Art. 17 (1)–(c) and (d).[86]

Inaction in this sense, albeit an empirical not normative concept,[87] is not limited to factual inaction but also extends to "*normative*" *inaction*, i.e., situations where inactivity is due to normative (procedural) obstacles, in particular a blanket

---

Williams/Schabas, in Triffterer (ed.) 2008, article 17, mn 23; Stahn (2008) 19 *CLF* 87, at 105–6; Carnero Rojo (2005) 18 *LJIL* 829, at 833; Ambos, in Ambos/Large/Wierda (eds.) 2009, at 72 para. 37; crit. however Schabas (2008) 6 *JICJ* 731, at 757.

[80]*Cf.* Seils/Wierda, *ICC and conflict mediation* (2005) 1, 6; *see* also Burke-White (2008) 49 *HarvIntLJ* 53, at 78; regarding the Darfur investigation *see* Pichon (2008) 8 *ICLR* 185, at 219–20.

[81]*See*, for instance, ICC-OTP, *Eight Report Security Council* (2008), para. 13: "All three Prosecution cases remain admissible. There are no proceedings in the Sudan against Ahmad Harun and Ali Kushayb, against Omar Al Bashir, or against the three rebel commanders of the Haskanita attack". *See* also Sheng, (2006) 1249 bepress Legal Series 1, at 5; Schabas, in Stahn/Sluiter (eds.) 2009, 229, at 236–37.

[82]*Prosecutor v. Lubanga and Ntaganda* (n 19 in Chap. 4), para. 41. *See* on this case Smith (2008) 8 *ICLR* 331, at 335–36; El Zeidy, *Complementarity* (2008), at 228 et seq.

[83]*Prosecutor v. Kony* et al. (*supra* n 2 in Part II), para. 44.

[84]*Ibid.*, para. 49 et seq. (52). For a discussion of the Ugandan situation *see* Burke-White/Kaplan, in Stahn/Sluiter (eds.) 2009, 17, at 79 et seq., 103 et seq. It is important to note in this respect that the Amnesty Act 2000 (Laws of Uganda vol. XII ch. 294, available at www.c-r.org/our-work/accord/northern-uganda/documents/2000_Jan_The_Amnesty_Act.doc (last visited 7 October 2009) is in fact a blanket amnesty since it is granting full immunity from prosecution to any LRA rebel who "renounces and abandons involvement in the war or armed rebellion" (sect. 4 (1)) and this abandoning of the fighting is an inherent condition of any amnesty deal.

[85]*See* already Ambos, in Bohlander (ed.) 2007, 429, at 448; *see* also El Zeidy, *Complementarity* (2008), at 161.

[86]*Prosecutor v. Katanga and Chui*, Motifs (n 20 Chap. 4), paras. 21, 81.; *Prosecutor v. Katanga and Chui* [25 September 2009], Judgment on the Appeal of Mr. Germain Katanga against the Oral Decision of Trial Chamber II of 12 June on the Admissibility of the Case (ICC-01704-01/07 OA 8), para. 73 et seq., 96–7, 111–13.

[87]Ambos, in Ambos/Large/Wierda (eds.) 2009, at 72 (para. 37).

amnesty (which is generally inadmissible).[88] In this situation there are two possibilities: First, a (substantive) investigation is *a limine* precluded since the investigative organs are only authorized to apply the respective procedural obstacle to the case at hand and terminate the proceedings if it is applicable; this case can be considered as one of (*a priori*) inaction.[89] Secondly, some investigative steps are undertaken and it is then decided not to prosecute the case (*a posteriori* inaction).[90] This case falls under Art. 17 (1)–(b)[91] and its admissibility depends on the unwillingness or inability test to be analyzed below (Sect. 5.2.2).

5.2.1.2 Application to the situation in Colombia

The very existence of the Justice and Peace Procedure demonstrates that the Colombian State is undertaking considerable efforts to deal with the crimes committed by illegal armed groups. In addition, while Law 975 is a new and innovative instrument in Colombia's long lasting peace process, it is not the only one but part of a broader normative and political framework which, notwithstanding its shortcomings and deficits, amounts to a great deal of State activity in order to come to terms with the violence related to the armed conflict. It is fair to say that the general commitment to protect human rights and to counter impunity in today's Colombia is due to a great extent to the proactive jurisprudence of the IACourtHR and the Colombian High Courts. The Constitutional Court itself acknowledges that the Colombian State has an obligation to investigate and punish international crimes and that this obligation also results from the international community's commitment, expressed by the principle of complementarity, to punish these crimes.[92] In a similar vein, the Supreme Court has repeatedly stressed this obligation in its decisions about extraditions and Law 975.[93]

---

[88] *See* for a discussion Ambos, in Ambos/Large/Wierda (eds.) 2009, at 54 et seq. (para. 24 et seq.) distinguishing between blanket (inadmissible) and conditional (potentially admissible) amnesties. For a similar approach with five criteria to evaluate amnesties Stigen, *Relationship* (2008), at 451 et seq.; also Razesberger, *Complementarity* (2006), at 171–72, 182 arguing that "self-issued amnesties" cannot block admissibility; Olásolo, in Almqvist/Espósito (eds.) 2009, at 268 et seq.

[89] Ambos, in Ambos/Large/Wierda (eds.) 2009, at 75–76, para. 40; *see* also Stigen, *Relationship* (2008), at 322; Kleffner, *Complementarity* (2008), at 264; Razesberger, *Complementarity* (2006), at 160; Burke-White/Kaplan, in Stahn/Sluiter (eds.) 2009, 17, at 104 (regarding Uganda); Olásolo, in Almqvist/Espósito (eds.) 2009, at 270.

[90] For the *a priori-a posteriori* distinction *see* Olásolo, *Triggering procedure* (2005), at 149–50, 166; *id.*, in Almqvist/Espósito (eds.) 2009, 260–61.

[91] *See* also Benzing (2003) 7 *MPUNYB* 591, at 601 with fn. 50; Kleffner, *Complementarity* (2008), at 264; Werle, in Müller et al. (eds.) 2009, 791, at 804; Olásolo, in Almqvist/Espósito (eds.) 2009, at 271 et seq.

[92] Constitutional Court [20 January 2003] judgment C-004, MP. Eduardo Montealegre Lynett, para. 26.

[93] *See* e.g. Supreme Court [31 July 2008] Rad. 28503, MP Javier Zapata Ortiz; *id.* [23 September 2008] Rad. 29298, MP María del Rosario González de Lemos; *id.* [19 July 2009] Rad. 30451, MP Yesid Ramírez Bastidas; *id.* [21 September 2009] Rad. 32022, MP Yesid Ramírez Bastidas.

While, against this background, it is impossible to speak of a total inactivity in a *factual* sense on the part of the Colombian State, it must nevertheless be critically examined if there exist *normative* (procedural) *mechanisms* which impede the initiation of proceedings or facilitate their irregular termination. Thus, *in casu*, the extradition of paramilitary commanders and the application of the opportunity principle to low-level group members raise the question if these mechanisms unduly limit or even undermine the duty to investigate and prosecute within the framework of Law 975. In other words, is it reasonable to argue that these mechanisms lead to the neutralization of the objectives of justice and peace and thus promote state inactivity in concrete and grave cases covered by Law 975?

While it may well be argued, admittedly from a quite formalistic perspective, that the *extraditions* do no affect the participation of the extradited commanders in the process of Law 975 since they have not been excluded from that process, it is difficult to deny that, in practical terms, the absence of these "most responsible" affects the process adversely in multiple ways.[94] The crucial question is whether the extradition of the commanders amounts to a *de facto* exclusion from the Justice and Peace process and thus turns into a decisive obstacle for the process as a whole. While according to the coordinator of the UJP the extradition has neither impeded the access to the extradited commanders nor their continued presence during the (free version) hearings,[95] others have stressed the climate of intimidation and other difficulties which hamper the continued participation of the extradited commanders and which may lead progressively to an increasing decline of declarations finally causing the death of the process because of the "removal of the subject matter".[96] In a similar vein the Supreme Court recently warned that extraditions impede the achievement of truth, justice and reparation; they especially paralyze the discovery of the truth and obstruct the work of the Colombian justice.[97] The Court's appreciation has been affirmed by the declarations of paramilitary commanders who have denounced multiple problems concerning their continuous participation in the process.[98] In sum, it is fair to conclude that while the access to the extradited commanders has become certainly more difficult and ultimately depends on the generousity of the US authorities it is equally true that none of the commanders has formally been excluded from Law 975 and they are, in fact, more or less actively participating. It would thus be premature to argue that the extraditions have

---

[94]*See* already *supra* n 39 et seq. in Chap. 3 and main text and Ambos et al., *Justicia y Paz* (2010), para. 319.

[95]Interview with Luis González, Bogotá, 13 August 2009.

[96]*See* http://www.verdadabierta.com/web3/justicia-y-paz/1588-ila-ley-del-silencio-semana ("por sustracción de materia"; last visited 8 October 2009).

[97]Supreme Court, *supra* n 41 in Chap. 3 (Concepto de la Corte, 10. Fundamentos para emitir concepto desfavorable a la solicitud de extradición).

[98]*See* http://www.verdadabierta.com/web31/justicia-y-paz/extraditados/1695-cartas-de-don-berna-y-de-el-mellizo-desde-estados-unidos (last visited 8 October 2009); http://www.verdadabierta.com/web31/justicia-y-paz/versiones/1705-mancuso-suspende-confesiones-en-justicia-y-paz (last visited 8 October 2009).

amounted to a state of inactivity towards the extradited paramilitaries. A different matter is, though, a possible lack of willingness or ability expressed by these extraditions. This will be discussed later.

As to the *opportunity principle* it must be asked whether its concrete application turns out to be an impediment for the investigation of international crimes subject to the ICC Statute. From a pure formal perspective this is certainly not the case since the corresponding provision requires that there are no other pending investigations against the group member going beyond his membership and his sworn declaration to that effect.[99] Additionally, the provision contains an explicit prohibition to apply the opportunity principle to serious violations of human rights and IHL. Thus, again, the issue is more of a practical nature and comes down to the question if the (future) beneficiaries of the opportunity principle have received the benefit lawfully only for membership or unlawfully for (additional) serious crimes thereby bypassing the justice and peace procedure. In the latter case the question of a lack of willingness and ability arises but it must be borne in mind that the investigation against the respective persons could and should be reopened.[100]

In sum, it can be concluded that there is *neither a factual nor normative scenario of State inactivity.*[101] The existing (factual) procedural obstacles do not amount to inactivity or a substantial deactivation of the institutional apparatus available to investigate and prosecute international core crimes. Procedural difficulties or obstacles must not be confused with the concept of total inactivity, be it for factual or normative reasons. It is in the context of unwillingness or inability where these obstacles must be revisited taking into account the political, operational, administrative and management-related conditions of the criminal proceedings under Law 975.

5.2.2 Inadmissibility due to State action (Art. 17 (1) (a)–(c) and 20 (3))

5.2.2.1 General considerations

By distinguishing between investigation (Art. 17 (1) (a)), prosecution (Art. 17 (1) (b)) and trial (Art. 17 (1) (c) referring to Art. 20 (3)) the provision aims to cover *all procedural stages* from investigation to a court trial. The criteria are considered to be exhaustive.[102] The distinction in the various procedural stages corresponds to the

---

[99] *See supra* n 24 in Chap. 1 and main text.

[100] *Supra* n 25 in Chap. 1 and main text.

[101] For the same result Olásolo, in Almqvist/Espósito (eds.) 2009, at 282.

[102] At first sight, the text does not point in either direction. However, no open wording – like "including" – was used that would have clarified an open nature, and, moreover, the word "considers" has been interpreted as deliberately limiting the criteria to the mentioned factors, Benzing (2003) 7 *MPUNYB* 591, at 606; Meißner, *Zusammenarbeit* (2003), at 72–3; Gropengießer/Meißner (2005) 5 *ICLR* 267, 282; Kleffner, *Complementarity* (2008), at 104.

different moment of application of possible exemptions from prosecution or punishment. An amnesty, for example, normally impedes, as just discussed, a prosecution (subpara. (b)) or even already an investigation (subpara. (a)), while a pardon is a typical post-conviction exemption only applicable after a trial (subpara. (c));[103] such a post-conviction measure can hardly constitute a ground for admissibility since it will be difficult to demonstrate that it was taken to shield the person concerned from criminal responsibility (Art. 17 (1) (c) in connection with Art. 20 (3) (a)).[104] The implicit *temporal distinction* as to the *procedural stage* of the investigation[105] is of secondary importance since ultimately the admissibility depends on the unwillingness and inability test referred to in both subparas. (a) and (b) and also in subpara. (c) by way of the reference to the "upwards" *ne bis in idem*[106] in Art. 20 (3).[107]

The provision presupposes some *State action*,[108] more concretely that the case is "being investigated or prosecuted" (Art. 17 (1) (a)) and, if there is enough evidence, ultimately tried.[109] The investigation and prosecution requirements must be read together[110] since, in any case, once an investigation is finished a decision to prosecute or not to prosecute must be taken. In other words, while an investigation in the sense of subpara. (a) may block the intervention of the ICC for a certain period of time (namely, as long as the case is "being investigated"), afterwards a decision in favor or against prosecution must be taken and in this precise moment Art. 17 (1) (b) becomes applicable.[111] In case of a decision in favour of prosecution

---

[103] Ambos, in Ambos/Large/Wierda (eds.) 2009, at 74 para. 39; *see* also Stigen, *Relationship* (2008), at 429–30 (discussing amnesty).

[104] *See* also Stigen, *Relationship* (2008), at 334–35; Kleffner, *Complementarity* (2008), at 266–67 criticizing the respective lacuna of article 17 in case of clemency measures without retroactive effect as to the validity of the conviction.

[105] *See* Ambos, in Ambos/Large/Wierda (eds.) 2009, at 73, para. 38.

[106] El Zeidy (2002) 32 *MichJIntL* 869, at 931; Kleffner, *Complementarity* (2008), at 118–9; Meyer (2006) 6 *ICLR* 549, 554; van den Wyngaert/Ongena, in Cassese/Gaeta/Jones (eds.) 2002, 705, at 724 et seq.

[107] I made this point less forcefully earlier in Ambos, in Ambos/Large/Wierda (eds.) 2009, at 74, para. 39. For this reason it is, for example, of secondary importance if the investigation must be completed (*see* Kleffner, *Complementarity* (2008), at 117) or, with regard to para. (1)(c), the local remedies be exhausted (*ibid.*, at 124–25).

[108] Benzing (2003) 7 *MPUNYB* 591, at 600–1 with fn. 48; Kleffner, in Kleffner/Kor (eds.) 2006, at 79, 82.

[109] HRW, *Benchmarks* (2007), 4 et seq. requires, apart from credible, impartial and independent investigation and prosecution and penalties that reflect the gravity of the crimes also the rigorous adherence to international fair trial standards. The trial conditions are however irrelevant for the question of admissibility, *cf.* recently *Prosecutor v. Katanga and Chui*, Motifs (n 20 Chap. 4), paras. 83 et seq. (84).

[110] *See* already Ambos, in Ambos/Large/Wierda (eds.) 2009, at 74, para. 39.

[111] This temporal aspect has apparently been overlooked by Cárdenas, *Zulässigkeitsprüfung* (2005), at 159 et seq. who distinguishes too artificially between investigation and prosecution and therefore applies Art. 17 (1) (a) too schematically to an amnesty.

the decision-making authority shifts to the trial judge[112] and Art. 17 (1) (c) becomes applicable.

While the trial requirement of subpara. (c) poses little problem (apart from the upwards *ne bis in idem* test of Art. 20 (3) which refers back to the unwillingness standard of Art. 17 (2) to be dealt with below), it is controversial and crucial how (strictly) the terms "investigations" and "prosecutions" in subpara. (a) and (b) are to be interpreted. As to the *investigation requirement*, it is debatable whether a criminal investigation by the respective criminal justice organs is necessary or alternative, even non-judicial forms of investigation,[113] in particular a (effective) Truth and Reconciliation Commission ("TRC"),[114] would suffice.[115] A literal interpretation does not clarify the issue since, on the one hand, the term "investigation" only implies a systematic and careful inquiry[116] and, on the other hand, the ICC Statute neither states that a "criminal" investigation is necessary[117] nor does it deal with alternative forms of accountability.[118] It seems clear, though, that the "investigation" must be carried out by state organs, i.e., non judicial organs like a TRC must at least be set up and supported by the state,[119] since the duty to investigate and prosecute rests upon the state (see Sect. 5.2.1). Apart from that, a systematic and teleological interpretation of Art. 17 indicates that the *objective* of any "investigation" is criminal prosecution or adjudication, namely to avoid that the suspect be shielded "from criminal responsibility" (Art. 17 (2) (a)) and "to bring the person concerned to justice" (Art. 17 (2) (b) and (c)).[120] While this does not exclude a *preliminary* investigation by a TRC with respective powers (i.e. to recommend criminal proceedings)[121] and indeed the wording of Art. 17 (1) (a) ("being investigated")

---

[112]Meißner, *Zusammenarbeit* (2003), at 77.

[113]On these *see* Ambos, in Ambos/Large/Wierda (eds.) 2009, at 40 et seq. (para. 12 et seq.).

[114]On the criteria that such an effective TRC must fulfill *see* Ambos, in Ambos/Large/Wierda (eds.) 2009, at 40 et seq. (46) (para. 13 et seq. [16]).

[115]The question is left open by Robinson (2003) 14 *EJIL* 481, at 499–500, but his general flexible approach indicates that he takes the "slightly broader approach" discussed by himself; undecided also Benzing (2003) 7 *MPUNYB* 591, at 602 and El Zeidy, *Complementarity* (2008), at 315; for Stigen, *Relationship* (2008), at 211 punishment must be "an option".

[116]*See* for a definition Stigen, *Relationship* (2008), at 203.

[117]Stahn (2005) 3 *JICJ* 695, at 697; Scharf (1999) 32 *CornJIntL* 507, at 525; Bartelt (2005) 43 *AVR* 187, 206; Majzub (2002) 3 *MelbJIntL* 247, 267; Razesberger, *Complementarity* (2006), at 180.

[118]Meyer, (2006) 6 *ICLR*, at 565.

[119]*See* also Cárdenas, *Zulässigkeitsprüfung* (2005), at 177, 183; for a judicial investigation also El Zeidy, *Complementarity* (2008), at 315.

[120]In this sense also Gavron (2002) 51 *ICLQ* 91, at 111 arguing that "to bring someone to justice" is to be interpreted in the legal, not wider moral sense. Stricter even Holmes, in Lee (ed.) 1999, 41, at 77: "Statute's provisions on complementarity are intended to refer to criminal investigations". In the same vein Kleffner, *Complementarity* (2008), at 268 et seq. (270).

[121]A good example is a Commission of Inquiry as the Israeli Kahan Commission established to investigate the responsibility of Israeli government and military officials, including the then Minster of Defense Ariel Sharon, for the atrocities committed in the Sabra and Shatila refugee camps in Lebanon in September 1982 since it had, pursuant to the Israeli Commissions of Inquiry

leaves room for such alternative investigations,[122] their ultimate objective must always be a criminal prosecution *stricto sensu*[123] where the legal and factual prerequisites of such a prosecution are fulfilled.[124] In turn, this means that investigations of a general nature about past events which do not individualize responsibility and therefore cannot serve as basis for a criminal prosecution or adjudication do not satisfy the investigation requirement of Art. 17. In sum, as a minimum, a *systematic inquiry* into the facts and circumstances of the case,[125] the already mentioned initial or *minimal investigative steps*,[126] with a view to a criminal prosecution are required. For this reason, it seems to be more adequate to evaluate alternative justice mechanisms within the framework of the interest of justice clause of Art. 53 (1) (c) and (2) (c).

This interpretation is confirmed by the second requirement, the *decision to prosecute*.[127] Such a decision can only be taken if a substantial investigation of *concrete* acts and *individual* suspects has been carried out. In other words, a decision to prosecute presupposes a criminal or at least individualized investigation, which precedes and prepares it.[128] Clearly, prosecution refers to criminal prosecution[129] but not the prosecution itself, only the "decision" to prosecute is

Law of 1968 (reprinted in English in (1983) 22 *ILM*, at 658), the authority to recommend criminal prosecution.

[122] *See* also Seibert-Fohr (2003) 7 *MPUNYB* 553, at 569 and Stahn (2005) 3 *JICJ* 695, at 697, 711 arguing against the requirement of a criminal investigation since it is not expressly contained in Art. 17. In a similar vein Cárdenas, *Zulässigkeitsprüfung* (2005), at 58–9, 101; *id.*, in Kleffner/Kor (eds.) 2006, 115, at 129; Razesberger, *Complementarity* (2006), at 180–81. Too restrictive Meißner, *Zusammenarbeit* (2003), at 76 requiring investigations within the framework of criminal proceedings; also Schomburg/Nemitz, in Schomburg/Lagodny/Gleß/Hackner (eds.) 2006, 1730 against an upward *ne bis in idem* effect (towards international courts).

[123] In this sense also Seibert-Fohr (2003) 7 *MPUNYB* 553, at 569 linking the investigation to the prosecution requirement; also Stigen, *Relationship* (2008), at 203; Kleffner, *Complementarity* (2008), at 269 and Gropengießer/Meißner (2005) 5 *ICLR* 267, at 287 arguing that "proceedings which do not have the *quality of a criminal proceeding* cannot rule out prosecution by the Court" (emphasis added); similarly Cárdenas, *Zulässigkeitsprüfung* (2005), at 137 stressing the need of criminal prosecutions after the TRC's work has been finished; conc. (modifying his earlier position) Robinson, (2003) 14 *EJIL*, at 144–5 (possibility of a criminal prosecution after investigation).

[124] *See* also Stahn (2005) 3 *JICJ* 695, at 711–12.

[125] Cárdenas, *Zulässigkeitsprüfung* (2005), at 58; *id.*, in Kleffner/Kor (eds.) 2006, 115, at 117, 119; Murphy (2006) 3 Eyes on the ICC 33, at 44. *See* also Stahn (2005) 3 *JICJ* 695, at 710; Seibert-Fohr (2003) 7 *MPUNYB* 553, at 588; Stigen, *Relationship* (2008), at 203.

[126] *See supra* n 78 and main text.

[127] *See* already Ambos, in Ambos/Large/Wierda (eds.) 2009, at 76, para. 41.

[128] *See* also Stahn (2005) 3 *JICJ* 695, at 712.

[129] *Cf.* Cárdenas, *Zulässigkeitsprüfung* (2005), at 58, 101; Stigen, *Relationship* (2008), at 205; Kleffner, *Complementarity* (2008), at 268–69.

required. This presupposes that the organ that takes this decision must at least have two options, namely either to prosecute or not to prosecute.[130]

5.2.2.2 Application to the situation in Colombia

There seems to be little doubt that the procedure under Law 975 complies with both the *investigation/prosecution* and *trial* requirements of Art. 17.[131] As shown above in the first part of this study, Law 975 provides for a full-fledged criminal procedure whose main difference with the ordinary criminal procedure consists of its inquisitorial nature and reliance on the demobilised person's full confession as the starting point and basis of the subsequent verification procedure. In any case, the facts of the case must be investigated by the UJP. The Supreme Court even requires extending the investigation beyond the concrete case to the structural aspects (context of the crimes, structure of the group involved etc.).[132] On the basis of the factual findings emerging from the confession and its subsequent verification the charges will be formulated and the person concerned tried by the competent judges.

In addition, it must not be overlooked that the special Justice and Peace procedure does not foreclose the possibility of subjecting the persons concerned to an ordinary procedure. In fact, the person may be excluded from the Justice and Peace procedure if the prosecutor or the judges consider that he did not comply with its requirements. While this exclusion will only be taken as ultimate resort, its mere possibility shows that the State is ultimately ready and willing to "do justice" by ordinary means. Whether this – despite the multiple problems and difficulties of the process identified above[133] – ultimately satisfies the complementarity requirements is a question of the *unwillingness* and *inability* test to be analyzed in the following section.

5.2.3 Admissibility due to unwillingness or inability (Art. 17 (2) and (3))

5.2.3.1 Preliminary remarks

If one understands, as suggested here, complementarity *stricto sensu* in a threefold way, all state action mentioned in Art. 17 (1) (a)–(c) only creates a presumption of inadmissibility which may be refuted by the establishment of unwillingness or inability pursuant to Art. 17 (2) and (3). This also holds true for subpara. (1) (c)

---

[130]Robinson, (2003) 14 *EJIL*, at 500; *see* also Stahn (2005) 18 *LJIL* 425, at 463.

[131]Conc. as to the investigation requirement Valiñas, in Stahn/van den Herik (eds.) 2010, at 281.

[132]*Supra* n 48 and main text.

[133]*See* Chap. 3.

since it introduces the criteria of subpara. 2 (a)–(c) by taking recourse to Art. 20 (3). Thus, in sum, to declare a situation or case admissible ultimately requires the establishment of unwillingness (subpara. 1 (a)–(c) in connection with para. 2) or inability (subpara. 1 (a), (b) in connection with para. 3) on the part of the respective national justice system. The burden of proof rests, as a rule, on the Prosecutor, i.e., he must prove the unwillingness or inability.[134] Yet, the Court depends on the respective State's cooperation in providing the information regarding the action taken by its national justice system (Rules 51, 55 (2) RPE); in fact, in light of the inaction scenario (Sect. 5.2.1) and the ensuing admissibility, one may even argue that it is in the best interest of the State concerned to provide compelling evidence demonstrating that it is acting accordingly;[135] in this sense, the burden falls on this State.[136]

The interpretation of the criteria contained in paras. 2 and 3 is controversial and unsettled, not the least because they are highly normative and open to value judgment.[137] Some scholars propose an alternative approach merging unwillingness and inability into one requirement.[138] There was and is also a controversy whether the criteria are to be understood objectively, subjectively or both.[139] It seems to be clear, though, that the term "*genuinely*" (para. (1) (a), (b)) – "the least objectionable word" – was inserted to give the unwillingness/inability test a more concrete and objective meaning.[140] Yet, the term also requires – rather subjectively – good faith and seriousness[141] on the part of the respective State with regard to

---

[134]*See* El Zeidy, *Complementarity* (2008), at 163; also OTP, *Complementarity* (2003), para. 55, 56, which however, as the rule, propose to impose the burden on the party raising a specific issue (para. 54).

[135]Razesberger, *Complementarity* (2006), at 53–4 (but later, at 55–6, arguing for the deletion of Rule 51); Burke-White/Kaplan, in Stahn/Sluiter (eds.) 2009, 17, at 110.

[136]El Zeidy, *Complementarity* (2008), at 163; OTP, *Complementarity* (2003), paras. 54 and 56 indicating examples of a shifting of the burden.

[137]*See* already Ambos, in Ambos/Large/Wierda (eds.) 2009, at 76 para. 42 with further references; in the same vein El Zeidy, *Complementarity* (2008), at 236; Bothe (2008) 83 *Friedenswarte* 59, at 65.

[138]*See* Kleffner, *Complementarity* (2008), at 161, 342 suggesting the "effectiveness of the national proceedings" as an overall criterion.

[139]*See* on the drafting process of the OTP policy paper Dicker, Session 1: Transcript, in ICC-OTP, *First public hearing* (2003). On the subjective–objective approach also Wu Wei, *Rolle des Anklägers* (2007), 73. On some States' opposition to subjective elements Holmes, in Lee (ed.) 1999, 41, at 49; El Zeidy (2002) 32 *MichJIntL* 869, at 899. Crit. on the term's substance Kleffner, *Complementarity* (2008), at 115–16.

[140]*Cf.* Holmes, in Lee (ed.) 1999, 41, at 50; *id.*, in Cassese/Gaeta/Jones (eds.) 2002, 667, at 674; *see* also El Zeidy, *Complementarity* (2008), at 163 et seq. (166); *id.*, (2002) 32 *MichJIntL* 869, at 900; Cárdenas, *Zulässigkeitsprüfung* (2005), at 110.

[141]Holmes, in Cassese/Gaeta/Jones (eds.) 2002, 667, at 674; Benzing (2003) 7 *MPUNYB* 591, at 605; Cárdenas, *Zulässigkeitsprüfung* (2005), at 110–11; *id.*, in Kleffner/Kor (eds.) at 168–9; El Zeidy, *Complementarity* (2008), at 164–5; Razesberger, *Complementarity* (2006), at 52. On possible standards also Stigen, *Relationship* (2008), at 218 et seq.

investigation and prosecution.[142] From human rights jurisprudence follows that the State has "the obligation to use all the legal means at its disposal" to conduct a serious and effective investigation and process leading to the identification and punishment of the responsible;[143] only such an investigation, complying with the applicable human rights standards, can be qualified as a genuine one.[144] Against this background, it would be difficult to argue, for example, that a State, which opts for an effective TRC with the ultimate goal of peace in mind, is "genuinely" unwilling.[145] In any case, the term implies a double objective-subjective test[146] and is indirectly defined by paras. 2 and 3.[147] In addition, one may identify a *structural distinction* between unwillingness and inability in the following sense: While in the former case an, in principle, functioning judicial system is politically manipulated to generate impunity for powerful and influential perpetrators, in the latter case such a system does, in the worst case, physically not even exist or is substantially collapsed or unavailable.[148]

---

[142]It does not refer to the preceding "unwilling or unable", *cf.* El Zeidy, *Complementarity* (2008), at 165; Stigen, *Relationship* (2008), at 216 with fn. 701. The French version of the Statute expresses this more unequivocally ("*véritablement à bien*"), *see* Morel, *Complémentarité* (2005), 99–100; Kleffner, *Complementarity* (2008), at 115. The (non authentic) German version speaks similarly of "die Ermittlungen oder die Strafverfolgung ernsthaft durchzuführen".

[143]IACtHR, for example Paniagua Morales et al [8 March 1998] Judgement, paras. 173; *see* also IACtHR, Zambrano-Vélez vs. Ecuador [4 July 2007] Judgement, para. 123; Escué-Zapata vs. Colombia [4 July 2007] Judgement, para. 106. Extensively on applicable human rights standards in this context Stigen, *Relationship* (2008), at 219 et seq.; El Zeidy, *Complementarity* (2008), at 175 et seq.

[144]In a similar vein van der Wilt/Lyngdorf (2009) 9 *ICLR* 39 et seq. arguing that the ECHR's case law on the duty to properly investigate flagrant human rights violations and its concrete assessment of state practice serves as useful guideline as to these or other States' unwillingness or inability. *See* also El Zeidy, *Complementarity* (2008), at 167 implying incorrectly however that the said human rights jurisprudence explicitly defines the term "genuine".

[145]Seibert-Fohr (2003) 7 *MPUNYB* 553, at 570.

[146]Stigen, *Relationship* (2008), at 216.

[147]*Cf.* Stigen, *Relationship* (2008), at 218.

[148]For a general analysis *see* Benzing (2003) 7 *MPUNYB* 591, at 613 et seq.; for a similar distinction Seils/Wierda, *ICC and conflict mediation* (2005), at 6; *see* also Cárdenas, *Zulässigkeitsprüfung* (2005), at 138 et seq.; for a concrete proposal and analysis of inability criteria with regard to the DRC *see* Burke-White (2005) 18 *LJIL* 559, at 576 et seq. who suggests (at 576) four criteria "to judge the effectiveness of judicial systems in states recovering from a total or substantial judicial collapse", namely availability of experienced and unbiased judicial personnel, a viable legal infrastructure, adequate operative law and a sufficient police capability. For Arsanjani/Reisman, in Sadat/Scharf (eds.), 2008, 325, at 329, inability exists if "the system (...) in unable to obtain the accused or the necessary evidence and testimony or (is) otherwise unable to carry out its proceedings".

5.2.3.2 Unwillingness

a) General considerations

Unwillingness is not defined in the Statute, Art. 17 (2) only spells out the criteria that have to be considered: (1) the purpose of shielding, (2) unjustified delay, and (3) the lack of independence and impartiality. The list is exhaustive[149] and is to be applied – as follows from the wording ("one or more of the following") – in the alternative.[150] Yet, the existence of one of these criteria does not necessarily lead to a finding of unwillingness, the Court "shall consider" them to determine unwillingness (Art. 17 (2)); thus, they are necessary but not sufficient factors to determine unwillingness.[151]

On another note it is important to stress that the obligation to investigate rests on the State. It cannot be substituted by non-State and/or international entities.[152] Consequently, the unwillingness must also be attributed to the State,[153] it must reflect – contrary to inability (*infra* Sect. 5.2.3.3) – its policy.[154] Yet, as States are not monolithic but pluralist and complex entities composed of different organs with sometimes opposing objectives and interests there may not exist a uniform policy of promoting or blocking criminal investigations and prosecutions.[155] It may well be possible that one State organ (e.g. the national government) intends to block an investigation while another organ (e.g. the Attorney General) is willing to carry out the very same investigation. In this scenario, the situation or case must still be considered admissible if, on the basis of an overall assessment, the unwillingness of only one organ frustrates the whole investigation. In other words, a State cannot hide behind the positive actions of one organ if other organs boycott the investigation.[156]

As to the first element – "*purpose of shielding the person concerned from criminal responsibility*" (para. 2 (a)) – the term "purpose" suggests a *subjective* interpretation in the sense of the State's specific intention, objective or desire to protect the individual responsible from (criminal) justice.[157] This must not be the

[149] *See* Stigen, *Relationship* (2008), at 257–8, 314; Kleffner, *Complementarity* (2008), at 104; El Zeidy, *Complementarity* (2008), at 168; Pichon (2008) 8 *ICLR* 185, at 191; *see* for further references Ambos, in Ambos/Large/Wierda (eds.) 2009, at 76 para. 42 with fn. 376; contrary, Morel, *Complémentarité* (2005), at 117; also Razesberger, *Complementarity* (2006), at 42–3, 57 (but confusing).

[150] Morel, *Complémentarité* (2005), at 116; Kleffner, *Complementarity* (2008), at 134.

[151] Stigen, *Relationship* (2008), at 258, 290 (as to "unjustified delay").

[152] *See* Kleffner, *Complementarity* (2008), at 109–10.

[153] For a discussion *see* Stigen, *Relationship* (2008), at 253 et seq.

[154] Stigen, *Relationship* (2008), at 275.

[155] *See* Kleffner, *Complementarity* (2008), at 106–07.

[156] Kleffner, *Complementarity* (2008), at 107.

[157] Arbour/Bergsmo, in van Hebel/Lammers/Schukking (eds.), 1999, 129, at 131 ("devious intent"); Cárdenas, *Zulässigkeitsprüfung* (2005), at 115–6; El Zeidy, *Complementarity* (2008), at 316; Razesberger, *Complementarity* (2006), at 43. For Kleffner, *Complementarity* (2008), at 135,

only or ultimate intention.[158] It constitutes, at the same time, an expression of *bad faith* of the respective state with regard to the intention to bring the person(s) responsible to justice.[159] Clearly, such a high subjective threshold raises the difficult question of the correct standard of proof[160] and necessarily requires recourse to *indicia* from which the "bad faith purpose" may be inferred (*circumstantial evidence*).[161] Such indicia may constitute, for example,[162] the bypassing of the normal legal procedure by appointing a special investigator who is politically close to the accused, the transfer of a case to secret or special (military) tribunals,[163] the inadequate allocation of resources or the lack of support and cooperation with the investigators. Some of these indicia may also serve as an expression of unavailability in the sense of para. 3, for example, the limited access to the justice system,[164] the decision to grant blanket amnesties and immunities[165] or a considerable mitigation of punishment.[166] While the former examples entail a total shielding, the latter implies a partial shielding.[167] In this sense, the Colombian Constitutional Court, while accepting amnesties that comply with the standards of IHL, excludes those that "are the product of decisions which do not offer effective access to justice".[168] Yet, while an amnesty may demonstrate bad faith under certain

---

the purpose-requirement resembles *dolus directus* and he refers to State intention in the sense of Art. 16 of the ILC Draft on State Responsibility (135–36).

158Kleffner, *Complementarity* (2008), at 137–38. *See* also El Zeidy, *Complementarity* (2008), at 170 pointing out that the drafters introduced "shielding" as an objective criterion.

159El Zeidy, *Complementarity* (2008), at 175.

160Kleffner, *Complementarity* (2008), at 135; Benzing (2003) 7 *MPUNYB* 591, at 609–10; Stigen, *Relationship* (2008), at 261–2; Bekou, in Ulrich (ed.) 2005, 61, 73–4; Meißner, *Zusammenarbeit* (2003), at 84; Evans (2005) 1 *Human Rights Law Commentary* 1, at 2–3; Gavron (2002) 51 *ICLQ* 91, at 111; Morel, *Complémentarité* (2005), at 120 ("[...] une des tâche les plus ardues du Procureur"); Bothe (2008) 83 *Friedenswarte* 59, at 65.

161Stigen, *Relationship* (2008), at 252, 259, 262; Kleffner, *Complementarity* (2008), at 136–7.

162For a thorough discussion *see* Stigen, *Relationship* (2008), at 262 et seq.

163Holmes, in Cassese/Gaeta/Jones (eds.) 2002, 667, at 675.

164*See* for a discussion *infra* Chap. 5, Sect. 5.2.3.3 with n 275 et seq. In this context *see* Stigen, *Relationship* (2008), at 266–67.

165Kleffner, *Complementarity* (2008), at 136; Pichon (2008) 8 *ICLR* 185, at 194–195 (considering however that amnesties are rather a case of unavailability in the sense of article 17 (3), *see infra* n 279). Against blanket amnesties in this context also El Zeidy, *Complementarity* (2008), at 175 ("clear-cut example" of shielding); Stahn (2005) 3 *JICJ* 695, at 714; Gropengießer/Meißner (2005) 5 *ICLR* 267, at 285.

166Kleffner, *Complementarity* (2008), at 137 ("sentence ... manifestly insufficient in light of the gravity of the crime(s) in question and the form of participation of the accused"), yet also pointing to the "large margin of appreciation" with regard to sentencing. *See* also with regard to Uganda's regime of alternative sentences Burke-White/Kaplan, in Stahn/Sluiter (eds.) 2009, 17, at 106, 111.

167On this distinction Stigen, *Relationship* (2008), at 260 mentioning explicitly an inferior penalty as a form of partial shielding.

168Constitutional Court of Colombia [30 July 2002] Judgment C-578, MP Cepeda Espinosa, sect. 4.1.2.1.7: "... que son producto de decisiones que no ofrezcan acceso efectivo a la justicia". ("which are product of decisions which do not offer an effective access to justice").

circumstances, this is not always and necessarily the case.[169] Imagine a situation where a State pursues the higher objective of peace and it grants, in good faith, an amnesty as a necessary means to achieve this higher end; then a "bad faith purpose" can hardly be assumed.[170] Similarly, if one recognizes the right to a peaceful transition it would be contradictory to argue that the granting of exemptions in order to assure this transition can be considered as shielding a person and thus as demonstrating unwillingness in the sense of Art. 17(2) (a).[171] Consequently, the fact that impunity will be a certain side effect of an exemption measure is not *per se* sufficient to qualify this measure as pursuing a bad faith purpose.[172] Apart from that, the decision or procedure entailing impunity must be undertaken "for the purpose of shielding" (Art. 17 (2) (a)) or, in other words, the non-prosecution must have "resulted from" (Art. 17 (1) (b)) this decision or procedure. Thus, there must be some causal link between the State's action (purpose) and the consequence (shielding).[173]

While subpara. (a) of Art. 17 (2) calls for a rather subjective interpretation, *subparas. (b) and (c)* are to be interpreted *more objectively*.[174] Although the notion of "intent", present in both subparas, normally carries a subjective meaning it must be read in context and this context, referring to such objective criteria like "unjustified delay", independence and impartiality and the "circumstances", implies an overall objective reading, albeit always indicating bad faith.[175] An "*unjustified*" *delay* requires less from the State than an "undue" delay in that it gives the State the possibility to forward justifications for the delay and thereby avoid the unwillingness verdict for this reason; in fact, the drafters wanted to give State parties this possibility and therefore preferred "unjustified" over "undue".[176] As the Statute does not define the concept, recourse must be taken to the due process rules of human rights instruments,[177] taking into account the complexity of the case,[178] the

---

[169]For a flexible approach also Stigen, *Relationship* (2008), at 424 et seq. (426, 463 et seq.); too strict Cárdenas, *Zulässigkeitsprüfung* (2005), at 117, 164, 183, 184; *id.*, in Kleffner/Kor (eds.) 2006, 115, at 130.

[170]Seibert-Fohr (2003) 7 *MPUNYB* 553, at 570; on this transitional justice dilemma *see* also Stigen, *Relationship* (2008), at 420 et seq., 429 et seq., 463 et seq.

[171]But *see* Gavron (2002) 51 *ICLQ* 91, at 111–2.

[172]Stricter Cárdenas, in Kleffner/Kor (eds.) 2006, 115, at 131 arguing that impunity as certain "collateral damage" must be considered part of the purpose.

[173]*See* also Stigen, *Relationship* (2008), at 260.

[174]Benzing (2003) 7 *MPUNYB* 591, at 610; *see* also El Zeidy, *Complementarity* (2008), at 168, 316; *id.* (2002) 32 *MichJIntL* 869, at 901.

[175]Stigen, *Relationship* (2008), at 290.

[176]Benzing (2003) 7 *MPUNYB* 591, at 610–1; Stigen, *Relationship* (2008), at 289; *see* also Holmes, in Lee (ed.) 1999, 41, at 54; El Zeidy, *Complementarity* (2008), at 181; *id.* (2002) 32 *MichJIntL* 869, at 900; Razesberger, *Complementarity* (2006), at 45; Morel, *Complémentarité* (2005), at 121.

[177]Benzing (2003) 7 *MPUNYB* 591, at 610–1; *see* also Morel, *Complémentarité* (2005), at 122; Bekou, in Ulrich (ed.) 2005, 61, at 74; Kleffner, *Complementarity* (2008), at 140 et seq.; El Zeidy, *Complementarity* (2008), at 183 et seq.

[178]El Zeidy, *Complementarity* (2008), at 187–88.

conduct of the parties[179] and the (comparative) length of ordinary criminal proceedings in the respective State;[180] the latter also follows from Rule 51 RPE according to which the Court may consider information provided by the respective State as to the practice of its courts meeting "internationally recognized norms and standards."[181] Yet, a delay in this sense is only relevant if it runs counter to the very purpose of Art. 17, i.e., to bring the suspect to justice.[182] A delay may be "unjustified" in particular if it could have been avoided by employing the adequate care,[183] economic or administrative restraints are no justification. In any event, the decision cannot be taken *in abstracto* but only on a case by case basis taking due account of the circumstances of the respective case.[184]

Subpara. 2 (c) – requiring *independent and impartial proceedings* – is based on Art. 10 (2) ICTY Statute and 9 (2) ICTR Statute, which use the terms in the context of *ne bis in idem* (see also Art. 20 (3) (b) ICC Statute). The case would be admissible because of unwillingness if national proceedings, including the respective investigations,[185] were either not independent *or* not impartial. The concepts can be defined by taking recourse in particular to (European) human rights case law.[186] For the European Court of Human Rights ("ECtHR") both concepts are closely linked.[187] For independence "regard must be had, *inter alia*, to the manner of appointment of the members and their term of office, the existence of guarantees against outside pressures and the question whether the body presents an appearance of independence".[188] As to impartiality the ECtHR distinguishes between the freedom from personal bias of the respective tribunal and – objectively – the existence of sufficient guarantees for impartiality.[189] Impartiality has been defined

---

[179]El Zeidy, *Complementarity* (2008), at 188 et seq.

[180]El Zeidy, *Complementarity* (2008), at 194; Pichon (2008) 8 *ICLR* 185, at 195; Razesberger, *Complementarity* (2006), at 45.

[181]*See* also El Zeidy, *Complementarity* (2008), at 194.

[182]El Zeidy, *Complementarity* (2008), at 183, 317.

[183]*Cf.* Cárdenas, *Zulässigkeitsprüfung* (2005), at 119–20.

[184]*See* Kleffner, *Complementarity* (2008), at 140; El Zeidy, *Complementarity* (2008), at 182, 184; Bekou, in Ulrich, (ed.) 2005, 61, at 75; van der Wilt/Lyngdorf (2009) 9 *ICLR*, at 60.

[185]*Cf.* Stigen, *Relationship* (2008), at 300, 308–09.

[186]Benzing (2003) 7 *MPUNYB* 591, at 612; Razesberger, *Complementarity* (2006), at 47; Stigen, *Relationship* (2008), at 300 et seq. Examining the jurisprudence in more detail, *see* Van der Wilt/Lyngdorf (2009) 9 *ICLR*, at 51 et seq.; Kleffner, *Complementarity* (2008), at 145 et seq.; El Zeidy, *Complementarity* (2008), at 196 et seq.

[187]ECtHR, *Findlay v. United Kingdom* [25 February 1997] Judgement (22107/93), para. 73 ("First, the tribunal must be subjectively free of personal prejudice or bias. Secondly, it must also be impartial from an objective viewpoint, that is, it must offer sufficient guarantees to exclude any legitimate doubt in this respect."); *Pullar v. United Kingdom* [10 June 1996] Judgement (22399/93) para. 30.

[188]ECtHR, *Langborger v. Sweden* [22 June 1989] Judgement (11179/84) para. 32; *Findlay v. United Kingdom* (n 184), para. 73.

[189]*Findlay v. United Kingdom* (n 184), para. 73 ("First, the tribunal must be subjectively free of personal prejudice or bias. Secondly, it must also be impartial from an objective viewpoint, that is,

similarly by the ICTY in *Furundzija* stating that "there is a general rule that a Judge should not only be subjectively free from bias, but also that there should be nothing in the surrounding circumstances which objectively gives rise to an appearance of bias."[190] In sum, independence refers to external influence on the tribunals and proceedings, whereas impartiality is concerned with possible bias of the judicial personnel itself.[191] An "effective", i.e., *inter alia*, independent and impartial TRC[192] may refute a lack of independence and impartiality.[193]

Both subparas. (b) and (c) require that the unjustified delay and lack of independence or impartiality are "inconsistent with an intent to *bring the person concerned to justice*". This requirement, which operates in addition to the former ones[194] and adds an element of subjectivity,[195] refers back to subpara. (a) in that it confirms that the person concerned must not be shielded from but brought to justice, i.e., criminally investigated and prosecuted.[196] If one defends a broad concept of justice, as this author,[197] a quasi-judicial procedure, albeit with a possibility of a subsequent criminal process and sanction, conducted, for example, by an effective TRC, would suffice in this regard.[198] It is controversial, however whether the corresponding judicial procedure must satisfy *due process* standards.[199] While the wording of Art. 17, especially the reference to "principles of due process recognized by international law" (para. (2)) but also the references to unjustified delay (para. 2 (b)) and independence/impartiality (para. 2 (c)), seems to suggest just that,[200] the drafting history and the *rationale* of Art. 17 speak against it.[201] Proposals that would have

---

it must offer sufficient guarantees to exclude any legitimate doubt in this respect."); *Pullar v. United Kingdom* (n 184), para. 30.

[190] *Prosecutor v. Furundžija* [21 July 2000] Appeal's judgement (IT-95-17/1) para. 189.

[191] Razesberger, *Complementarity* (2006), at 46.

[192] On the criteria of "effectiveness" *see* already the reference in *supra* n 112.

[193] *See* Ambos, in Ambos/Large/Wierda (eds.) 2009, at 78 (para. 43); also Razesberger, *Complementarity* (2006), at 181.

[194] *Cf.* Kleffner, *Complementarity* (2008), at 143, 149–50.

[195] Carnero R. (2005) 18 *LJIL* 829, at 835.

[196] *See* already *supra* n 120 and main text.

[197] Ambos, in Ambos/Large/Wierda (eds.) 2009, at 22–23 (para. 2) with further references. *See* also Stigen, *Relationship* (2008), at 433 et seq., 446 et seq.

[198] *See* Ambos, in Ambos/Large/Wierda (eds.) 2009, at 78 (para. 43) with further references.

[199] *See* for a convincing critique of this "due process thesis" Heller (2006) 17 *CLF* 255, at 260 et seq. *See* also Carnero R. (2005) 18 *LJIL* 829, at 836 et seq. (852 et seq.); Pichon (2008) 8 *ICLR* 185, at 192 et seq.

[200] Heller (2006) 17 *CLF* 255, 258–9; also Kleffner, *Complementarity* (2008), at 127 et seq.; El Zeidy, *Complementarity* (2008), at 169; contrary Carnero R. (2005) 18 *LJIL* 829, at 837–8, 852 considering a literal interpretation "not decisive" and stressing the ambivalent meaning of "justice" as "trial" (process) or "accountability" (resulting).

[201] For a more detailed interpretation and discussion *see* Carnero R. (2005) 18 *LJIL* 829, at 838 et seq., 840 et seq. concluding that the drafting history clearly shows that the drafters favoured the intervention of the ICC only when the unfair domestic proceedings was intended to shield the

included procedural fairness were rejected during the negotiations.[202] The function of Art. 17 is not to guarantee due process – the respective rights are explicitly provided for in Art. 67 – but to avoid impunity by putting pressure on States to prosecute and punish international core crimes and, in the negative, refer these cases to the ICC.[203] This clearly follows from the "intent to bring the person concerned to justice"-requirement contained in both subpara. (b) and (c) at the end. With this requirement it is made plain that bringing the person to justice is – *in addition* ("and") to expedite, independent and impartial proceedings – the main purpose of both subparas.[204] Thus, the situation under subparas. (b) and (c) differs from the situation under human rights law in that the purpose of Art. 17 is primarily to avoid impunity and not the protection of procedural rights. Article 17 is about admissibility, not due process. The ICC is a criminal, not a human rights court. In fact, within the framework of admissibility, it is more important to make sure that the person be brought to justice than to preserve his due process rights. For the existence of these rights would make it more difficult to convict the accused and thus operate in favour of admissibility while the absence of these rights would make conviction easier and thus operate against admissibility in favour of the national jurisdiction.[205] From the perspective of complementarity then the absence of due process is the preferred option. Another reading of Art. 17 (2) (b) and (c) is only possible if the due process criteria and the intent-to-bring-the person-to-justice-requirement were to be phrased disjunctive ("or") instead of conjunctive ("and").[206] Or one would have to interpret the due process clause in a broader sense as referring to principles and standards with regard to duly investigate, prosecute and punish international crimes.[207]

Comparing subparas. (a), (b) and (c) it may be concluded that *bad faith* lies at the core of the unwillingness test.[208] The crucial point is whether the proceedings are not "genuine" in the sense explained above, i.e., whether the deviation from a genuine proceeding is such that it must be considered as an expression of the State's bad faith and thus unwillingness.[209] Consequently, the "unwillingness" test is about

person from justice (852). *See* also Heller (2006) 17 *CLF* 255, at 262–3, 270 et seq.; Pichon (2008) 8 *ICLR* 185, at 193.

[202]Heller (2006) 17 *CLF* 255, at 272–3; Carnero R. (2005) 18 *LJIL* 829, at 849; Pichon (2008) 8 *ICLR* 185, at 193.

[203]*See* also Stigen, *Relationship* (2008), at 221.

[204]*See* also Pichon (2008) 8 *ICLR* 185, at 193; Kleffner, *Complementarity* (2008), at 152 ("blind spot vis-à-vis unfair proceedings").

[205]*See* also Benzing (2003) 7 *MPUNYB* 591, at 612–13; Pichon (2008) 8 *ICLR* 185, at 193–4, 196; Van der Wilt/Lyngdorf (2009) 9 *ICLR*, at 63–64, 67 et seq.; Heller (2006) 17 *CLF* 255, at 257, 261–62.

[206]*See* Heller (2006) 17 *CLF* 255, at 279–80 with a further reform proposal for article 14.

[207]*See* for this, clearly untypical interpretation Kleffner, *Complementarity* (2008), at 131 et seq.

[208]Cárdenas, *Zulässigkeitsprüfung* (2005), at 113; Stigen, *Relationship* (2008), at 290; El Zeidy, *Complementarity* (2008), at 168, 236.

[209]Stigen, *Relationship* (2008), at 252.

the quality of the proceedings, its seriousness and good-faith with a view to bring the person to justice, it is not about passing moral judgments about the national justice system concerned.[210] There may be legitimate reasons not to investigate, prosecute or convict, for example a lack of evidence, no public interest or policy considerations.[211] In addition, the threshold of subpara. (a) is considerably higher than the ones of subparas. (b) and (c). Thus, it seems as if subpara. (a) encompasses subparas. (b) and (c)[212] so that it may be advisable for the Prosecutor to first examine these criteria and only if they are satisfied then subpara. (a).[213] In any case, the threshold of para. 2 is in general high.[214]

b) Application to the situation in Colombia

Evaluating the criterion of *unwillingness* in a concrete situation is extremely difficult since it implies strong value judgments with regard to the judicial system of a State in general and its treatment of international crimes in particular. As to the Colombian situation it is, first of all, important to recognize the numerous efforts made to tackle the violence and the crimes subject to Law 975; efforts going well beyond Law 975 in temporal and substantive terms. In any case, to reach a final judgment, the analysis of (un)willingness must not only focus, in an isolated manner, on the sub-criteria mentioned in Art. 17 (2) ICC-Statute (purpose of shielding the person concerned from criminal responsibility, unjustified delay and lack of independent and impartial proceedings), but put them in context, i.e., attempt to undertake a comprehensive assessment of the multiple efforts of the national authorities taking into account the real and concrete context of the Colombian situation.

aa) Purpose of shielding

As to the purpose of shielding the gist of the issue lies in the assessment of the so-called "alternative sentence" between 5 and 8 years. While Law 975, providing for criminal proceedings and ultimately a sanction, does not constitute an (disguised) amnesty or pardon,[215] the question arises whether the alternative sentence may be qualified as an expression of bad faith that ensues a lack of willingness and thus, at least indirectly, a purpose of shielding. The Colombian Constitutional Court, while admitting that the sentence may appear disproportionately low for the serious crimes in question, does not see a disproportionality with regard to the right to

---

[210] *Cf.* Stigen, *Relationship* (2008), at 252.

[211] *See* for a discussion of these reasons Stigen, *Relationship* (2008), at 309 et seq.

[212] *See* also El Zeidy, *Complementarity* (2008), at 170.

[213] Pichon (2008) 8 *ICLR* 185, at 195–6.

[214] El Zeidy, *Complementarity* (2008), at 170.

[215] *See* Constitutional Court (n 8 in Chap. 1) (Consideraciones de la Corte VI.3.3.).

justice, given that the ordinary sentence is not replaced but only suspended under certain conditions to be fulfilled by the beneficiary. Against this background, it is not to be expected that the judgments pursuant to Law 975 will be invalidated by the ICC; rather, more importance may be given – in the sense of a more comprehensive restorative justice approach[216] – to the demobilized person' effective contribution to truth and reconciliation and his reintegration into society.

bb) Unjustified delay

The criterion of unjustified delay can be evaluated from an *absolute perspective* by considering the time needed to investigate, prosecute and convict demobilized members under Law 975, or from a *relative perspective* by comparing the Law 975 with the ordinary criminal proceedings. In any case, this evaluation must take various factors into consideration, in particular the complexity of the investigated facts and the conduct of the state authorities and the demobilized persons. The relative perspective faces the problem that almost no reliable data on the duration of ordinary criminal proceedings is available. Empirical information of the "Higher Council of the Judiciary" (*Consejo Superior de la Judictarura)* indicates that a trial for homicide lasted 16.4 months under the old CCP (Law 600 of 2000) and 3.9–5.3 months (2007 and 2008) under the current one (Law 906 of 2004)[217]; despite this apparent improvement in terms of speediness of the trial the impunity rate for homicides remains with 97% still extremely high under the new procedure.[218] In the case of criminal investigations of crimes committed against trade-unionists which form part of the notorious Case No. 1787 of the International Labour Organization,[219] 82 sentences in 68 cases involving 134 convicted persons were issued between 2002 and 2007;[220] in other words, 1.1 cases per month were resolved.[221]

---

[216]In this sense Valiñas, in Stahn/van den Herik (eds.) 2010, at 283 et seq. (286) discusses Law 975 under "restorative-guided alternative forms of justice" and recognizes that it serves "certain restorative interests".

[217]Judiciary Control Council, Administrative Chamber, figures available at: http://www.ramajudicial.gov.co/csj_portal/assets/INFORME%20SAP%202.doc (last visited 8 October 2009) and http://www.ramajudicial.gov.co/csj_portal/assets/INTERVENCION%20%20DEL%20DR.%20TORRES%20COMISION%20PRIMERA.pdf (last visited 8 October 2009).

[218]*See* Rivera/Barreto, *Impunidad* (without date), at 11.

[219]The case includes about 1,400 cases of violence against trade unions and their members. The cases have been filed by various trade unions due to the lack of action by the Government. They include, *inter alia*, cases of murder, death threats, disappearances and kidnappings. Arising from Case No. 1787, the Special Unit for Human Rights and IHL of the Office of the Prosecutor General has been assigned a total of 1,354 cases; *see* HRW, *US-Colombia Free Trade Agreement* (2009)

[220]Figures available at: www.usleap.org/files/MSPSentencesMarch08.doc (last visited 8 October 2009).

[221]Juidiciary Control Council, *Resumen del Informe al Congreso (2007*), available at: http://www.ramajudicial.gov.co/csj_portal/assets/Resumen%20Informe%20al%20Congreso%202007.doc (last visited 8 October 2009).

From an *absolute perspective* it is also extremely difficult to make a reasoned judgment. First of all, it is to be noted that not one member of an irregular group has been finally convicted since the entry into force of Law 975 (25 July 2005). In the most advanced case of *Wilson Salazar Carrascal*[222] the Higher Tribunal's Justice and Peace Chamber issued a judgment on 19 March 2009, 3 years after the demobilization of the accused (3 March 2006). Although this period does not seem to be excessively long, it must not be overlooked that the case only dealt with few offences and has not terminated yet since the Court had to suspend the execution of the alternative sentence due to the incomplete charging of the prosecutor, *inter alia*, leaving out the crime of aggravated conspiracy.[223] The insufficient investigation and the incomplete indictment caused the Supreme Court of Justice to annul the proceedings, including the hearing on the formulation of charges.[224] The case has also served as a test case for the debate and solution of judicial controversies concerning the correct interpretation of the procedurals stages of Law 975 by lodging several appeals to the Supreme Court of Justice. Thus, the delay has not only been caused by a too slow investigation of the SJUP. In the second most advanced case against *Gian Carlo Gutiérrez Suárez*, who belonged as a foot soldier to the Calima block and has confessed 26 crimes, the free version hearings took place between May and December 2007. Yet, in a recent decision the Supreme Court invalidated the acceptance of charges by the Higher Tribunal of Justice and Peace, arguing that the substantive control of the charges accepted by the defendant has been inadequate and without proper participation of the victims.[225] In three other cases the Higher Tribunal granted leave to appeal to the Supreme Court of Justice, where the cases are currently pending.[225a]

The evaluation of the sub-criterion of unjustified delay depends also on the *techniques and strategies of investigation* applied by the UJP. The Supreme Court's demands to investigate the patterns of widespread and systematic violations of human rights and IHL and the respective harm caused individually or collectively to victims[226] convert each investigation in a highly complex exercise. This requires a *comprehensive investigation and prosecution strategy* as well as *criteria for case selection and prioritization* in order to deal with the high numbers of crimes, victims and offenders. While the use of partial (successive) imputations (*imputaciones parciales*), as discussed above,[227] may be an important tool in this regard,

---

[222]Tribunal Superior de Bogotá (n 32 in Chap. 1); *see* also *supra* n 69 in Chap. 2 and main text.

[223]*See* Tribunal Superior de Bogotá (n 32 in Chap. 1), para. 163. On the conspiracy offence *see supra* n 19 in Chap. 1 and main text.

[224]Supreme Court [31 July 2009] Rad. 31539, MP Augusto Ibánez Guzmán.

[225]Supreme Court (n 29 in Chap. 3), Consideraciones de la Corte, 5. El caso concreto: "(...) la Sala de Decisión de Justicia y Paz, no ejerció el control material (...). Nada resolvió sobre las inquietudes de los representantes de las víctimas, señalando que un pronunciamiento previo al respecto implicaría un anticipo al juicio de tipicidad planteado por la Fiscalía. Así, dejó huérfana de sustento material la diligencia, impidiendo que su objeto central y finalidades fuesen cumplidos (...)".

[225a]*See* Tribunal Superior de Bogotá (n 50b in Chap. 2).

[226]Supreme Court, *supra* n 46 et seq. in Chap. 2 and main text.

[227]*Supra* Chap. 3 (vi) with n 28 and main text.

it can offer only a partial (incomplete) response and does not make a comprehensive strategy superfluous.

cc) Independent and impartial proceedings

As to the third sub-criterion of independent and impartial proceedings, it must first be noted that the adoption of Law 975 was the result of a broad public discussion among and between many institutions of the public sector and many civil society groups between 2003 and 2005.[228] Subsequently, Law 975 was reviewed by the Constitutional Court in several judgments,[229] of which judgment C-370 of 2006 is the most important one demanding some substantial changes, *inter alia*, as to the right to truth and reparation for the victims. In this regard, the government's subsequent regulation of Law 975 by executive decrees has been criticized as an attempt to bypass the Constitutional Court's ruling adopted.[230] Notwithstanding the accuracy of this critique it can be observed that the executive branch has adopted a very flexible approach as to the use of executive decrees in order to fill the normative gaps of Law 975. On the other hand, the interpretation of Law 975 by the Constitutional and the Supreme Court has been crucial for its application by the enforcement authorities and lower courts.[231] With regard to the ICC Statute, the Supreme Court has even explicitly recognized the ICC's jurisdiction over the Statute crimes committed on Colombian territory.[231a] It even reserved its right to inform the ICC if Colombian institutions obstruct the efficient administration of justice.[231b] Neither the interpretation nor the application has been influenced by the executive branch or other external actors to an extent that one could doubt the substantive independence of the judicial authorities.

As to the procedure in more concrete terms, it can be ascertained that the judicial authorities (*Fiscalía* and courts) take over the total control of the process when the administrative phase ends, i.e., with the passing of the list of postulated members of

[228] *See* Fundación Social, *Trámite de la ley de justicia y paz* (2006), at 114–15.

[229] Constitutional Court [25 April 2006] Judgment C-319, MP Alvaro Tafur Galvis; *id.* [18 May 2006], C-370 (n 8 in Chap. 1); *id.* [24 May 2006] C-400, MP Alfredo Beltrán Sierra; *id.* [31 May 2006] C-426, MP Humberto Antonio Sierra Porto; *id.* [7 June 2006] C-455, MP Jaime Araújo Rentería; *id.* [14 June 2006] C-476, MP Alvaro Tafur Galvis; *id.* [12 July 2006] C-531, MP Marco Gerardo Monroy Cabra; *id.* [25 July 2006] C-575, MP Alvaro Tafur Galvis; *id.* [9 August 2006] C-650, MP Alvaro Tafur Galvis; *id.* [16 August 2006] C-670, MP Rodrigo Escobar Gil; *id.* [23 August 2006] C-719, MP Jaime Araújo Rentería; *id.* [7 February 2007] C-080, MP Rodrigo Escobar Gil; *id.* [4 December 2008] C-1199, MP Nilson Pinilla Pinilla.

[230] CCJ, *Boletín No. 4* (2006).

[231] *See* Tribunal Superior de Bogotá (n 32 in Chap. 1) para. 204, with regard to the obligation of the Victims Trust Fund to pay economic and symbolic reparations ordered by the Higher Tribunal for Justice and Peace; *see also* Supreme Court (n 16 in Chap. 1) (Rad. 26945), where the Court rejects the application of Art. 71 Law 975 despite the provision set out in art 2 of Decree 4436 of 11 December of 2006 which refers to Art. 71.

[231a] Supreme Court [21 September 2009], Rad. 32022, MP Espinoza Perez.

[231b] Supreme Court [3 December 2009], Rad. 32672, section 11.3.

GAOML to the Prosecutor General.[232] The exclusion of the listed demobilized persons from its benefits cannot be ordered by the government, but must be decided by the Prosecutor or the Higher Tribunal for Justice and Peace, depending on the ground for exclusion.[233] The verification of the eligibility criteria lies exclusively in the competence of the judicial authorities.[234] The Higher Tribunal's judicial decisions concerning reparative measures for victims are binding on *Acción Social* as the trustee of the Victims Reparations Fund and their execution cannot be rejected invoking a lack of financial resources.[235] Finally, it is the exclusive competence of the Higher Tribunal to supervise the execution of the sentence and the other obligations imposed on the convicted persons.[236]

dd) General and paradigmatic aspects

As has been said at the beginning of this section, it is important – apart from the (isolated) evaluation of the sub-criteria – to consider some general and paradigmatic aspects for the global *evaluation* of the unwillingness standard. First, with Law 975 a *complex institutional framework* has been created with specific functions assigned to previously existing or newly established institutions.[237] Given the challenges and obstacles in the implementation and application of Law 975 it was necessary to gradually increase the personal, financial, institutional and operational resources. Attending the different hearings (free version, imputation, formulation of charges, control of the charges, reparations hearing) one notes the *commitment* and *good will* of the judicial operators to comply with the international standards concerning the investigation and prosecution of international crimes.[238] The existing deficits in the process as to the *Fiscalia's* investigative capacity and strategy as well as to an adequate victims' participation[239] cannot be interpreted as an expression of bad faith or unwillingness of the judicial authorities to investigate and prosecute the perpetrators of international crimes properly.

With regard to the *extraditions* of high ranking commanders, already discussed previously,[240] it is clear that they have *objectively* not been shielded from criminal

---

[232]Supreme Court (n 75 in Chap. 2) (Rad. 28492), Consideraciones; *id.* (n 11 in Chap. 2) (Rad. 29472), Consideraciones. *See* also *supra* n 10 in Chap. 2 and main text.

[233]Supreme Court (n 11 in Chap. 2) (Rad. 29472), Consideraciones. On the grounds for exclusion *see supra* n 12–15 in Chap. 2 with main text.

[234]Supreme Court (n 11 in Chap. 2) (Rad. 29472), Consideraciones.*; see also* Art. 8 (1) of Decree 4760 of 2005.

[235]Constitutional Court (n 8 in Chap. 1) (Consideraciones de la Corte, 6.2.4.3.1.3.).

[236]*See* Art. 32 (1) Law 975.

[237]For a detailed critical analysis of this framework *see* Ambos et al., *Justicia y Paz* (2010), para. 73 et seq.

[238]With regard to the imputation of the crimes committed by members of illegal armed groups as war crimes or crimes against humanity, *see* CitPax, *Imputación de crímenes internacionales* (2009).

[239]*See supra* Chap. 3 espec. (iv)–(vi).

[240]*Supra* Chap. 3 (vii) n 39 et seq. with main text.

proceedings since they will indeed be prosecuted in the US, albeit not for international core crimes but for drug related offences. As to the *subjective* requirement of the purpose of "shielding the persons concerned from criminal responsibility", i.e. the specific intent of the competent State to protect them against criminal prosecution, there is hardly any evidence that would prove such an ultimate purpose of the extraditions. On the other hand, the absence of clear legal framework to guarantee the cooperation between the judicial authorities of Colombia and the US with a view to an unlimited access to the detainees and to facilitate the effective realization of hearings via video link and the appearance of the extradited paramilitaries as witnesses in the investigations and trials against Colombian politicians implicated in the so called "parapolitics" scandal,[241] raises doubts as to the government's good faith regarding the extraditions. Moreover, the delays caused because of the absence of a clear legal framework could be interpreted as an unjustified delay in the investigation and prosecution of the commanders, taking into account that any further delay remains the Colombian State's responsibility. Last but not least, it is also true that the extraditions impede or at least hamper the possibility of prosecutions by the ordinary criminal justice system if the commanders withdraw from the Justice and Peace procedure or are excluded from it.[241a]

The application of the *opportunity principle* to the so called *foot soldiers,* already discussed extensively above,[242] cannot be interpreted as a purpose to shield these persons from criminal responsibility for the simple reason that the application is only envisaged for mere membership in an irregular group and international core crimes are explicitly excluded.[243] In fact, the opportunity principle operates, conceptually, with regard to a certain offence (*in casu* membership in a group) and not with regard to a certain offender as such, i.e., its application depends on the offence in question (membership) and does not cover serious crimes if committed during the membership of the person covered (notwithstanding that there may be a factual connection between the offence and the offender in that mid- or high-level offenders are normally not mere members). It is worthwhile mentioning in this context that the Supreme Court granted in several decisions the benefits of Law 782[244] to members of GAOML on the basis of their mere membership applying the controversial Art. 71 of Law 975,[245] which declares the political offence of rebellion (*sedición*) applicable to all GAOML but was later declared unconstitutional for formal reasons.[246]

---

[241]*See infra* n 254 with main text.

[241a]For a critical analysis in this respect, *see* International Human Rights Law Clinic Berkeley, *Truth Behind Bars* (2010).

[242]*See supra* n 22 et seq. in Chap. 1, 12 et seq. in Chap. 3 and 68 in this Chap., always with main text.

[243]*See* Art. 324 no. 17 para. 3 CCP as quoted *supra* n 26 in Chap. 1.

[244]*See supra* n 13 in Chap. 1 with main text.

[245]*See* Supreme Court [18 October 2005] Rad. 24311, MP Alfredo Gómez Quintero; *id.* [18 October 2005] Rad. 2431), MP Marina Pulido de Barón; *id.* [27 October 2005] Rad. 24526, MP Alfredo Gómez Quintero.

[246]*See* Constitutional Court, Judgement C-370 (n 229).

As has been explained above[247] the postulation, which serves as the first filter during the administrative phase of Law 975 with regard to its *ratione personae* application, has mainly been defined during or shortly after the collective demobilizations of the paramilitary blocks, i.e., at the moment when the demobilized members are included in the postulation lists. Yet, at that moment, there existed only little information about the crimes committed by the demobilised, often there was just not enough information available to take an informed decision. In general terms, the demobilization and postulation procedure has not been carried out in a reasonable way but was fraught with irregularities with regard to, *inter alia*, the actual paramilitary background of the demobilized and their quantitative and qualitative involvement in crimes.[248] In several cases demobilized members were included in the postulation lists without having full knowledge of the implications of this decision. For example, in the case of a collective demobilization of a paramilitary block, which operated in the Caribbean coast, about 500 persons were included in the list (just to fill out all the forms which have been handed out by the competent State agency), although only 25 persons demobilised voluntarily, while the rest acted upon orders of their commanders.[249] The high numbers of non-ratifications of postulated persons, for example in the cases of the North and the Tayrona Blocks,[250] can only be explained by the lack of an adequate control over the inclusion of persons in the postulation lists. In the cases of other paramilitary blocks only very few members were postulated. For example, while 3,200 persons demobilized belonging to the paramilitary apparatus of the notorious commander "Don Berna" (blocks of Cacique Nutibara, Héroes de Granada and Héroes de Tolová),[251] only about 50 postulates have been actively taking part in the Law 975 proceedings.[252] The inadequate and sometimes arbitrary realization of the postulation procedure makes the respective proceedings highly unreliable. This means that when deciding on the application of the opportunity principle the Prosecutor would need to examine previously the criminal record of a potential beneficiary in each and every case, independent of its inclusion if the postulation lists.[253]

---

[247]Part I Chap. 2.1.

[248]*See* already Chap. 3 (iii) with n 19 et seq.

[249]Interview with a demobilized paramilitary member, Bogotá, 16 August 2009.

[250]These blocks operated in the departments of Guajira, Magdalena, Atlántico and Cesar in the North of Colombia.

[251]*See* Alto Comisionado para la Paz, *Proceso de Paz* (without date).

[252]*See* Huber, *¿Qué quieren las víctimas?* (2009).

[253]According to the Special Unit for Justice and Peace of the Office of the Prosecutor General, 24,304 demobilized persons have fully been identified and their criminal records have been examined (FGN-UJP, *Oficio 012896* (2009), at 8 and 19). One must not overlook, however, that in many cases complaints have not been filed by victims for fear of reprisals or the complaints do not indicate the responsible persons.

The criminal proceedings have not been limited to members of the AUC. In the course of the *parapolitics scandal*, the judicial authorities, especially the Supreme Court and the Prosecutor General, made great efforts to investigate the connections between the political elite and the paramilitary movement of the AUC. The Prosecutor General also initiated or re-opened investigations against members of the armed forces.[254] In this sense, Law 975 can be understood as a special criminal procedure for members of illegal armed groups, including the broader context of powerful political, military and economic sectors with links to the paramilitary movement. Insofar the special criminal proceedings under Law 975 and the ordinary proceedings complement each other mutually. Thus, the UJP has collected informations, arising from the free versions, with regard to *third parties*[255] not (formally) belonging to the paramilitary groups (e.g. politicians, members of the armed forces etc.). This entailed criminal proceedings against 218 politicians (among them 128 mayors, 28 Councilmen, 44 Congressmen and 18 Governors), 140 members of the armed forces, 44 public servants and 4,371 additional investigations against other individuals.[256] The Prosecutor General and the Supreme Court have initiated 83 investigations against Congressmen until 20 June 2009 (29 are in the preliminary phase, 18 in the investigation phase and 9 in the trial phase). At least 10 Congressmen have been convicted so far for their ties with paramilitary groups.[257]

Against this background, it is fair to conclude that there is *no general unwillingness* of the Colombian State to investigate and prosecute international crimes. This is not to deny that the Justice and Peace procedure is riddled with problems and deficits, in particular with a view to the lack of a global strategy of the UJP, the (unintended) consequences of the extradition of the paramilitary commanders and the adequate application of the opportunity principle. Nevertheless, a *global evaluation* of the States activities in terms of the *good/bad faith dichotomy* as a normative expression of the criterion of unwillingness taking into account the sub-criteria of Art. 17 (2) ICC-Statute leads to the conclusion that Colombia is currently complying with its obligations under Art. 17 ICC Statute.[258]

[254] *See* for example the case of the former military commander Rito Alejo del Rio Ríos, accused of links to paramilitary groups (Supreme Court [11 March 2009] Rad. 30510, MP Yesid Ramírez Bastidas).

[255] To be distinguished from the investigations by other units than UJP against the demobilized members *themselves*, *see supra* Chap. 3 (ii) with n 17.

[256] FGN-UJP, *Aplicación Ley 975* (2009).

[257] *See* Corporación Nuevo Arco Iris, *Observatorio* (2009).

[258] In such cases, the Prosecutor of the ICC, according to the *positive complementarity principle*, should try to encourage a State to prosecute cases in an adequate way; *see* Ryngaert, in Ryngaert (ed.), 2009, 146, at 171.

5.2.3.3 Inability

a) General considerations

While the inability concept is more objective and factual than its counterpart of unwillingness,[259] its correct interpretation is still controversial.[260] Inability is determined by three disabling events: (1) a "total" collapse, (2) a "substantial" collapse, or (3) the "unavailability" of the national judicial system.[261] The said events must entail the State's inability[262] "to obtain the accused or the necessary evidence and testimony or otherwise (...) to carry out its proceedings". (Art. 17 (3)).[263]

A *total collapse* presupposes that the judicial system as a whole – not only temporarily or partially – does not function anymore.[264] In this sense, a total collapse may be equated with inaction as discussed above (Sect. 5.2.1)[265] This is for example the case if the State authorities have lost control over their territory to an extent that the administration of justice has broken down completely, or where the authorities, while still exercising (some) effective (military or police) control over the territory, do not perform such administration.[266] Thus, the total collapse may be defined as "a complete breakdown of the national administration of justice, either due to the State's loss of control over the territory or due to the national decision to efface the national administration of justice".[267]

As to a *substantial collapse*, it is controversial whether the provision embraces a quantitative and/or qualitative assessment.[268] It must be taken into account that the original term "partial" was replaced by "substantial" in order to increase the admissibility threshold and reinforce the primacy of national jurisdictions.[269]

---

[259]Holmes, in Cassese/Gaeta/Jones (eds.) 2002, 667, at 677; Wei, *Rolle des Anklägers* (2007), at 74; Evans, (2005) 1 *Human Rights Law Commentary* 1, at 4; Morel, *Complémentarité* (2005), at 129; Kleffner, *Complementarity* (2008), at 152–53; El Zeidy, *Complementarity* (2008), at 222.

[260]*See* El Zeidy, *Complementarity* (2008), at 227 with references for both positions.

[261]Arsanjani/Reismann, in Sadat/Scharf (eds.) 329; OTP, Complementarity, *supra n* 77 in Chap. 5, para. 49; El Zeidy (2002) 32 *MichJIntL* 869, at 903; Philips (1999) 10 *CLF* 61, at 79. – For the practically little relevant question if the qualifier "total or substantial" also refers to unavailability *see* Kleffner, *Complementarity* (2008), at 153.

[262]"Judicial system" must be understood broadly, *see* Kleffner, *Complementarity* (2008), at 154.

[263]For a discussion *see* Stigen, *Relationship* (2008), at 326 et seq.

[264]Cárdenas, in Kleffner/Kor (eds.) 2006, 115, at 125; *id.*, *Zulässigkeitsprüfung* (2005), at 126; Stigen, *Relationship* (2008), at 314–5 ("could arguably be temporary, albeit not too brief, [. . .]").

[265]*Cf.* Kleffner, *Complementarity* (2008), at 154, 160.

[266]Benzing (2003) 7 *MPUNYB* 591, at 614; Meißner, *Zusammenarbeit* (2003), at 86; Greppi, in Politi/Gioia (eds.) 2008, 63, at 64.

[267]Pichon (2008) 8 *ICLR* 185, at 196; Razesberger, *Complementarity* (2006), at 48; Ellis (2002) 15 *Fla. J. Int'l L.* 215, 238 et seq.

[268]For "relevant facts and evidence" *see* ICC-OTP, *Complementarity in practice* (2003), para. 50.

[269]Arsanjani/Reismann, in Sadat/Scharf (eds.), at 330–1; Hoffmeister/Knoke (1999) 59 *ZaöRV* 785, at 798; Philips (1999) 10 *CLF*, at 79; Morel, *Complémentarité* (2005), at 132; El Zeidy, *Complementarity* (2008), at 224 et seq., Razesberger, *Complementarity* (2006), at 48–9.

Also, there must remain a scope of application for the unavailability criterion. This means that a strict interpretation is called for. The collapse is "substantial" if it has a great or significant impact on the functioning of the national justice system.[270] This system must be damaged to an extent that it is generally not capable anymore of ensuring the investigation of the case and the prosecution of the individuals.[271] A geographically limited collapse may suffice, i.e., if the State's effective control does not extend to the whole territory but fails in some parts;[272] a good example is the situation in the Ituri region of the Democratic Republic of the Congo.[273] If, however, such a partial (substantial) collapse can be compensated by shifting the resources and proceedings to another venue the threshold is not reached.[274]

The determination of *unavailability* is more difficult,[275] not least because it partly overlaps with the substantial collapse requirement.[276] A wide literal interpretation may reveal three potential facets: the non-existence of something, the non-accessibility of something, and the non-usefulness of a remedy, irrespective of its existence and accessibility.[277] This broad literal reading[278] is confirmed by systematic (Art. 88 uses the term "availability" in a broader sense than existence of legislation only) and teleological arguments ("unavailability" must be construed broad enough to reduce the number of situations the ICC must refer to national proceedings despite the State's actual inability to carry out proceedings).[279] Such a broad reading would also allow for including situations under unavailability where a legal system is generally in place but *in concreto* does not provide for effective judicial remedy or access to the courts, be it for political, legal or factual reasons (capacity overload), or is not able to produce the desired result (bring the

---

[270]Stigen, *Relationship* (2008), at 316; El Zeidy, *Complementarity* (2008), at 226.

[271]Benzing (2003) 7 *MPUNYB* 591, at 614; Stigen, *Relationship* (2008), at 316.

[272]Hall, *Suggestions concerning ICC prosecutorial policy and strategy* (2003), at 17; El Zeidy (2002) 32 *MichJIntL* 869, at 903–04; Kleffner, *Complementarity* (2008), 32–3; Razesberger, *Complementarity* (2006), at 48–9; differentiated Stigen, *Relationship* (2008), at 315–6.

[273]Wouters/Verhoeven, in Ankumah/Kwakwa (eds.) 2005, 133, 138.

[274]*Cf.* Kleffner, *Complementarity* (2008), at 155; El Zeidy, *Complementarity* (2008), at 225.

[275]Crit. of the lack of clarity Morel, *Complémentarité* (2005), at 133.

[276]*Cf.* Kleffner, *Complementarity* (2008), at 155, 160.

[277]Stigen, *Relationship* (2008), at 316–7.

[278]In contrast Cárdenas, in Kleffner/Kor (eds.) 2006, 115, at 124; *id.*, *Zulässigkeitsprüfung* (2005), at 128 argues – based on the authentic Spanish version of article 17 (3) ("al hecho de que carece ") – that a system is *only* unavailable when it is non-existent. *See* also Burke-White (2008) 19 *CLF* 59, 74 ("lack of judicial infrastructure"); contrary, Hall, *Suggestions concerning ICC prosecutorial policy and strategy* (2003), at 17; El Zeidy, *Complementarity* (2008), at 226–7.

[279]*See* ICC-OTP, *Complementarity in practice* (2003), para. 49 with fn. 15: "It is suggested that the term 'unavailability' should be given a broad interpretation, so as to cover the various 'inability' scenarios in the latter part of Article 17(3) and to cover typical cases of inability". *See* also Stigen, *Relationship* (2008), at 317–8; Kleffner, *Complementarity* (2008), at 153 ("any unavailability") and Meißner, *Zusammenarbeit* (2003), at 87 arguing that a functioning judiciary exists but it cannot deal with the particular case for normative or factual reasons.

responsible to justice).[280] If this is accepted, human rights case law as to an effective judicial remedy against serious human rights violations can provide important guidelines for the complementarity test.[281] In this sense *exemption provisions* conceded in processes of transition may not only be considered as a problem of unwillingness[282] but also as one of inability in the sense of "*human rights unavailability*", i.e., a lack of an effective judicial remedy or access to the courts.[283] Also, the absence or inadequacies of national legislation regarding international criminal law (for lack of implementation of the ICC Statute) could render a national system unavailable.[284] As a consequence, the ICC would qualify a State's legal system – for lack of implementation of the ICC Statute – as "unavailable" in the sense of Art. 17 (3). The opposite view rejects such quality judgments about a national justice system.[285] It argues that the drafters did not consider the scenario of an over-burdened justice system since, *inter alia*, this is an assessment which is ultimately up to the State concerned.[286] Thus, one cannot demand more

[280] For a detailed discussion *see* Stigen, *Relationship* (2008), at 319 et seq.; *see* also Benzing (2003) 7 *MPUNYB* 591, at 614: "capacity overload"; El Zeidy, *Complementarity* (2008), at 227–8; Razesberger, *Complementarity* (2006), at 49.

[281] This argument has been recently developed by van der Wilt/Lyngdorf (2009) 9 *ICLR*, at 39 et seq. arguing that the ECHR's case law on the duty to properly investigate flagrant human rights violations and its concrete assessment of state practice serves as useful guideline as to these or other States' unwillingness or inability. *See* also Stigen, *Relationship* (2008), at 222 et seq., 318.

[282] *Cf.* Gropengießer/Meißner (2005) 5 *ICLR* 267, at 282 et seq.; Kreicker, in Eser/Sieber/Kreicker (eds.) 2006, at 305.

[283] In this sense O'Shea, *Amnesty* (2002), at 126 arguing that a failure to prosecute based on amnesty would amount to an inability to prosecute owing to the unavailability of the state's national judicial system; for inability due to a blanket amnesty also Burke-White (2005) 18 *LJIL* 559, at 582; Stigen, *Relationship* (2008), at 322 (law not "at disposal"); Razesberger, *Complementarity* (2006), at 160–61. *See* also Pichon (2008) 8 *ICLR* 185, at 195 arguing that "amnesties have to be subsumed in general under the notion of unavailability, since it would contradict the whole purpose of an amnesty if it could easily be lifted in a concrete case" and concluding with regard to Sudan (at 223) that immunity "leads to unavailability". *See* also Kleffner, *Complementarity* (2008), at 106 (regarding amnesty) 157–58 ("statutory limitations", "bar to carrying out the proceedings"); El Zeidy, *Complementarity* (2008), at 227.

[284] Kleffner (2003) 1 *JICJ* 86, 89; *id.*, *Complementarity* (2008), at 156–7; El Zeidy, *Complementarity* (2008), at 227; Razesberger, *Complementarity* (2006), at 49 et seq.; Bekou, in Ulrich (ed.) 2005, 61, at 78. – An example provides the ICTR decision in the case of *Prosecutor v. Bagaragaza*: though not in the context of the ICC Statute, the ICTR had to decide on a comparable issue when the Norway requested a referral of the just mentioned case to its authorities based on rule 11*bis* ICTR RPE. Since Norway had not implemented the crime of genocide into its national criminal law, the ICTR's Trial Chamber came to the conclusion that Norway lacked jurisdiction *ratione materiae* over the crimes as charged in the indictment, and consequently "Bagaragaza's alleged criminal acts cannot be given their full legal qualification under Norwegian criminal law, and the request for the referral to the Kingdom of Norway falls to be dismissed" (*Prosecutor v. Bagaragaza* [19 May 2006] Decision on the Prosecution's motion for referral to the Kingdom of Norway, ICTR-2005-86-R11, para. 16).

[285] Arsanjani/Reismann, in Sadat/Scharf (eds.), at 329 et seq.; Philips (1999) 10 *CLF*, at 79; Holmes, in Lee (ed.) 1999, 41, at 48.

[286] Arsanjani/Reismann, in Sadat/Scharf (eds.), at 331 et seq.

than "some existent national infrastructure" and the fulfillment of some minimum international standards with a view to ensure the security for victims, witnesses, judges and defendants.[287] As to the existence of international crimes in the national legislation it is, following this view, sufficient that the concrete acts can be appropriately punished, be it on the basis of international or national crimes.[288]

A convincing and sensible interpretation should be based on a compromise between the broad and narrow interpretations. A too narrow interpretation would make the "total or substantial collapse" criteria superfluous and must therefore be rejected. On the other hand, a too broad interpretation would ignore that by using the term "substantial" instead of "partial" (collapse), the mere inefficient functioning of a judicial system, its internal deficiencies, should not fall under the unavailability concept.[289] Thus, in the result, the existence of substantial legal or factual obstacles entailing a lack of effective remedies may only constitute unavailability if this qualification can be made by an external observer without entering into value (quality) judgments regarding the *internal* functioning of the national justice system concerned. The qualification must be based on objective (quantitative) factors which are easily verifiable from outside of the system, for example empirical information indicating that that there is no effective remedy for human rights violations. Under these circumstances it is possible that a capacity overload might render the judicial system unavailable, either due to the sheer magnitude of the crimes committed or due to a lack of personal or other resources.[290]

b) Application to the situation in Colombia

For the implementation of Law 975 a *complex institutional framework* has been established:[291] new institutions[292] and specialized units within existing judicial institutions[293] have been created and existing institutions have been vested with

---

[287] Burke-White (2005) 18 *LJIL* 559, at 579.

[288] Pichon (2008) 8 *ICLR* 185, at 197; Stigen, *Relationship* (2008), at 319 et seq. (321), 336; Razesberger, *Complementarity* (2006), at 51, 153 et seq.; in the result also Kleffner, *Complementarity* (2008), at 119 et seq. (123); for a different interpretation stressing the difference between ordinary and international crimes El Zeidy, *Complementarity* (2008), at 290 et seq.; similarly (albeit too superficial) Sedman, in Stahn/van den Herik (eds.) 2010, at 265–66.

[289] Stigen, *Relationship* (2008), at 323 (limiting factual obstacles to external ones).

[290] *Cf.* Stigen, *Relationship* (2008), at 329–30.

[291] *See* already *supra* n 237 with main text.

[292] *Inter alia* the CNRR and the Regional Commissions for Property Restitution (*Comisiones Regionales para la Restitución de Bienes*).

[293] *Inter alia* the UJP, three Pre-Trial Chambers and a Trial Chamber for Justice and Peace in the Higher Tribunals of Barranquilla, Medellín and Bogotá, a specialized Unit for Justice and Peace in the *Procuraduría* and two special units of the Office of the Human Rights Ombudsman (*Defensoría del Pueblo*).

new functions.[294] Against this background it is not possible to speak of a *total collapse* of the judicial system in Colombia.

Given the concrete functioning of the Justice and Peace procedure it is not possible to speak of a *substantial collapse* of the judicial system either. Up to November 2009, the UJP has set up three main offices (in Bogotá, Medellín and Barranquilla) and additional satellite offices in 42 cities; it employed more than 680 officials.[295] The Special Unit for Human Rights and IHL of the Prosecutor General consisted of 258 officials. Between 2004 and 2008, approximately 207,000 millions Colombian pesos (approx. 69 million €) were invested to guarantee an adequate implementation and application of Law 975.[296] The judicial authorities have, in theory, the possibility to carry out investigative activities in the whole territory of the country. Exhumations and victims' sessions have been realized in all departments, including the ones characterized by their difficult access due to the geographical situation or the presence of (new) illegal armed groups.[297] Thus, as to the substantial collapse test, requiring a restrictive interpretation and a quantitative and/or qualitative evaluation with a view to the guarantee of investigations or prosecutions, it is fair to conclude that, despite the said difficulties, the investigations necessary within the framework of Law 975 can be carried out, either directly in the regions concerned or by means of the displacement of resources and proceedings to other places.[298] Several institutions, like the Office of the Prosecutor General, the *Procuraduría*, the *Defensoría*, *Acción Social* and the CNRR[299] have offered assistance to the victims so that these are able to report the crimes. The judicial hearings are realized before the Higher Tribunal's Justice and Peace Chamber and the Supreme Court composed of judges with lengthy experience in the criminal justice system.

With regard to the third sub-criterion of inability (*lack or non-availability of a national justice system*), Colombia understands the expression "otherwise unable" as the clear absence of the necessary objective conditions to investigate and try a

---

[294] *See* e.g. for *Acción Social, supra* n 64 in Chap. 2.

[295] *See* FGN-UJP, *Oficio 012896* (2009), at 17.

[296] *See* http://www.dnp.gov.co/PortalWeb/Portals/0/archivos/documentos/GCRP/Presentaciones_Renteria/ CR_Justicia_2019(27_oct_08).pdf (last visited 9 October 2009).

[297] *See* the map drawn by the FGN-UJP, Sub-Unidad de Búsqueda de Desaparecidos, available at: http://www.fiscalia.gov.co/justiciapaz/EXH/imagenes/mapa-de-colombia.jpg (last visited 23 November 2009); FGN, *Informe de Gestión* (2009), at 109; *id.*, '20 grupos satélites de la Policía Judicial', available at: http://www.fiscalia.gov.co/justiciapaz/Despachos.htm (last visited 9 October 2009).

[298] *See* the nationwide presence of the CNRR through its 12 regional offices, available at: http://www.cnrr.org.co (last visited 9 October 2009). Also, between 2006 and 2009, the UJP has organized events for victims in 352 municipalities, which were attended by 70,957 persons (*cf.* FGN-UJP, *Aplicación Ley 975* (2009)).

[299] *See supra* n 25 in Chap. 3.

person.[300] Based on this declaration, the Constitutional Court adopted a similar restrictive position as to the inability standard of Art. 17 (3) ICC Statute.[301] Accordingly, "otherwise unable" refers to a clear absence of necessary objective conditions to carry out proceedings and must be comparable with the concrete examples mentioned in Art. 17 (3) ICC Statute (i.e., "to obtain the accused or the necessary evidence and testimony"), which are easily verifiable and deal with objective prerequisites to carry out the proceedings. Obviously, if one follows this view (that corresponds to the restrictive interpretation explained in the previous section), a non-availability of the national justice system does not exist, for the Colombian judicial system is generally functioning well, notwithstanding its limitations and shortcomings.[302]

This conclusion is confirmed by the advances, albeit small but real, in the *prosecution of international crimes* pursuant to the criminalization of IHL violations in Art. 135–164 of the Criminal Code of 2000 (Law 599). While prior to the demobilization of the AUC the Prosecutor had managed to identify only 350 of its members and the number of convicted paramilitaries amounted to not more than a hundred, the information obtained through Law 975 has – notwithstanding the fair trial problems pointed out above[303] – made possible the identification of a large part of the demobilized members and led during the last 4 years to the conviction of about 1880 of them under the ordinary criminal justice system.[304] Under Law 975, 707 postulated persons have been heard so far by the prosecutors during the free version hearings.[305] The UJP has formulated successive imputations against 165 demobilized persons and presented charges against 74 of them; 54 cases involving 9 paramilitaries have advanced to the hearing on the legalization of charges.[306] These figures show that the identification of the members of the paramilitary groups made it possible to attribute certain crimes to certain persons. For these reasons, an

[300] *See* para. 3 of the interpretative declaration of 5 August 2002 to Art. 17 ICC Statute: "Concerning article 17 (3), Colombia declares that the use of the word 'otherwise' with respect to the determination of the State's ability to investigate or prosecute a case refers to the obvious absence of objective conditions necessary to conduct the trial". (available at: http://www.icrc.org/ihl.nsf/NORM/909EEAAE157FBD43412566E100542BDE?OpenDocument, last visited 9 October 2009).

[301] Constitutional Court (n 165) (V.4.3.2.1.5. La regulación del principio de complementariedad).

[302] *See also* Castillo/García Villegas/Soledad Granada, in García Villegas (ed.) 2008, 168 ("Sin embargo, la violencia no ha impedido el funcionamiento de un sistema judicial que, cuando se compara con los de otros países latinoamericanos, tiene una sorprendente autonomía respecto del sistema político y una notoria estabilidad institucional.").

[303] Chapter 3 (ii) with n 17.

[304] Iguarán (n 51).

[305] During the free version hearings 32,909 crimes have been confessed (among them 26,163 homicides and 2,282 cases of forced disappearance) involving 47,054 victims; 14,612 of the confessed crimes, involving more than 16,000 victims, have been described in more detail (among them 9,214 homicides and 1,278 forced disappearances) (*cf.* FGN-UJP, *Aplicación Ley 975* (2009)).

[306] Comité Interinstitucional de Justicia y Paz, *Matriz* (2009).

external observer, avoiding a value judgment about the internal functioning of the Colombian criminal justice system, hardly comes to the conclusion that there exists a "clear absence of necessary objective conditions to carry out proceedings", neither in general terms nor in the specific context of Law 975.[307] However, doubts remain, again, with regard to the commanders extradited to the US, since the difficult and uncertain access to them by the Colombian authorities[308] may be compared to the situation mentioned explicitly in Art. 17 (3) ICC Statute regarding the inability "to obtain the accused or the necessary evidence and testimony".[309]

Clearly, a *broader interpretation* of the criterion of inability which focuses on the concrete effectiveness of a judicial remedy in a particular case might lead to a different conclusion arguing that the deficits in the application of Law 975, along with the enormous caseload and the lack of personal, financial and institutional resources, constitute a denial of an effective legal remedy entailing the inability of the judicial system as a whole.[310] Yet, it is quite clear that the number of crimes, perpetrators and victims to be dealt with under Law 975 would overload probably any national justice system. Until 30 September 2009, 257,089 victims had been registered.[311] The 707 persons – a small number compared to the more than 50.000 demobilized[311a] – who so far have ratified their willingness to be investigated and prosecuted according to Law 975 and are actively taking part in the free version hearings, have confessed 32,909 crimes (which are related to 47,054 victims), 26,163 of them dealing with homicides. The UJP has been able to verify and investigate the details of the confessed crimes in (only) 14,612 cases.[312] It has been widely acknowledged (and also witnessed by this author) that the UJP, despite the commitment of its officials and its attempts to improve the investigative activities, lacks sufficient resources and works beyond its capacity limits.

While the said relative inefficiency does not necessarily lead to an overall inability-judgment, at least if one does not follow the broader interpretation just

[307] *Cfr.* Burbidge (2008) *ICLR* 8, 557, at 586 ("Nevertheless the process is beginning to produce some results. It is difficult not to be impressed by a visit to the Fiscalia's Justice and Peace web-site where the photographs of all the paramilitary accused are displayed. The calendar throughout 2007–2008 is thick with public hearings in which the accused have their appointments to make a full confession.").

[308] *See supra* Chap 3 (vii) with n 44 and in this Chap. n 94 et seq. with main text (in this Chap.).

[309] Since the extradition of the paramilitary commanders in May 2008, only a few cases have slowly advanced, e.g. those of Salvatore Mancuso, Diego Murillo Bejerano (aka don Berna), Ramiro Vanoy (aka Cuco Vanoy) and Guillermo Pérez Alzate (aka Pablo Sevillano), *see* Caracol, Extradición de paramilitares estancó sus procesos judiciales en Colombia, 13 de mayo de 2009, available at: http://www.caracol.com.co/nota.aspx?id=811096 (last visited 9 October 2009).

[310] Concerning the case load of the Special Unit for Human Rights and International Humanitarian Law of the Prosecutor General, *see* FGN, *Informe de Gestión* (2009), at 112.

[311] FGN-UJP, *Aplicación Ley 975* (2009).

[311a] According to police figures 51.921 GAOML members have demobilized (among them approx. 16.000 members of guerilla groups), see Policía Nacional de Colombia, *Desmovilizados colectivos e individuals* (2009).

[312] *Ibid.*

described, it clearly demonstrates the need for a *comprehensive and integral strategy* for the selection and prioritization of paradigmatic situations and cases focusing on the most responsible blocks and persons of the illegal armed groups. Only such a strategy allows for the clarification of the systematic and widespread character of the crimes committed and the discovery of the macro-criminal structures. In contrast, the most advanced cases currently under investigation are characterized by their heterogeneity: Among the 159 demobilised against which the "imputation" has been formulated and the 51 accused (at the subsequent stage of the formulation of charges) are most of the not (yet) extradited high-level paramilitary commanders[313] but also some of the extradited commanders[314]; as well as a considerable number of mid-level commanders, but also numerous low-level paramilitaries.[315] In addition, there are also many persons who had already been detained or convicted prior to the demobilization of their paramilitary block or others who have been tried and convicted in the ordinary criminal justice system after their demobilization.

[313]Namely the commanders of the blocks of Cundinamarca, Montes de María, Autodefensas Campesinas de Meta y Vichada, Autodefensas Campesinas de Puerto Boyacá, Autodefensas Campesinas del Magdalena Medio, Frente Julio Peinado Becerra, Frente Héroes de los Llanos y el Guaviare and Élmer Cárdenas; *see* http://www.fiscalia.gov.co/justiciapaz/Audiencias.asp (last visited 9 October 2009)

[314]Salvatore Mancuso (Catatumbo and Cordoba blocks), Ramiro "Cuco" Vanoy (Minerso block) and Guillermo Perez Alzate (Libertadores del Sur block).

[315]The most advanced cases are those of Wilson Salazar Carrascal (n 32 in Chap. 1, n 311) and Gian Carlo Gutiérrez Suárez (main text after n 220), i.e. cases of mere foot soldiers (*patrulleros*).

Chapter 6
Conclusion: Classifying the Colombian Case with a View to Different Transitional Justice Scenarios

Among the *five scenarios of transitional justice* developed elsewhere,[1] the Colombian case can be located in the fourth group of "*measures that do not amount to full exemptions of criminal responsibility*", since Law 975 does not completely extinguish the punishment, but only grants a considerable reduction of the sentence.[2] As shown before,[3] such measures comply with the requisites of Art. 17(1) (b) ICC Statute. As to the Justice and Peace procedure it has already been demonstrated (*supra* Sect. 5.2.2.2) that both the investigation/prosecution and trial requirements are also complied with since they are all provided for by Law 975. Additionally, as expressed by the Constitutional Court, the judicial benefits granted by Law 975 depend on the cooperation (full confession) by the respective member of the irregular armed group and the subsequent verification of this confession by the investigators of the UJP. If he does not cooperate fully he may be subjected to an ordinary criminal process.

The assessment of *unwillingness or inability* (*supra* Sect. 5.2.3) depends on the seriousness of the commitment (good faith) of the government and the judicial authorities to achieve peace as the purpose of the (transition) process on the one hand, and justice for the victims on the other. The government's commitment can be evaluated by the comprehensiveness of the measures, i.e. if they are designed to apply to all groups involved in the conflict in an equal manner or if one group is excluded or (de facto) privileged, which would imply a verdict of unwillingness with regard to that group. This is not so much a legal-normative, but practical question. Be that as it may, at this moment it seems rather difficult to affirm Colombia's unwillingness or inability to investigate and prosecute international crimes and, on this basis, to justify the ICC's (formal) intervention. One may come

---

[1] *See* Ambos, in Ambos/Large/Wierda (eds.), 2009, at 78 (para. 44) distinguishing between a blanket self-amnesty, a conditional amnesty with a TRC, a conditional amnesty without a TRC, measures not amounting to full exemptions and *ex post* exemptions, in particular pardons.

[2] Concurring Olásolo, in Almqvist/Espósito (eds.) 2009, at 279.

[3] Ambos, in Ambos/Large/Wierda (eds.), 2009, at 80 (para. 47).

K. Ambos, *The Colombian Peace Process and the Principle of Complementarity of the International Criminal Court*,
DOI 10.1007/978-3-642-11273-7_6, © Springer-Verlag Berlin Heidelberg 2010

to a different conclusion with regard to concrete cases, though, in particular the cases against the most important, high-level commanders (including the extradited ones). Insofar one may argue that Colombia has not done everything possible and necessary with regard to Art. 17 ICC Statute but this does not change the global evaluation defended here.

To be sure, the deficits and problems of the Justice and Peace process must be resolved as soon as possible to avoid an intervention of the ICC. The recourse to *alternative justice mechanisms*, in particular, an effective Truth Commission and (other) non-punitive sanctions, could help to overcome or at least mitigate some of the practical problems in the implementation of Law 975.[4] Without such mechanisms, it will be difficult to reconcile the demobilization process with the justice element of transitional justice. Especially the establishment of an effective Truth Commission[5] and a major commitment of the other institutions and entities involved in the process[6] would help the *Fiscalía* to concentrate more exclusively on its actual task of criminal investigation and prosecution instead of assuming additional functions, especially with regard to victims' assistance.[7] The design and implementation of reparation mechanisms going beyond the limited framework of criminal proceedings may help to facilitate an easier and less discriminatory access to reparations for victims. Finally, returning to the starting point of this second part, it should be recalled that the complementarity test is an ongoing process which may be revisited periodically, i.e., there may come a point where the ICC's Prosecutor is no longer prepared to maintain the Colombian situation under observation in the preliminary phase of proceedings but go a step further and submit it to the Pre-Trial Chamber for further consideration pursuant to Art. 15(3) ICC Statute.[8]

---

[4]*See* in this sense also for a broader restorative-based alternative justice approach Valiñas, in Stahn/van den Herik (eds.) 2010, at 280 et seq (287–88).

[5]On its absence see already crit. Chap. 3. (vi) with n 30.

[6]On the complex institutional framework see already *supra* n 237 and 291 et seq. in Chap. 5 and main text.

[7]*See* on this issue already Chap. 3. (iv).

[8]Art. 15(3) ICC Statute: "If the Prosecutor concludes that there is a reasonable basis to proceed with an investigation, he or she shall submit to the Pre-Trial Chamber a request for authorization of an investigation, together with any supporting material collected...". In this context it is worthwhile mentioning that the OTP invoked this provision on 26 November 2009 in requesting the authorization of Pre-Trial Chamber II to open the investigation into crimes allegedly committed in Kenya in relation to the post-election violence of 2007–2008, *see* http://www.icc-cpi.int/NR/rdonlyres/AC13413D-D097-4527-B0AE-60CF6DBB1B68/281313/LM OINTROstatement26112009_2_2.pdf (last visited 10 March 2010).

Chapter 7
Some Recommendations for the Further Application of Law 975

The following recommendations relate, to a great extent, to the intermediate conclusions drawn above from the analysis of the Justice and Peace Procedure.[1]

(i) Given the large number of crimes, perpetrators and victims it is of utmost importance that the Prosecutor General develops a *global and comprehensive strategy of investigation with clear prosecution objectives and targets,* taking into account the macrocriminal context of the crimes committed. Such a strategy presupposes a *policy of selecting and prioritizing crimes, suspects and cases* focusing on the most responsible and on the paradigmatic cases which make the real dimensions and magnitude of the violence visible. Indeed, the investigation of system or collective criminality of the magnitude existing in Colombia requires going beyond a mere adding up of the individual crimes committed by the low- and mid-rank members of illegal armed groups. Rather, what is needed is an inquiry into the patterns of the violence, into the motivations, interests and rationales of those most responsible and the circumstances which allowed that those acts could be perpetrated in a coordinated manner in the first place.

(ii) This strategy must, on the level of substantive law, be complemented by the development of *uniform and stringent criteria* as to what *crimes and forms of imputation* (participation) should be applied in identical or similar cases. Indeed, the strategy deficit is worsened by the almost chaotic state of the Colombian substantive criminal law, characterized by continuous legislative amendments, the incomplete incorporation of international crimes, the lack of a consolidated jurisprudence concerning these crimes and a widespread confusion regarding the interplay between international and domestic criminal law. There is a clear need for expert advice in this area.

---

[1]*See supra* Chap. 3. For more detailed recommendations see Ambos et al., *Justicia y Paz* (2010), para. 412 et seq.

K. Ambos, *The Colombian Peace Process and the Principle of Complementarity of the International Criminal Court*,
DOI 10.1007/978-3-642-11273-7_7,

(iii) Notwithstanding a holistic approach in terms of prosecutorial strategy, the *figure of successive ("partial") imputations*[2] and – as a logical consequence – successive proceedings should not be dismissed in its entirety but be used in a more effective, rationale and coherent way. Investigations and, on that basis, imputations should be structured along *historical, geographical, material or personal criteria and circumstances*, focusing on the most responsible and the most serious crimes. Concretely speaking, investigations so structured should focus, *inter alia*, on crimes committed during certain periods of time (e.g. during the incursion of an illegal armed group into a region, the consolidation of its control and the exercise of undisputed power over the population), in determined regions of the country, in the context of certain forms of victimization (e.g. the use of massacres to intimidate the population, acts of social cleansing, sexual violence against women, recruitment of children, violence against political opponents or other vulnerable groups, like displaced persons, homosexuals, trade-unionists or human rights defenders) or by particular individual or collective perpetrators (e.g. by specialized units of illegal armed groups). The recourse to successive imputations in a reasonable and rational manner is unavoidable in order to cope with macro-criminality. In fact, in such investigations imputations are necessarily "partial" in that each and every crime and suspect can never be investigated and, even less probably, prosecuted or tried. Indeed, the necessary selection and prioritization entails, almost automatically, a "partialisation" of the truth but this is the price of a rational and realistic prosecution strategy.

(iv) The growing practice of collective free version hearings with several suspects has considerably accelerated the proceedings, so that a *wider use of collective judicial hearings and joinders of trial proceedings* can be recommended. With these measures it is possible to reduce the congestion of the criminal justice system, the backlog of cases and the delay of proceedings. In order to avoid unnecessary repetitions during proceedings, successive imputations and collective hearings could be used simultaneously when investigating and prosecuting crimes which have been perpetrated by several suspects through a division of tasks, e.g. in the case of massacres or other crimes with a sophisticated preparation and the participation of several persons. Additionally, it seems convenient to reconsider the procedural framework with a view to reducing the number of hearings during the criminal proceedings. The current practice of realizing two preliminary hearings (on the formulation of imputations and the formulation of charges) before the actual hearing on the legalization of charges could be replaced through a judicial reform which provides for only one hearing in which the Prosecutor – after having completed his investigation – presents the charges before the Higher Tribunal's Justice and Peace Chamber. The Chamber has then to decide on the legalization of charges and the fulfilment of the eligibility requirements.

[2] *See* on the issue of partial/successive imputations already Part I, Chap. 2.3 and Chap. 3 (vi).

(v) The different hearings during the judicial phase of Law 975 usually commence with the prosecutor' presentation of the *general context of the crimes committed*, i.e. the history, structure and chains of command of the illegal armed group, its areas of influence and control, its financial sources and ties with political, military or social sectors.[3] Given the importance and, at the same time, complexity of the clarification of this context, it is recommendable that other institutions and persons, i.e., the Group for the Historical Memory of the CNRR, victims and their organizations, NGOs, academics and experts, are adequately consulted and heard as (expert) witnesses, especially during the hearings on the legalization of the acceptance of charges and the reparations before the Special Justice and Peace Chamber of the Higher Tribunal. Given the absence of a "real" Truth and Reconciliation Commission in Colombia the broad participation of these institutions and individuals is particularly important with a view to the establishment of the truth. This may also contribute to a comprehensive evaluation of the eligibility requirements, facilitate reconciliation by giving victims the right to present their views and guarantee the determination of adequate reparations.

(vi) One of the biggest challenges is to *improve the inter-institutional* between *and intra-institutional cooperation* within the institutions involved in the Justice and Peace procedure (i.e. especially the Special Unit for Justice and Peace of the Office of the Prosecutor, the Higher Tribunals' Special Chambers of Justice and Peace, the Special Units for Justice and Peace of the *Procuraduría General de la Nación*, the *Defensoría del Pueblo* and the national and regional offices of the CNRR). The inter-institutional cooperation should focus on the access to information about the suspects and victims, the smooth exchange of information regarding ongoing and future proceedings, the scheduling of hearings, the assignation of legal representatives to victims of cases dealt with during the hearings and the adoption of preliminary measures to protect victims, witnesses or to secure the demobilized persons' assets necessary for the reparation of victims. *Intra-institutional cooperation* refers to the relationship between different units within the said institutions. Generally, this cooperation suffers from the lack of continuity of the personnel working in all institutions, especially in the Special Units for Justice and Peace of the Office of the Prosecutor General. The lack of a public and transparent *concours* to enter most public institutions means that officials have no job security and can be sacked almost at will by their superiors. The high fluctuation has the consequence that the accumulated experience and knowledge of more experienced officials is getting lost and that the new officials have serious problems to catch up in ongoing proceedings. *Thus, a professionalisation of public service and institutions* in Colombia is, not only in the area of our concern, overdue. In the case of the *Defensoría del Pueblo* it is important to guarantee an adequate legal representation, not only in the

[3] *See supra* Chap. 3 (v).

preliminary phase of the proceedings, but also before the Justice and Peace Chamber of the Higher Tribunal in Bogota. Given the concentration of this phase of the proceedings in Bogotá it is important to make sure that the regional offices of the Defensoría pass on the case file to the public defenders in Bogotá. On the other hand, it must be assured that victims' requests for legal representation and participation lodged in the ordinary local offices of the Defensoría del Pueblo will be transmitted to the Special Units for Justice and Peace of the Defensoría.

(vii) The problems of coordination between and within governmental entities are also a result of the geographic *centralization of the Justice and Peace proceedings*. While the free version hearings are taking place in several cities throughout the country, only three major cities (Bogotá, Medellín and Barranquilla) host the judicial hearings regarding the imputation and formulation of charges. Even worse, the hearings for the legalization of charges, on reparations and for sentencing lie in the exclusive competence of the Higher Tribunal's Special Justice and Peace Chamber which currently only operates in Bogotá. As a consequence, access to the judicial hearings is difficult, if not impossible for most victims, their legal representatives and even postulated persons since they normally live in the areas where the crimes have been committed and these are far away from the major cities. Thus, it is highly advisable to *decentralize the criminal proceedings*, in order to, at least, remove this obstacle for the participation of, especially, the victims. In this regard it is worthwile recalling that these disadvantages of a centralized judicial structure might be mitigated by an adequate *outreach program* which facilitates the access to the hearings through modern forms of communication (technology), e.g. online transmissions of hearings, electronic access to the case files and sufficiently in advance information regarding the scheduling and content of prospective hearings.

(viii) In any case, the access to the hearings is just one problem related to the deficient *victims' participation* in the justice and peace procedure.[4] Many practical steps are needed to improve the security and mobility of the victims and thus effectively enable them to participate in the proceedings. The Trust Fund for Reparations lacks sufficient resources to adequately compensate victims. Many victims are not properly informed and thus ignorant of their rights. Given the complexity of the legal framework of Law 975 the efforts made to *adequately inform victims about their rights* to justice, truth and reparation and the existing remedies established under national law should be increased.

(ix) Last but not least, the *extraditions* of several leading members of the paramilitary movement occurred without the establishment of a comprehensive and detailed cooperation agreement between Colombia and the U.S.A., especially securing the continued access to these persons by the

---

[4] *See supra* Chap. 3 (iv).

Colombian authorities.[5] Thus, at the moment, it is the exclusive decision of the U.S. authorities to grant access or not. Yet, the *de facto* exclusion of these persons from the Justice and Peace procedure entails the loss of essential informations with regard to the establishment of the truth. Thus, with a view to Colombia's (international) obligations *vis-à-vis* the victims, this situation should be corrected as soon as possible and this presupposes, as already said, an agreement between Colombia and the U.S.A. on judicial cooperation.

[5] *See supra* Chap. 3 (vii).

Documents and Materials

1. Bibliography

1.1 Monographs and Books

Alonso Espinal, Manuel Alberto/Valencia Agudelo, Germán Darío *et al. Estudio sobre el proceso de desmovilización, desarme y reinserción en Antioquia: anotaciones desde lo local,* Medellín, Comisión Departamental de seguimiento y acompañamiento al Proceso de Desmovilización, Desarme y Reinserción en Antioquia, 2007.

Ambos, Kai. *El marco jurídico de la justicia de transición: especial referencia al caso Colombiano,* Bogotá, Ed. Temis, 2008.

Ambos, Kai, with the assistance of Florian Huber/Rodrigo A. González Fuente-Rubilar/John Zuluaga. *Procedimiento de la Ley de Justicia y Paz (Ley 975 de 2005) y derecho penal internacional - Estudio sobre la facultad de intervención complementaria de la Corte Penal Internacional a la luz del denominado proceso de "justicia y paz" en Colombia,* Bogotá, Ed. Temis, 2010; available at www.department-ambos.uni-goettingen.de/index.php/en/Forschung/friedensprozess-in-kolumbien-aufgrund-des-gesetzes-975-v-2272005.html.

Beck, Katharina. *Der Demobilisierungsprozess der Paramilitärs in Kolumbien unter Alvaro Uribe,* Saarbrücken, VDM Verlag Dr. Müller, 2008.

Cárdenas, Claudia. *Die Zulässigkeitsprüfung vor dem Internationalen Strafgerichtshof,* Berlin, Berliner Wissenschafts-Verlag, 2005.

Douglas, Sarah/Farr, Vanessa/Hill, Felicity/Kasuma, Wenny. *Getting it right, doing it right: gender and disarmament, demobilization and reintegration,* UNIFEM, 2004.

Gaitán, Olga Lucía. *Mecanismos para impulsar el esclarecimiento de la verdad en los procesos penales por el delito de desaparición forzada de personas en Colombia, en aplicación de la Ley 975 de 2005,* Bogotá, Fundación Social, 2006.

Huber, Florian. *La ley de justicia y paz: desafios y temas de debate,* Bogotá, Fundación Ed. Cerec, 2007.

McAuliffe de Guzman, Margaret. *Gravity and the legitimacy of the ICC,* Yale Law School Student Scholarship Series, 2008 (paper 69), 30; available at http://lsr.nellco.org/yale/student/papers/69 (last visited 3 September 2009).

Meißner, Jörg. *Die Zusammenarbeit mit dem internationalen Strafgerichtshof nach dem römischen Statut,* Munich, C.H.Beck, 2003.

Morel, Sophie. *La mise en œuvre du principe de complémentarité par la cour pénale internationale le case particulier des amnisties,* Lausanne, Editions bis et ter, 2005.

Olásolo, Héctor. *The triggering procedure of the International Criminal Court,* Leiden et al., Nijhoff, 2005.

O'Shea, Andreas. *Amnesty for Crime in International Law and Practice,* Londres-Nueva York-La Haya, Kluwer, 2002.

Otero, Diego. *Las cifras del conflicto colombiano,* Bogotá, Indepaz, 2007; available at: http://www.indepaz.org.co/attachments/191_cifras%201964%20-2007.pdf (last visited 31 October 2009).
Pérez, Luis Carlos, *Tratado de Derecho Penal*, 4 vol., Bogotá, Temis, 2nd ed. 1978.
Razesberger, Florian. *The ICC. The principle of complementarity*, Frankfurt am Main, Peter Lang, 2006.
Redepaz (La Red Nacional de Iniciativas Ciudadanas por la Paz y contra la Guerra), *Víctimas del conflicto armado en Colombia: perfil, escenarios, autores y hechos,* 2008.
Schabas, William. *An introduction to the International Criminal Court*, 3rd ed., Cambridge, CUP, 2007.
Schiff, Benjamin. *Building the International Criminal Court*, Cambridge, CUP, 2008.
Schomburg, Wolfgang/Lagodny Otto/Gleß, Sabine/Hackner, Thomas: *Internationale Rechtshilfe in Strafsachen*, Munich, C.H.Beck, 4th ed. 2006.
Stigen, Jo. *The relationship between the International Criminal Court and national jurisdictions,* Leiden Boston, Martinus Nijhoff Publishers, 2008.
Wei, Wu. *Die Rolle des Anklägers eines internationalen Strafgerichthofs*, Frankfurt a. M., Peter Lang, 2007.

1.2 Articles in journals/books

Agirre Aranburu, Xabier. Gravity of crimes and responsibility of the suspect, in M. Bergsmo (ed.) *Criteria for Prioritizing and Selecting Core International Crimes Cases*, FICHL Publication Series N° 4, Oslo, PRIO, 2009, 147–166; available at http://www.prio.no/ficjc.
Ambos, Kai. The structure of International Criminal Procedure: 'Adversarial', 'Inquisitorial' or Mixed?, in M. Bohlander (ed.) *International Criminal Justice: A critical analysis of institutions and procedures*, London, Cameron May, 2007, 429–503.
Ambos, Kai. Zum heutigen Verständnis von Akkusationsprinzip und –verfahren aus historischer Sicht, in *JURA* 30, 2008, 586–594; spanish version: El principio acusatorio y el proceso acusatorio: un intento de comprender su significado actual desde la perspectiva histórica, in L. Bachmaier Winter (ed.) *Proceso penal y sistemas acusatorios*, Madrid, Marcial Pons, 2008, 49–72.
Ambos, Kai. Article 25. Individual criminal responsibility, in O. Triffterer (ed.) *Commentary on the Rome Statute of the ICC*, Munich, C.H. Beck, 2nd ed. 2008.
Ambos, Kai. The Legal framework of Transitional Justice, in Ambos/Large/Wierda (eds.) *Building a Future on Peace and Justice. Studies on Transitional Justice, Peace and Development. The Nuremberg Declaration on Peace and Justice,* Berlin, Springer, 2009, 19–103.
Arbour, Louise/Bergsmo, Morten. "Conspicious absence of jurisdictional overreach", in H. van Hebel/J.G. Lammers/J. Schukking (eds.) *Reflections on the ICC*, The Hague, T.M.C. Asser Press, 1999, 129–140.
Arsanjani, Mahnoush/Reisman, Michael. The International Criminal Court and the Congo: From theory to reality, in L. Sadat/M. Scharf (eds.) *The theory and practice of International Criminal Law. Essays in honour of M. Cherif Bassiouni*, Leiden, Martinus Nijhoff, 2008, 325–347.
Bartelt, Sandra. Die Zulässigkeit von Wahrheitskommissionen im Lichte des neuen Internationalen Strafgerichtshof, in *AVR* 43, 2005, 187–217.
Bastidas, William. Demobilisierung: Das Ende des Paramilitarismus in Kolumbien?, in *Autoritärer Staat und paramilitärische Machtnahme in Kolumbien. Die Regierung Uribe und der Krieg gegen die soziale Bewegung,* Berlin, FDCL e.V. & Kolumbienkampagne Berlin (ed.) 2007, 22–29.
Bekou, Olympia. Complementarity and the ICC: a dangerous gamble? in G. Ulrich (ed.) *The International Criminal Court: challenges and prospects*, Proceedings of an international

conference organised by the European Inter-University Centre for Human Rights and Democratisation (EIUC), Venecia, Marsiolio Editori, 2005, 61–81.

Benzing, Markus. The complementarity regime of the ICC: International criminal justice between state sovereignty and the fight against impunity, in *MPYbUNL* 7, 2003, 591–632.

Bothe, Michael. Complementarity: ensuring compliance with international law though criminal prosecutions – whose responsibility?, in *Friedenswarte* 83, 2008, 59–72.

Burbidge, Peter. Justice and Peace?, The role of law in resolving Colombias civil conflict, in *ICLR* 8, issue 3, 2008, 581–588.

Burke-White, William. Complementarity in practice: The International Criminal Court as part of a system of multi-level global governance in the Democratic Republic of Congo, in *LJIL* 18, 2005, 559–590.

Burke-White, William. Implementing a policy of positive complementarity in the Rome system of justice, in *CLF* 19, 2008, 59–85.

Burke-White, William. Proactive complementarity: The International Criminal Court and national courts in the Rome system of international justice, in *HarvIntLJ* 49, 2008, 53–108.

Burke-White, William/Kaplan, Scott. The ICC and an admissibility challenge in the Uganda situation, in Stahn/Sluiter (eds.) *The emerging practice of the International Criminal Court*, Leiden – Boston, Martinus Nijhoff, 2009, 79–114 (also published in (2009) 7 *JICJ* 257–279).

Cárdenas, Claudia, in G. Werle (ed.) *Justice in transition – prosecution and amnesty in Germany and South Africa*, Berlin, Berliner Wissenschaftsverlag, 2006, 239–255.

Cárdenas, Claudia. "The admissibility test before the ICC under special considerations of amnesties and truth commissions", in J. K. Kleffner/G. Kor (eds.) *Complementary views on complementarity*, La Haya, TMC Asser Press, 2006, 115–139.

Cárdenas, Claudia. Wann darf der Internationale Strafgerichtshof ermitteln oder verfolgen?, in G. Hankel (ed.) *Die Macht und das Recht. Beiträge zum Völkerrecht und Völkerstrafrecht am Beginn des 21. Jahrhunderts* Hamburgo, Hamburger Institut für Sozialforschung, 2008, 127–156.

Carnero Rojo, Enrique. The role of fair trial considerations in the complementarity regime of the International Criminal Court: from "no peace without justice" to "no peace without victor's justice"?, in *LJIL* 18, 2005, 829–869.

Castillo, Camilo/García Villegas, Mauricio/Granada, Soledad/Villoamárin, Adriana. La justicia en zonas de conflicto armado, in García Villegas (ed.) *Jueces sin Estado, La Justicia colombiana en zonas de conflicto armado*, Bogotá, Siglo del Hombre Editores, 2008, 165–196.

De Greiff, Pablo. DDR and reparations: establishing links between peace and justice instruments, in Ambos/Large/Wierda (eds.) *Building a Future on Peace and Justice. Studies on Transitional Justice, Peace and Development. The Nuremberg Declaration on Peace and Justice,* Berlin, Springer-Verlag, 2009, 321–355.

Díaz, Catalina. Colombia´s Bid for Justice and Peace, in Ambos/Large/Wierda (eds.) *Building a Future on Peace and Justice. Studies on Transitional Justice, Peace and Development. The Nuremberg Declaration on Peace and Justice,* Berlín, Springer-Verlag, 2009, 469–501.

Easterday, Jennifer. Deciding the Fate of Complementarity: A Colombian Study, in *Ariz. J. Int´l & Comp. L.* 26, 2009, 49–110.

El Zeidy, Mohamed. The principle of complementarity: a new machinery to implement international criminal law, in *MichJIntL*, 32, 2002, 869–975.

Ellis, Mark. The International Criminal Court and its implication for domestic law and national capacity building, in *15 Fla. J. Int'l L.*, 2002, 215–242.

Evans, Rhys David. Amnesties, pardons and complementarity: does the International Criminal Court have the tools to end impunity?, in *Human Rights Law Commentary* 1, 2005, 1–10.

Faltas, Sami. DDR without camps: the need for decentralized approaches, in Bonn Int'L Centre for Conversion (BICC), *Conversion Survey 2005: Global disarmament, demilitarization, and demobilization*, Baden-Baden, Nomos-Verlag, 2005; available at: http://www.sweden.gov.se/content/1/c6/06/54/02/5d16fcf2.pdf (last visited 15 November 2009).

Figari Layus, Rosario/Kintzel, Yvonne. Der Demobilisierungprozeß in Kolumbien: ein Beispiel für Transitional Justice?, in *MenschenRechtsMagazin* 13 Jahrgänge, Universität Postdam, 2008, Heft 2, 253–262.

Gavron, Jessica. Amnesties in the light of developments in international law and the establishment of the International Criminal Court, in *ICLQ* 51, 2002, 91–117.

Gómez Pardo, Jorge Enrique. The content of Colombian Justice and Peace Law accomplishes the ICC standards, in *Revista Debate Interamericano* (Ministerio de Relaciones Exteriores) 2009, 123–154.

Gómez Quintero, Alfredo. La administración de justicia en el marco del proceso de paz colombiano, in Almqvist/Espósito (eds.) Justicia transicional en Iberoamérica, Madrid, Centro de Estudios Políticos y Constitucionales, 2009, 157–178.

Greppi, Edoardo. Inability to investigate and prosecute under article 17, in M. Politi/F. Gioia (eds.) *The International Criminal Court and national jurisdictions,* Hampshire, Ashgate, 2008, 63–70.

Gropengießer, Helmut/Meißner, Jörg. Amnesties and the Rome Statute of the ICC, in *ICLR* 5, 2005, 267–300.

Guariglia, Fabricio. The selection of cases by the Office of the Prosecutor of the International Criminal Court, in Stahn/Sluiter (eds.) *The emerging practice of the International Criminal Court*, Leiden – Boston, Martinus Nijhoff, 2009, 209–217

Gutiérrez, Francicso. The peace process with the paramilitaries in Colombia: sustainability, proportionality and the allocation of guilt, in Bergsmo/Kalmanovitz (eds.) *Law in Peace Negotiations*, FICHL Publications Series No. 5, Oslo, PRIO, 2009, 99–121; available at: http://www.prio.no/ficjc.

Hall, Christopher Keith. Developing and implementing an effective positive complementarity prosecution strategy in Stahn/Sluiter (eds.) *The emerging practice of the International Criminal Court*, Leiden – Boston, Brill, 2009, 290.

Heller, Kevin Jon. The shadow side of complementarity: the effect of article 17 of the Rome Statute on national due process, in *CLF* 17, 2006, 255–280.

Heller, Kevin Jon. Situational gravity under the Rome Statute, in: C. Stahn/L. van den Herik (eds.) *Future Perspectives on International Criminal Justice*, The Hague, Asser Press, 2010, 227–253.

Holmes, John T. The principle of complementarity, in R. S. Lee (ed.) *The international Criminal Court: The Making of the Rome Statute. Issues, Negotiations, Results,* The Hague et al., Kluwer, 1999, 41–78.

Holmes, John T. Complementarity: national courts *versus* the ICC, in Cassese/Gaeta/Jones (eds.) *The Rome Statute of the ICC: a commentary,* Vol. I, Oxford, OUP, 2002, 667–686.

Hoffmeister, Frank/Knoke, Sebastian. Das Vorermittlungsverfahren vor dem Internationalen Strafgerichtshof – Prüfstein für die Effektivität der neuen Gerichtsbarkeit im Völkerstrafrecht, in *ZaöRV* 59, 1999, 785–808.

Kalmanovitz, Pablo. Introduction, in Bergsmo/Kalmanovitz (eds.) *Law in Peace Negotiations*, FICHL Publications Series No. 5, Oslo, PRIO, 2009, 7–20; available at http://www.prio.no/ficjc.

Kleffner, Jann K. Complementarity as a catalyst for compliance, in Kleffner/Kor (eds.) *Complementary views on complementarity*, The Hague, TMC Asser Press, 2006, 79–104.

Kleffner, Jann K. The impact of complementarity on national implementation of substantive international criminal law, in *JICJ* 1, 2003, 86–113.

Kreicker, Helmut. Völkerstrafrecht im Ländervergleich, in Eser/Sieber/Kreicker (eds.) *Nationale Strafverfolgung völkerrechtlicher Verbrechen/National Prosecution of International Crimes, Vol. VII.* Berlin & Freiburg, Duncker & Humblot, 2006.

Laplante, Lisa J./Theidon, Kimberly. Transitional Justice in Times of Conflict: Colombia's Ley de justicia y paz, in *MichJIntL*, 28, 2007, 50–108.

Majzub, Diba. Peace and Justice? Amnesties and the International Criminal Court, in *MelbJIntL* 3, 2002, 247–279.

Meyer, Frank. Complementing complementarity, in *ICLR* 6, 2006, 549–583.
Mohan, Mahdev. The Paradox of Victim-Centrism: Victim Participation at the Khmer Rouge Tribunal, in *ICLR* 9, 2009, 733–775.
Mora Sarasti, Roberto. Ley de justicia y paz y justicia transicional: un avance significativo, in *International Law: Revista Colombiana de Derecho Internacional* N. 6, Bogotá, Jul-Dic 2005, 119.
Murphy, Robin. Establishing a Precedent in Uganda: The Legitimacy of National Amnesties under the ICC, in *Eyes on the ICC* 3, 2006, 33–56.
Ohlin, Jens. Peace, security, and prosecutorial discretion, in Stahn/Sluiter (eds.) *The emerging practice of the International Criminal Court*, Leiden – Boston, Martinus Nijhoff, 2009, 185–208.
Olásolo, Héctor. The Prosecutor of the ICC before the initiation of investigations: a quasi judicial or political body?, in *ICLR* 3, 2003, 87–150.
Olásolo, Héctor. The lack of attention to the distinction between situation and cases in national laws on co-operation with the International Criminal Court with particular reference to the Spanish case, in *LJIL* 20, 2007, 193–261.
Olásolo, Héctor. Admissibilidad de situaciones y casos objeto de procesos de justicia de transición ante la Corte Penal Internacional, in Almqvist/Espósito (eds.) *Justicia transicional en Iberoamérica*, Madrid, Centro de Estudios Políticos y Constitucionales, 2009, 255–289.
Osiel, Mark. How should the ICC Office of the Prosecutor choose its cases? The multiple meanings of 'situational gravity', in *The Hague Justice Portal*, 2009, 1–7; available at: http://www.haguejusticeportal.net/eCache/DEF/10/344.html (last visited 3 September 2009).
Osiel, Mark. When Law 'expresses' more than it cares to admit: Comments on Heller, in: C. Stahn/ L. van den Herik (eds.) *Future Perspectives on International Criminal Justice*, The Hague, Asser Press, 2010, 254–258.
Philips, Ruth. The International Criminal Court Statute: Jurisdiction and admissibility, in *CLF* 10, 1999, 61–85.
Pichon, Jakob. The principle of complementarity in the cases of the Sudanese nationals Ahmad Harun and Ali Kushayb before the International Criminal Court, in *ICLR* 8, 2008, 185–228.
Pizarro, Eduardo, La hora de las víctimas, http://www.verdadabierta.com/web3/reconciliacion/45-reparaciones-a-victimas/231-la-hora-de-las-victimas?format=pdf (last visited 8 October 2009).
Rastan, Rod. What is a 'case' for the purpose of the Rome Statute?, in *CLF* 19, 2008, 435–448.
Robinson, Darryl. Serving the interests of justice: amnesties, truth commissions and the International Criminal Court, in *EJIL* 14, 2003, 481–505.
Rodman, Kenneth. Is Peace in the Interest of Justice? The Case for Broad Prosecutorial Discretion at the International Criminal Court, in *LJIL* 22, 2009, 99–126.
Ryngaert, Cedric. The Principle of Complementarity: A Means of Ensuring Effective International Criminal Justice, in Cedric Ryngaert (ed.) *The Effectiveness of International Criminal Justice*, Antwerpen, Intersentia, 2009, 146–172.
Saffon, María Paula/Uprimny, Rodrigo. Transitional justice in Colombia, in Bergsmo/Kalmanovitz (eds.) *Law in Peace Negotiations*, Oslo, PRIO, 2009, 217–244; available at http://www.prio.no/ficjc.
Saffon, María Paula. Problematic selection and lack of clear prioritization: the Colombian experience, in Morten Bergsmo (ed.) *Criteria for Prioritizing and Selecting Core International Crimes Cases*, FICHL Publication Series No. 4, Oslo, PRIO, 2009, 93–101; available at http://www.prio.no/ficjc.
Schabas, William. Complementarity in practice: some uncomplimentary thoughts, in *CLF* 19, 2008, 5–33.
Scharf, Michael. The amnesty exception to the jurisdiction of the International Criminal Court, in *Cornell Journal of International Law* 32, 1999, 507–527.
Schüller, Andreas. Gravity under the Rome Statute: Procedural filter or instrument of shaping criminal policy?, in *HuV-I*, 21, 2008, 73–81.

Sedman, David, Should the prosecution of ordinary crimes in domestic jurisdictions satisfy the complementarity principle?, in: C. Stahn/L. van den Herik (eds.) *Future Perspectives on International Criminal Justice*, The Hague, Asser Press, 2010, 259–266.

Seibert-Fohr, Anja. The relevance of the Rome Statute of the International Criminal Court for amnesties and truth commissions, in *MPYbUNL* 7, 2003, 553–590.

Seils, Paul. The selection and prioritization of cases by the Office of the Prosecutor of the ICC, in Bergsmo (ed.) *Criteria for Prioritizing and Selecting Core International Crimes Cases*, FICHL Publication Series 4, Oslo, PRIO, 2009, 55–60; available at http://www.prio.no/ficjc.

Seils, Paul/Wierda, Marieke. The International Criminal Court and conflict mediation, in *ICTJ*, junio 2005, 1–20; available at: http://www.ictj.org/en/news/pubs/index.html (last visited 2 September 2009).

Sheng, Ada. Analysing the International Criminal Court complementarity principle through a Federal Courts lens, in *bepress Legal Series* 1249, 2006, 1–30.

Smith, Stephen E. Inventing the laws of gravity: the ICC's initial Lubanga decision and its regressive consequences, in *ICLR* 8, 2008, 331–352.

Stahn, Carsten. The geometry of transitional justice: choices of institutional design, in *LJIL* 18, 2005, 425–466.

Stahn, Carsten. Complementarity, amnesties and alternative forms of justice: some interpretative guidelines for the International Criminal Court, in *JICJ* 3, 2005, 697.

Stahn, Carsten. Complementarity: a tale of two notions, in *CLF* 19, 2008, 87–113.

Stegmiller, Ignaz. Complementarity thoughts, in *CLF* 21, 2010, issue 1 (forthcoming).

Uprimny, Rodrigo/Saffon, María Paula. ¿Al fin, ley de justicia y paz? La Ley 975 tras el fallo de la Corte Constitutional, in Uprimny (ed.) *Justicia transicional sin transición*, Bogotá, DeJuSticia, 2006, 201.

Valiñas, Marta, Interpreting complementarity and interests of justice in the presence of restorative-based alternative forms of justice, in: C. Stahn/L. van den Herik (eds.) *Future Perspectives on International Criminal Justice*, The Hague, Asser Press, 2010, 267–288.

Van den Wyngaert, Christine/Ongena, Thérèse. *Ne bis in idem* principle, including the issue of amnesty, in A. Cassese/P. Gaeta/J. Jones (eds.) *The Rome Statute of the ICC: a commentary*, Vol. I, Oxford, OUP, 2002, 705–729.

Van der Wilt, Harmen/Lyngdorf, Sandra. Procedural obligations under the European Convention on Human Rights: Useful guidelines for the assessment of "unwillingness" and "inability" in the context of the complementarity principle, in *ICLR* 9, 2009, 39–75.

Werle, Gerhard. Transitional Justice – Der juristische Rahmen, in H.E. Müller et al. (eds.) *Festschrift für Ulrich Eisenberg*, Munich, Beck, 2009, 791–806.

Williams, Sharon/Schabas, William, Art. 17, in O. Triffterer (4 *Commentary on the Rome Statute of the ICC*, Munich et al., Beck 2ª ed. 2008, 605–625.

Wouters, Jan/Verhoeven, Sten. Cases identified for investigation and prosecution by the International Criminal Court, in E. Ankumah/E. Kwakwa (eds.) *African Perspectives on International Criminal Justice*, African Legal Aid Special Series Vol. 3, Accra, Océ Business Services, 2005, 133–160.

Zulaga Lopéz, Lorena. Ley de justicia y paz: ¿camino idóneo para la acción de paz?, in *Divergencia* N. 7, Bogotá, Universidad Externado de Colombia, Dic 2007, 10–13.

1.3 Papers and other documents

Alto Comisionado para la Paz. Proceso de Paz con las Autodefensas, Presentación General, without date; available at: http://www.altocomisionadoparalapaz.gov.co/web/g_autodefensa/dialogos.htm (last visited 23 November 2009).

Amnesty International (AI). 'Leave us in Peace'. Targeting Civilians in Colombia´s Internal Armed Conflict, 2008; available at: http://www.amnesty.org/es/for-media/press-releases/colombia-paz-conflicto-armado-datos-cifras-20081028 (last visited 3 September 2009).

Centro Internacional de Toledo para la Paz (CitPax). Observatorio Internacional sobre el proceso de DDR y la aplicación de la Ley de Justicia y Paz en Colombia, Area de Justicia, *Segundo Informe sobre las formulas de imputación de crímenes internacionales en el marco de Justicia y Paz,* July 2009.

Comisión Colombiana de Juristas (CCJ).*Anotaciones sobre la Ley de Justicia y Paz: : Una mirada desde los derechos de las víctimas,* Bogotá, 2007.

Comisión Colombiana de Juristas (CCJ). A pesar de los cambios, el Gobierno sigue desconociendo sentencia de Corte Constitucional en reglamentación, *Boletín No. 4*, 4 October 2006; available at: http://www.coljuristas.org/LinkClick.aspx?fileticket=sRBPuzF3IBs=&tabid=126&mid=522 (last visited 8 October 2009).

Comisión Nacional de Reparación y Reconciliación, Plan área de memoria histórica. Aprobado por el pleno de la CNRR del 20 de febrero de 2007; available at: http://memoriahistorica-cnrr.org.co/index.php?option=com_content&task=view&id=12&Itemid=28. (last visited 9 October 2009).

Comité Interinstitucional de Justicia y Paz, Matriz de Justicia y Paz, 31 December 2009 (document on file with the author).

Corporación Nuevo Arco Iris. *Observatorio del Conflicto Armado, Los expedientes de la parapolítica*, Bogotá 2009; available at: http://www.nuevoarcoiris.org.co/sac/files/oca/analisis/parapolitica_legislativa_JUNIO_2009.pdf (last visited 23 November 2009).

Fiscalía General de la Nación (FGN). *Informe de Gestión 2007-2008,* Bogotá 2008; available at http://fgn.fiscalia.gov.co:8080/Fiscalia/archivos/InformedeGestion/infgesfis07-08.pdf. (last visited 23 November 2009).

Fiscalía General de la Nación (FGN). *Informe de Gestión 2008-2009,* Bogotá 2009; available at: http://fgn.fiscalia.gov.co:8080/Fiscalia/archivos/RendiciondeCuenta/informe_de_gestion_09.pdf (last visited 23 November 2009).

Fiscalía General de la Nación (FGN)-Unidad de Justicia y Paz (UJP), Documento interno sobre la aplicación de la Ley 975, 15 October 2009 (on file with the author).

Fiscalía General de la Nación (FGN)-Unidad de Justicia y Paz (UJP). *Oficio 012896*, Bogotá 9 November 2009 (Comments on preliminary versión of Ambos et al., Justicia y Paz (2010)) (on file with the author).

Fundacíon Social. *Observatorio de opinión sobre la "Ley de alternatividad penal". Comentarios y recomendaciones de los actores más importantes en la materia,* Bogotá, FS-ICTJ, 2003.

Fundacíon Social. *Trámite de la Ley de justicia y paz: elementos para el control ciudadano al ejercicio del poder político*, Bogotá, 2006.

Fundacíon Social. *Ley de alternatividad penal y justicia transicional: documento de recomendaciones*, Bogotá, 2007.

Hall, Christopher Keith. Suggestions concerning International Criminal Court prosecutorial policy and strategy and external relations. Contribution to an expert consultation process on general issues relevant to the ICC Office of the Prosecutor, 28.3.2003; available at: http://www.icc-cpi.int/iccdocs/asp_docs/library/organs/otp/hall.pdf (last visited 15 November 2009).

Huber, Florian. ¿Qué quieren las víctimas como reparación y qué pueden esperar de los mecanismos de reparación diseñados por la Ley de Justicia y Paz? – Un balance crítico de la implementación de la Ley 975 de 2005 y su impacto práctico, Presentation during the conference 'Reparación en Colombia: Qué quieren las víctimas? Retos, desafíos y alternativas para garantizar la integralidad', Bogotá, 8 May 2009 (unpublished document).

Human Rights Watch. *Benchmarks for assessing possible national alternatives to International Criminal Court cases against LRA leaders*, May 2007, 1–10, 4 et seq.; available at: www.iccnow.org/documents/icc0507web[1].pdf (last visited 7 October 2009).

Human Rights Watch. *Breaking the Grip? Obstacles to Justice for Paramilitary Mafias in Colombia*, New York 2008.

Human Rights Watch. *Human Rights Watch comments to the Office of the US Trade Representative concerning the US-Colombia Free Trade Agreement*, 15 September 2009; available at: http://www.hrw.org/en/news/2009/09/15/human-rights-watch-comments-office-us-trade-representative-concerning-us-colombia-fr#_ftnref4 (last visited 29 October 2009).

ICC-OTP. Informal expert paper: the principle of complementarity in practice, 2003; available at: http://www.icc-cpi.int/iccdocs/doc/doc654724.PDF (last visited 3 September 2009).

ICC-OTP. First public hearing of the Office of the Prosecutor, The Hague 17/18 June 2003; available at http://www2.icc-cpi.int/Menus/ICC/Structure+of+the+Court/Office+of+the+Prosecutor/Network+with+Partners/Public+Hearings/First+Public+Hearing/First+public+hearing+of+the+Office+of+the+Prosecutor+++Session+6.htm (last visited 23 November 2009).

ICC-OTP. Third Report of the Prosecutor of the International Criminal Court, to the Security Council pursuant to UNSC 1593 (2005), 14 June 2006; available at: http://www.icc-cpi.int/NR/rdonlyres/E61D7F34-7D21-44B9-8840-53B254172AF7/0/OTP_ReportUNSC_3Darfur_English.pdf (last visited 3 September 2009).

ICC-OTP. Eight Report of the Prosecutor of the International Criminal Court, to the Security Council pursuant to UNSC 1593 (2005), 3 December 2008; available at: http://www.icc-cpi.int/NR/rdonlyres/BBA77B57-C81C-4152-988C-D8D953471453/279075/8thUNSCreportsenttoUNENG1.pdf (last visited 3 September 2009).

ICC-OTP. Update on communications received by the Office of the Prosecutor of the ICC, 10 February 2006; available at: http://www.iccnow.org (last visited 3 September 2009).

ICC-OTP. Criteria for Selection of Situations and Cases, draft for discussion, June 2006 (on file with the author).

ICC-OTP. Report on the activities performed during the first three years (June 2003–June 2006) 12 September 2006; available at http://www.iccnow.org/documents/3YearReport%20_06Sep14.pdf (last visited 3 September 2009).

ICC-OTP. Report on prosecutorial strategy, 14 September 2006; available at http://www.iccnow.org/documents/ProsecutorialStrategy_06Sep14.pdf (last visited 3 September 2009).

ICC-OTP. Second public hearing of the Office of the Prosecutor, The Hague 25/26 September 2006/New York 17/18 October 2006; available at http://www2.icc-cpi.int/Menus/ICC/Structure+of+the+Court/Office+of+the+Prosecutor/Network+with+Partners/Public+Hearings/Second+Public+Hearing/Second+public+hearing.htm (last visited 23 November 2009).

ICC-OTP. Prosecutorial Strategy 2009–2012, 1 February 2010; available at: http://www2.icc-cpi.int/Menus/ICC/Structure+of+the+Court/Office+of+the+Prosecutor/Reports+and+Statements/Statement/Prosecutorial+Strategy+2009+_+2012.htm (last visited 10 March 2010).

Instituto Nacional de Medicina Legal y Ciencias Forenses. *Forensis. Datos para la vida*, Bogotá, Internacional Print Ltda, 2008; available at http://www.medicinalegal.gov.co/index.php?option=com_wrapper&view=wrapper&Itemid=60.

Inter-American Commission on Human Rights (IACHR). *Report on the demobilization process in Colombia*, OEA/Ser.L/V/II.120, Doc. 60, 13 December 2004.

International Human Rights Law Clinic-University of California, Berkeley, *Truth Behind Bars – Colombian Paramilitary Leaders in U.S. Custody*, February 2010); available at http://www.law.berkeley.edu/files/IHRLC/Truthbehindbars.pdf (last visited 11 March 2010).

Landmine Monitor Report 2007; available at: http://www.icbl.org/lm/2007/ (last visited 8 October 2009).

Rivera, Sneider/Barreto Luis. Resumen ejecutivo. La impunidad en el sistema penal acusatorio en Colombia, without date; available at: http://www.mij.gov.co/econtent/library/documents/DocNewsNo4362DocumentNo2463.PDF (last visited 29 August 2009).

Policía Nacional de Colombia (DIJIN), Desmovilizados colectivos e individuals. Informe control y monitoreo a octubre 2009; available at http://www.altocomisionadoparalapaz.gov.co/web/noticias/2009/octubre/documentos/40%20CONTROL%20DESMOVILIZADOS%20OCTUBRE.pdf (last visited 10 March 2010).

Procuraduría General de la Nacíon, *Seguimiento a políticas públicas en materia de desmovilización y reinserción. Derecho a la verdad, memoria histórica y protección de archivos. Four volumes,* Bogotá, USAID, 2008.
Rivera, Sneider/Barreto Luis. Resumen ejecutivo. La impunidad en el sistema penal acusatorio en Colombia, without date; available at: http://www.mij.gov.co/econtent/library/documents/DocNewsNo4362DocumentNo2463.PDF (last visited 29 August 2009).
Uprimny, Rodrigo/Saffon, María Paula. Transitional Justice, Restaurative Justice and Reconciliation. Some Insights from the Colombian case, 2005; available at http://www.dejusticia.org/interna.php?id_tipo_publicacion=5?id_tipo_publicacion=5?id_tipo_publicacion=5?id_tipo_publicacion=5&id_publicacion=348 (last visited 23 November 2009).
War Crimes Research Office. The gravity threshold of the ICC, 2008; available at: www.wcl.american.edu/warcrimes/icc/icc_reports.cfm (last visited 7 October 2009).
War Crimes Research Office. The relevance of "a situation" to the admissibility and selection of cases before the International Criminal Court, Washington D.C., October 2009.

2. Additional Sources*

2.1 NORMATIVE FRAMEWORK

2.1.1 Legislation

Constitución Política de Colombia
Ley 1106 de 2006 – Prorroga Ley 782 de 2002.
Ley 1312 de 2009 – Reforma Ley 906 de 2004 respecto del principio de oportunidad.
Ley 1312 de 2009.
Ley 418 de 1997.
Ley 4488 de 2005 – Adquisición de tierras para trabajos de reincorporados.
Ley 599 de 2000 – Código Penal Colombiano.
Ley 600 de 2000 – Código Procesal Penal Colombiano, sistema mixto.
Ley 782 de 2002 – Desmovilización y reinserción de grupos al margen de la Ley.
Ley 890 de 2004 – Modificatoria de la Ley 599 de 2000.
Ley 906 de 2004 – Código Procesal Penal Colombiano, Sistema Acusatorio.
Ley 938 de 2004.
Ley 975 de 2005 – Ley de Justicia y Paz.

*The following list of additional sources shall serve as a basis for further research and represents all sources used for the elaboration of the original Spanish study. It includes all relevant norms (2.1.), the relevant jurisprudence by international and Colombian Tribunals (2.2.), official and NGO (unpublished) documents (2.3.), the original full bibliography (2.4.) and, last but not least, a list of the interviews and meetings carried out as part of the field work in Colombia (2.5.). The titles already contained in the bibliography prepared for this English version of the study (see doc. 1 before) have not been repeated here.

2.1.2 Executive Decrees

Decreto 0176 de 2008 – Objeto de las comisiones regionales para la restitución de bienes.
Decreto 0315 de 2007 – Intervención de las víctimas.
Decreto 0395 de 2007 – Condicionamiento de beneficios.
Decreto 0423 de 2007 – Certificación en las desmovilizaciones colectivas.
Decreto 0551 de 2007 – Criterios de reparación de las víctimas.
Decreto 1000 de 2003 – Corrige Ley 782 de 2002.
Decreto 1059 de 2008 – Desmovilización individual de miembros de grupos de guerrilla privados de la libertad.
Decreto 128 de 2003 – Política de reincorporación a la vida civil.
Decreto 1290 de 2008 – Programa de reparación individual por vía administrativa.
Decreto 1364 de 2008 – Adición al decreto 4760 de 2005.
Decreto 1733 de 2009.
Decreto 2012 de 2003 – Prevención y atención de desastres.
Decreto 2767 de 2004 – Beneficios en caso de desmovilización individual y colectiva.
Decreto 2816 de 2006 – Programa de protección de Derechos Humanos.
Decreto 2898 de 2006 – Grupo Armado organizado al margen de la Ley.
Decreto 3046 de 2006 – Creación Alta Consejería para la Reintegración.
Decreto 3360 de 2003 – Desmovilización Colectiva.
Decreto 3391 de 2006 – Aplicación de la Ley 975 de 2005.
Decreto 3460 de 2007 – Comité de coordinación interinstitucional de justicia y paz.
Decreto 35000 de 2007 – Intervención de vícitimas en etapa de investigación.
Decreto 3570 de 2007 – Protección para víctimas y testigos de la Ley 975 de 2005.
Decreto 4417 de 2006 – Plazo razonable previo a versión libre/indagación voluntad de sometimiento al proceso.
Decreto 4436 de 2006 – Beneficios.
Decreto 4719 de 2008 – Desmovilizados privados de la libertad.
Decreto 4760 de 2005 – Conductas delictivas.
Decreto 614 de 2009 – Reglamentación art. 62 Ley 975 de 2005.
Decreto 880 de 2008 – Reglamenta Artículo 61 Ley 975 de 2005.

2.1.3 Resolutions, agreements, memoranda and others

2.1.3.1 Resolutions and memoranda Fiscalía General de la Nación

Memorando Instructivo No. 8 de 22 de mayo de 2006 – Priorización de actividades.
Memorando Instructivo No. 17 de 11 de septiembre de 2006 – Priorización de casos.
Memorando Instructivo de 08 de julio de 2007 – Apoyo económico a la reintegración.
Memorando Instructivo No. 49 de 9 de agosto de 2007 – Entrevista previa a postulados.
Memorando Instructivo No. 23 de 21 de abril de 2008 – Atención a víctimas.

Memorando Instructivo No. 31 de 19 de mayo de 2008 – Estrategias para agilizar las versiones libres y confesión.
Memorando Instructivo No. 30 de 13 de mayo de 2009 – Representación judicial y atención psicosocial a las víctimas.
Memorando Instructivo No. 59 de 28 de agosto de 2009 – Estrategia para la reconstrucción de la verdad.
Memorando Instructivo No. 67 de 22 de octubre de 2009 – Intervención de las víctimas en la versión libre.
Resolución 0-0387 de 2007 – Procedimiento de transmisión de las versiones libres.
Resolución 0-0683 de 2007 – Unidad Nacional de Fiscalía para la Justicia y la paz/ distribución planta de cargos.
Resolución 0-0784 de 2007 – Grupos de criminalística.
Resolución 0-2296 de 2007 – Versión libre en la Ley de justicia y paz.
Resolución 0-2889 de 2007 – Búsqueda de desaparecidos/Exhumación.
Resolución 0-3998 de 2007 – Reglamentación versiones libres.
Resolución 0-4773 de 2007 – Objeto de las comisiones regionales para la restitución de bienes.
Resolución 29 de 2008 – Coordinador Medellín.
Resolución 3461 de 2005 – Crea Unidad Nacional de Justicia y Paz.
Resolución 35 de 2008 – Distribución de Fiscales.
Resolución 36 de 2008 – Fiscales de Apoyo.
Resolución 4010 de 2008 – Última planta.
Resolución 517 de 2006 – Sedes de funcionamiento Unidad Nacional de Justicia y Paz.
Resolución 648 de 2008 – Atención de solicitudes bajo Ley 782 de 2002.
Resolución 7178 de 2008 – Documentos de la UNFJP como parte del proceso penal.

2.1.3.2 Resolutions Presidencia de la República

Resolución 001 de 2006 – Establece zona para AUC Puerto Boyaca.
Resolución 002 de 2006 – Establece zona para AUC Magdalena Medio.
Resolución 008 de 2006 – Establece zona para Bloque Tayrona.
Resolución 016 de 2005 – Establece zona para Bloque Mojana.
Resolución 017 de 2006 – Establece zona para Bloque Norte.
Resolución 074 de 2006 – Establece zona para Bloque Elmer Cárdenas.
Resolución 08 de 2005 – Establece zona para Bloque Suroeste Antioqueño.
Resolución 091 de 2004 – Declara inicio proceso de paz AUC.
Resolución 092 de 2004 – Establece zona de ubicación temporal para las AUC.
Resolución 12 de 2005 – Reconcoce miembros de las AUC, Mancusso y otros.
Resolución 122 de 2005 – Establece zona para Bloque Héroes de Tolova.
Resolución 163 de 2005 – Establece zona para Bloque Montes de María.
Resolución 164 de 2005 – Establece zona para Bloque Héroes de Granada.
Resolución 174 de 2005 – Establece zona para AUC Meta y Vichada.
Resolución 189 de 2005 – Establece zona para Bloque libertadores del sur.

Resolución 216 de 2003 – Declara iniciación proceso de paz con Bloque Cacique Nutibara.
Resolución 217 de 2003 – Reconoce voceros Bloque Cacique Nutibara.
Resolución 223 de 2003 – Inicia proceso de paz con Bloque Ortega AUC.
Resolución 224 de 2003 – Reconoce miembros del Bloque Ortega.
Resolución 246 de 2004 – Establece zona de ubicación temporal para las AUC.
Resolución 250 de 2005 – Establece zona para Bloque Noroccidente Antioqueño.
Resolución 253 de 2005 – Establece zona para Bloque Central Bolívar.
Resolución 254 de 2005 – Establece zona para Bloque Mineros.
Resolución 260 de 2004 – Establece zona para Bloque Cacique Nutibara.
Resolución 271 de 2005 – Establece zona para Bloque Central Bolivar.
Resolución 285 de 2005 – Establece zona para Bloque Tolima.
Resolución 295 de 2004 – Establece zona para Bloque Cundinamarca.
Resolución 338 de 2005 – Establece zona para Bloque vencedores de Arauca.

2.1.3.3 Resolutions and agreements of governmental departments

Acuerdo 290 de 2005 – Ministerio de Protección Social, Distribución de recursos Fosyga.
Acuerdo 307 de 2005 – Ministerio de Protección Social, Modifica Acuerdo 290 de 2005.
Acuerdo 331 de 2006 – Ministerio de Protección Social, priorización beneficiarios desmovilizados.
Directiva n° 15 de 2007 – Ministerio de Defensa Nacional, implementación política de desmovilización.
Directiva n° 16 de 2007 – Ministerio de Defensa Nacional, bonificaciones económicas a desmovilizados.
Resolución 001 de 2005 – Ministerio de Defensa Nacional.
Resolución 2462 de 2005 – Ministerio del Interior y de Justicia, límites ayudas humanitarias.
Resolución 3579 de 2006 – Ministerio de Protección Social, ampliación de cobertura a subsidios de desmovilizados.
Resolución 513 de 2005 – Ministerio del Interior y de Justicia, condición para beneficios por reincorporación.
Resolución 908 de 2006 – Ministerio de Protección social, ampliación de cobertura a subsidios de desmovilizados.

2.1.3.4 Consejo Superior de la Judicatura

Acuerdo PSA A06-3275 de 2006 (19 de Enero), "por el cual se designan los Tribunales Superiores de Distrito Judicial que conocerán de las competencias de que trata la Ley 975 de 2005".
Acuerdo PSA A06-3275 de 2006 – Competencias Tribunales Justicia y Paz.
Acuerdo PSA A06-3276 de 2006 –Competencias Tribunales Justicia y Paz.

Acuerdo PSA A06-3549 de 2006 – Apoyo administrativo a Tribunales.

Acuerdo PSA A08-4641 de 2008 (12 de Marzo), "por el cual se modifican las competencias de que trata la Ley 975 de 2005, para los Tribunales Superiores de Bogotá y Barranquilla."

Sala Jurisdiccional Disciplinaria, auto del 06 de mayo de 2008, Rad. 110011102000200801403 01, MP Angelino Lizcano Rivera.

2.1.3.5 Procuraduría General de la Nación

Circular del 10 de octubre de 2006 – Garantías a los derechos de las víctimas.

Diretiva 008 de 2007 – Garantía de participación judicial de las víctimas.

Resolución 171 de 2006 – Coordinación interna justicia y paz.

2.1.3.6 Defensoría del Pueblo

Resolución 1113 de 2006 – Representación judicial de las víctimas.

Resolución 438 de 2007 – Procedimiento de orientación a las víctimas.

Resolución N° 1113 de 2005.

2.1.3.7 Others

Acuerdo 018 de 2006 – Fondo Reparación a las Víctimas, Reglamento interno.

Circular 10 de 2007 – DAS, instrucciones a directores.

Resolución 00927 de 2003 – DAS.

Resolución 0690 de 2003 – Registraduría Nacional del Estado Civil.

Procedimiento General, Unidad de Justicia y Paz, Fiscalía General de la Nación, Código: FGN-58000-P-01, 13 November 2009.

Participación de las víctimas en aplicación de la Ley 975 de 2005, Unidad de Justicia y Paz, Fiscalía General de la Nación, Código: FGN-58000-P-03, 30 September 2008.

2.2 JURISPRUDENCE

2.2.1 International Jurisprudence

2.2.1.1 International Criminal Court

ICC Prosecutor Presents Evidence on Darfur Crimes, The Hague, 27 February 2007, ICC-OTP-20070227-206-En

ICC-PTC I, *Prosecutor v. Harun and Kushayb*, Decision on the Prosecution application under article 58 (7) of the Statute, 27 April 2007 (ICC-02/05-01/07).

ICC-PTC I, *Prosecutor v. Lubanga and Ntaganda*, Annex II, Decision on the Prosecutor's application for warrants of arrest, article 58, 10 February 2006 (ICC-01/04-01/07).

ICC-PTC I, *Prosecutor v. Lubanga*, Decision on the applications for participation in the proceedings of VPRS-1, VPRS-2, VPRS-3, VPRS-4, VPRS-5, VPRS-6, 17 January 2006 (ICC-01/04-101-tEN-Corr).

ICC-PTC I, *Prosecutor v. Lubanga,* Decision on the Prosecutor's application for warrant of arrest, article 58, 10 February 2006 (ICC-01/04-01/07).

ICC-PTC II, *Prosecutor v. Kony et al.*, Decision on the admissibility of the case under article 19(1) of the Statute, 10 March 2009 (ICC-02/04-01/05).

Prosecutor v. Al Bashir, Decision on the Prosecutor's application for a warrant of arrest against Omar Hassan Ahmad Al Bashir, 4 March 2009 (ICC-02/05-01/09-3).

Prosecutor v. Bemba, Mandat d'arrêt à l'encontre de Jean-Pierre Bemba Gombo remplaçant le mandat d'arrêt décerné le 23 mai 2008, 10 June 2008 (ICC-01/05-01/08-15).

Prosecutor v. Chui, Decision on the evidence and information provided by the Prosecution for the issuance of a warrant of arrest, 6 July 2007 (ICC-01/04-02/07).

Prosecutor v. Katanga and Chui, Motifs de la décision orale relative à l'exception d'irrecevabilité de l'affaire (article 19 du Statut), 16 June 2009 (ICC-01/04-01/07-1213).

Prosecutor v. Katanga and Chui, Motion challenging the admissibility of the case by the Defence of Germain Katanga, pursuant to article 19(2) (a) of the Statute, 11 de marzo de 2007 (ICC-01/04-01/07-949).

Prosecutor v. Katanga and Chui, Public redacted version of the 19th March 2009 Prosecution response to motion challenging the admissibility of the case by the Defence of Germain Katanga, pursuant to article 19(2), 30 March 2009 (ICC-01/04-01/07-1007).

Prosecutor v. Thomas Lubanga Dyilo, sobre la decisión de la PTC I del 10 de febrero de 2006 y la incorporación de documentos en el registro del caso contra Mr. Thomas Lubanga Dyilo, 24 February 2006 (ICC-01/04-01/06).

Situation in DRC, Judgment on the Prosecutor's appeal against the decision of Pre-Trial Chamber I entitled "Decision on the Prosecutor's application for warrants of arrest, article 58", 13 July 2006 (ICC-01-04-169) [reclasificado y publicado el 23 de septiembre de 2008 conforme a la *Situation in DRC*, Decision on the unsealing of judgment of the Appeals Chamber issued on 13 July 2006, 22 September 2008 (ICC-01-04-538-PUB-Exp).

2.2.1.2 Inter-American Court of Human Rights

I/A Court H.R., Case of Escué-Zapata v. Colombia. Merits, Reparations and Costs. Judgment of July 4, 2007. Series C- No. 165.

I/A Court H.R., Case of the "White Van" (Paniagua-Morales et al.) v. Guatemala. Merits. Judgment of March 8, 1998. Series C- No. 37.
I/A Court H.R., Case of Zambrano-Vélez et al. v. Ecuador. Merits, Reparations and Costs. Judgment of July 4, 2007. Series C- No. 166.

2.2.1.3 Resolutions of other international courts

Findlay v. United Kingdom, ECtHR judgement, 25 February 1997 (22107/93).
Krnojelac (Appeals Chamber Judgment), 17 September 2003 (ICTY-97-25-A).
Langborger v. Sweden, ECtHR judgement, 22 June 1989.
Prosecutor v. Tadic (Appeals Chamber Judgment), 15 July 1999 (ICTY-94-1-A).
Prosecutor v. Bagaragaza, Decision on the Prosecution's motion for referral to the Kingdom of Norway, 19 May 2006 (ICTR-2005-86-R11).
Prosecutor v. Brima, Kamara and Kanu (AFRC trial), Sentencing judgement, 19 July 2007 (SCSL-04-16-T).
Prosecutor v. Deronjić, Trial judgement, Sentence, 30 March 2004 (IT-02-61-S).
Prosecutor v. Fofana and Kondawa (CDF trial), Judgement on the sentencing of Moinina Fofana and Allieu Kondawa, 9 October 2007 (SCSL-04-14-T).
Prosecutor v. Furundžija, Appeal's judgement, 2 July 2000 (IT-95-17/1).
Prosecutor v. Milutinović et al., Trial judgement, Volume 3 of 4, 26 February 2009 (IT-05-87-T).
Prosecutor v. Simić, Trial judgement, Sentence, 17 October 2002 (IT-95-9/2-S).
Pullar v. United Kingdom, ECtHR judgement, 10 June 1996 (22399/93).
Prosecutor vs. Issa Hassan Sesay, Morris Kallon and Augustine Gbao, Vasiljevic (Appeals Chamber Judgment), 25 February 2004 (ICTY-98-32-A).

2.2.2 Colombian Jurisprudence

2.2.2.1 Corte Constitucional

Sentencia C-412 de 1993, MP Cifuentes Muñoz.
Sentencia C-272 de 1999, MP Cifuentes Muñoz.
Sentencia SU-961 de 1999, MP Naranjo Mesa.
Sentencia C-774 de 2001, MP Escobar Gil.
Sentencia C-228 de 2002, MP Cepeda Espinosa y Montealegre Lynett.
Sentencia C-578 de 2002, MP Cepeda Espinosa.
Sentencia C-695 de 2002, MP Córdoba Triviño.
Sentencia C-004 de 2003, MP Eduardo Montealegre Lynett.
Sentencia T-249 de 2003, MP Montealegre Lynett.
Sentencia T-719 de 2003, MP Manuel José Cepeda Espinosa.
Sentencia C-923 de 2005, MP Córdoba Triviño.
Sentencia C-1154 de 2005, MP Cepeda Espinosa.

Sentencia C-928 de 2005, MP Araujo Renteria.
Sentencia C-979 de 2005, MP Córdoba Triviño.
Sentencia C-046 de 2006, MP Tafur Galvis.
Sentencia C-127 de 2006, MP Tafur Galvis.
Sentencia C-319 de 2006, MP Tafur Galvis.
Sentencia C-370 de 2006, MP Córdoba Triviño.
Sentencia C-454 de 2006, MP Córdoba Triviño.
Sentencia C-531 de 2006, MP Monroy Cabra.
Sentencia C-575 de 2006, MP Tafur Galvis.
Sentencia T-771 de 2006, MP Córdoba Triviño.
Sentencia C-209 de 2007, MP Cepeda Espinosa.
Sentencia C-516 de 2007, MP Córdoba Triviño.
Sentencia T-188 de 2007, MP Tafur Galvis.
Sentencia T-355 de 2007, MP Sierra Porto
Sentencia T-049 de 2008, MP Monroy Cabra.
Sentencia T-399 de 2008, MP Sierra Porto.
Sentencia T-496 de 2008, MP Córdoba Triviño.
Sentencia T-085 de 2009, MP Araujo Rentaría.

2.2.2.2 Corte Suprema de Justicia

Sentencia del 18 de octubre de 2005, Rad. 24310, MP Pulido de Barón.
Sentencia del 18 de octubre de 2005, Rad. 24311, MP Gómez Quintero.
Auto del 27 de octubre de 2005, Rad. 24526, MP Gómez Quintero.
Sentencia del 15 de febrero de 2006, Rad. 21330, MP Lombana Trujillo.
Sentencia del 11 de mayo de 2007, Rad. 26945, MP Ramírez Bastidas.
Sentencia del 23 de mayo de 2007, Rad. 27052, MP Pérez Pinzón.
Sentencia del 8 de junio de 2007, Rad. 27484, MP Pérez Pinzón.
Sentencia del 13 de junio de 2007, Rad. 27153, MP Espinosa Pérez.
Auto del 8 de julio de 2007, Rad. 27848, MP Pérez Pinzón.
Auto del 11 de julio de 2007, Rad. 26945, MP Ramírez Bastidas.
Auto del 23 de agosto de 2007, Rad. 28040, MP González de Lemos.
Auto del 27 de agosto de 2007, Rad. 27873, MP Socha Salamanca.
Auto del 25 de septiembre de 2007, Rad. 28040, MP González de Lemos.
Auto del 25 de septiembre de 2007, Rad. 28250, MP González de Lemos.
Auto del 26 de octubre de 2007, Rad. 28492, MP Ramírez Bastidas.
Sentencia del 5 de diciembre de 2007, Rad. 25931, MP González de Lemos.
Auto del 19 de diciembre de 2007, Rad. 26118 (without MP).
Auto del 31 de marzo de 2008, Rad. 28890, MP Ibáñez Guzmán.
Atuo del 2 de abril de 2008, Rad. 28643, MP Socha Salamanca.
Auto del 10 de abril de 2008, Rad. 29472, MP Ramírez Bastidas.
Auto del 22 de abril de 2008, Rad. 29559, MP Enrique Socha.
Auto del 16 de mayo de 2008, Rad. 26740, (without MP).
Auto del 28 de mayo de 2008, segunda instancia, Rad. 29560, MP Ibáñez Guzmán.

Auto del 23 de julio de 2008, Rad. 30120, MP Gómez Quintero.
Auto del 31 de julio de 2008, Rad. 28503, MP Zapata Ortiz.
Auto del 1 de agosto de 2008, Rad. 26470 (sin MP).
Auto del 8 de septiembre de 2008, Rad. 30360, MP Ramírez Bastidas.
Auto del 3 de octubre de 2008, Rad. 30442, MP Gómez Quintero.
Auto del 1 de noviembre de 2008, Rad. 28393, MP Zapata Ortiz.
Auto del 25 de noviembre de 2008, Rad. 26942 (without MP).
Auto del 9 de febrero de 2009, Rad. 30955, MP Leonidas Bustos.
Auto del 12 de febrero de 2009, Rad. 30998, MP Espinoza Pérez.
Auto del 18 de febrero de 2009, Rad. 30775, MP Quintero Milanés.
Auto del 24 de febrero de 2009, aprobado acta n° 48, MP Gómez Quintero.
Auto del 4 de marzo de 2009, Rad. 31235, MP Ramírez Bastidas.
Sentencia del 11 de marzo de 2009, Rad. 30510, MP Ramírez Bastidas.
Auto del 11 de marzo de 2009, Rad. 31162, MP Socha Salamanca.
Auto del 31 de marzo de 2009, Rad. 31491, MP Gómez Quintero.
Auto del 2 de abril de 2009, Rad. 31492, MP González de Lemos.
Auto del 13 de abril de 2009, Rad. 31527, MP Socha Salamanca.
Auto del 15 de abril de 2009, Rad. 31181, MP González de Lemos.
Auto del 16 de abril de 2009, Rad. 31115, MP Bustos Martínez.
Auto del 11 de mayo de 2009, Rad. 31290, MP Ibáñez Guzmán.
Auto del 12 de mayo de 2009, Rad. 31150, MP Ibáñez Guzmán.
Auto del 20 de mayo de 2009, Rad. 31495, MP Bustos Martínez.
Auto del 21 de mayo de 2009, Rad. 31620, MP Quintero Milanés.
Auto del 22 de mayo de 2009, Rad. 31582, MP González Lemos.
Auto del 29 de julio de 2009, Rad. 31539, MP Ibáñez Guzmán.
Auto del 19 de agosto de 2009, Rad. 30451, MP Ramírez Batidas.
Auto del 21 de septiembre de 2009, Rad. 32022, MP Sigifredo Espinoza Perez.
Sentencia del 3 de diciembre de 2009, Rad. 32672, sin MP.
Sentencia del 14 de diciembre de 2009, Rad. 32575, MP González Lemos.
Sentencia del 17 de febrero de 2010, Rad. 32568, MP Bustos Martínez.

2.2.2.3 Consejo de Estado

Sala de lo Contencioso Administrativo, Sección Cuarta, sentencia del 26 de julio de 2007, Rad. 250002324000200700290-01.

2.2.2.4 Tribunal Superior de Justicia y Paz de Bogota

Auto del 9 de junio de 2008, Rad. 82133, MP Eduardo Castellanos Roso.
Sentencia del 19 de marzo de 2009, Rad. 110016000253200680526, MP Castellanos Roso.
Sentencia del 15 de octubre de 2007, Rad. 2007 0006 01, MP Rivera Sierra.
Sentencia del 20 de Febrero de 2008, Aprobado acta n° 05, MP González Romero.

Sentencia del 15 de Febrero de 2008, Rad. 2008 0006, MP Cepeda Alvarado.
Sentencia del 22 de julio de 2008, Aprobado acta n° 012, MP Castellanos Roso.
Sentencia del 26 de Marzo de 2008, Aprobado acta n° 012, MP González Romero.
Sentencia del 7 de diciembre de 2009, Aprobado acta n° 013, Rad. 110016000253200680281, MP Jiménez López.
Sentencia del 25 de enero de 2010, Rad. 110016000253200680077, MP Jiménez López.

2.3 DOCUMENTS

2.3.1 Governmental documents

2.3.1.1 Oficina del Alto Comisionado para la Paz

"Discursos en Ceremonias de Desmovilizaciones". Available at: http://www.altocomisionadoparalapaz.gov.co/web/publicaciones/discursos/Discursos%20de%20baja%20res.pdf (accessed 3 September 2009).
"Fundamentos normativos de la aplicación del delito de sedición a las Autodefensas". Available at: http://www.altocomisionadoparalapaz.gov.co/web/publicaciones/fundamentos%20normativos/Fundamento%20normativo.pdf (accessed 3 september de 2009).
"Inspección, empadronamiento, traslado y destrucción del material de guerra entregado por las Autodefensas". Available at: http://www.altocomisionadoparalapaz.gov.co/web/noticias/2007/enero/documentos/Informe_Armas.pdf (accessed 3 September 2009).
"Proceso de paz con las Autodefensas. Informe ejecutivo". Available at: http://www.altocomisionadoparalapaz.gov.co/web/libro/Libro.pdf (accessed 3 September 2009).

2.3.1.2 Comisión Nacional de Reparación y Reconciliación

"Área de Memoria Histórica, Trujillo: una tragedia que no cesa". Available at: http://www.cnrr.org.co/new/interior_otros/Trujillo_informe.pdf (accessed 28 July 2009).
"Compilación Normativa: Justicia y Paz Procesos de Desmovilización, Reincorporación y Reconciliación Nacional". Available at: http://www.cnrr.org. co/new/interior_otros/LIBRO%20COMPILACION%20REINSERTADOS.pdf (accessed 28 June 2009).
"Continúa jornada de reparación individual por vía administrativa". Available at: http://www.cnrr.visiondirecta.com/09e/spip.php?article1733 (accessed 31 July 2009).

"Disidentes, Rearmados y Emergentes ¿Bandas Criminales o Tercera Generación Paramilitar?". Available at: http://www.cnrr.org.co/new/interior_otros/informeDDR.pdf (accessed 28 July 2009).

"Informe al Congreso, Proceso de reparación a las víctimas – balance actual y perspectivas futuras", 2007. Available at: http://www.cnrr.org.co/new/interior_otros/informe_congreso2007.pdf (accessed 28 July 2009).

"Informe de Gestión", 2005–2009. Available at: http://www.cnrr.org.co/new/interior_otros/InfGestion2005–2008.pdf (accessed 28 July 2009).

"Inicia entrega de reparación vía administrativa" Available at: http://www.cnrr.visiondirecta.com/09e/spip.php?article1685 (accessed 28 July 2009).

"Memoria Histórica". Available at: http://www.cnrr.org.co/memoria_historica.htm (accessed 21 May 2009).

"Plan área de memoria histórica. Aprobado por el pleno de la CNRR del 20 de febrero de 2007". Available at: http://memoriahistorica-cnrr.org.co/index.php?option=com_content&task=view&id=12&Itemid=28 (accessed 21 May 2009).

"Primera entrega de reparación vía administrativa". Available at: http://www.cnrr.visiondirecta.com/09e/spip.php?article1697 (accessed 31 July 2009).

"Proceso de Reparación a las vícitmas: balance actual y perspectivas futuras (2007)". Available at: http://www.cnrr.org.co/new/interior_otros/informe_congreso2007.pdf (accessed 3 September 2009).

"Recomendación de criterios de reparación y de proporcionalidad restaurativa", Bogotá, April 2007. Available at: http://www.cnrr.org.co/new/interior_otros/RCRPR.pdf (accessed 28 July 2009).

"Ruta de la reparación administrativa llegó a 521 familias antioqueñas". Available at: http://www.cnrr.visiondirecta.com/09e/spip.php?article1765 (accessed 31 July 2009).

"Todo esfuerzo que se haga por la reparación ayuda a que el dolor no se convierta en odio ni en venganza: Presidente Uribe." Available at: http://www.cnrr.visiondirecta.com/09e/spip.php?article1739 (accessed 31 July 2009).

"Turno de la reparación administrativa llega este domingo a Medellín". Available at: http://www.cnrr.visiondirecta.com/09e/spip.php?article1760 (accessed 31 July 2009).

Boletín CNRR n° 1 de noviembre de 2007; n° 2 de diciembre de 2007; 3 de febrero de 2008; n° 5 de junio de 2008; n° 6 de julio de 2008 (tres años de Ley de justicia y paz). Todos Available at: http://www.cnrr.org.co/ (accessed 3 September 2009).

2.3.1.3 Ministerio de Defensa

"Desmovilización Desarme & Reincorporación en Colombia". Available at: http://www.mindefensa.gov.co/descargas/Documentos_Descargables/espanol/Desmovilizacion%20Desarme%20&%20Reincorporacion%20en%20Colombia.pdf (accessed 3 September 2009).

2.3.1.4 Procuraduría General de la Nación

"Juez de paz. Su papel en los proceso de reinserción y derechos de las víctimas". Available at: http://www.procuraduria.gov.co/descargas/publicaciones/cartilla_juezdepaz.pdf (accessed 3 September 2009).

"La Oportunidad como principio complementario del proceso penal". Available at: http://iemp.procuraduria.gov.co/files/downloads//Principio.pdf (accessed 3 September 2009).

2.3.1.5 Defensoría del Pueblo

"Guía de orientación jurídica y psicosocial para la atención a las víctimas de la violencia generada por grupos armados organizados al margen de la Ley". Available at: http://www.defensoria.org.co/red/anexos/pdf/04/juspa4.pdf (accessed 3 September 2009).

2.3.1.6 Other govermental documents

Acción Social. Agencia Presidencial para la Acción Social y la Cooperación Internacional. Available at: http://www.accionsocial.gov.co/contenido/contenido.aspx?catID=297&conID=1736 (accessed 1 August 2009).

Acuerdo de Santa Fe de Ralito. Available at: http://www.altocomisionadoparalapaz.gov.co/acuerdos/acuerdos_t/jul_15_03.htm (accessed 13 July 2009).

Departamento Nacional de Planeación. Available at: http://www.dnp.gov.co/PortalWeb/Portals/0/archivos/documentos/DJS/DJS_Presentaciones/27_10_08_Paola_Buendia.pdf (accessed 29 July 2009).

Fiscalía General de la Nación. "20 grupos satélites de la Policía Judicial". Available at: http://www.fiscalia.gov.co/justiciapaz/Despachos.htm (accessed 28 August 2009).

Fiscalía General de la Nación. "Informe de Gestión 2008–2009", p. 109. Available at: http://fgn.fiscalia.gov.co:8080/Fiscalia/archivos/Rendicionde Cuenta/informe_de_gestion_09.pdf (accessed 28 August 2009).

Fiscalía General de la Nación. "Programa metodológico. Versión preliminar para trabajo", Bogotá, 2007.

Fiscalía General de la Nación. Unidad Nacional de Justicia y Paz. "Oficio 012896", Bogotá, 9 November 2009. Comentarios a la versión preliminar del estudio "Procedimiento de la Ley de Justicia y Paz (Ley 975 de 2005) y derecho penal internacional – Estudio sobre la facultad de intervención complementaria de la Corte Penal Internacional a la luz del denominado proceso de 'justicia y paz' en Colombia" (quoted as FGN-JyP, Comentarios, 2009).

Informe de Consultoría "La impunidad en el sistema penal colombiano", elaborado por la Unión Europea y presentado en febrero de 2009, como parte del proyecto

"Fortalecimiento del sector justicia para la reducción de la impunidad en Colombia."
Informes del Ministerio de Hacienda y Crédito Público de Colombia. Available at: http://web.presidencia.gov.co/sp/2009/junio/18/carta.pdf (accessed 31 June 2009).
Ponencia coordinada en Senado por Mario Uribe Escobar y en Cámara por Armando Benedetti y Roberto Camacho. Available at: la Gaceta 74 de 2004. Available at: http://www.fiscalia.gov.co/justiciapaz/Documentos/Gacetas/Gaceta_74_05.htm (accessed 2 April 2009).
Ponencia Coordinada en Senado por Rafael Pardo Rueda y en Cámara por Gyna Parody. Available at: Gaceta 77 of 2005. Available at: http://www.fiscalia.gov.co/justiciapaz/Documentos/Gacetas/Gaceta_77_05.htm (accessed 2 April 2009).
Ponencia del Fiscal General de la Nación en la conferencia "Simposio Internacional, Justicia Transicional en Colombia, 4 años de el contexto de la Ley de Justicia y Paz", Bogotá, 23 July 2009.
Proyecto de Ley N° 001 de 2009 Cámara, "por medio de la cual se dictan medidas de protección a las víctimas de la violencia", 20 July 2009. Available at: http://www.observatorio.derechoshumanosypaz.org/agenda.php (accessed 1 August 2009).
Proyecto de Ley N° 036 de 2009 Cámara, "por la cual se dictan medidas de protección a las víctimas de la violencia". Available at: http://www.observatorio.derechoshumanosypaz.org/agenda.php (accessed 1 August 2009).
Texto aprobado en la Comisión Primera de la H. Cámara de Representantes del Proyecto de Ley 044/08 –CÁMARA- 157/07. –SENADO- "por la cual se dictan medidas de protección a las víctimas de la violencia". Available at: http://prensa.camara.gov.co/camara/site/artic/20070730/asocfile/044_08ctexaproencomision.doc (accessed 27 June 2009).
Unidad de Justicia y Paz de la Fiscalía General de la Nación, Despachos. Available at: http://www.fiscalia.gov.co/justiciapaz/Despachos.htm (accessed 31 July 2009).
Unidad de Justicia y Paz de la Fiscalía General de la Nación, Memos (sobre imputaciones a terceros en versión libre): 80 de 2007, 09 de 2008, 17 de 2008, 28 de 2008, 50 de 2008, 031 de 2007.
Unidad de Justicia y Paz de la Fiscalía General de la Nación, Subunidad de Búsqueda de Desaparecidos. Available at: http://www.fiscalia.gov.co/justiciapaz/EXH/imagenes/mapa-de-colombia.jpg (accessed 29 August 2009).

2.3.2 International and non-governmental organizations

2.3.2.1 Inter-American Commission on Human Rights

"Condición Jurídica y Derechos de los Migrantes Indocumentados," Opinión Consultiva OC-18/03, 17 September 2003.

"Excepciones al Agotamiento de los Recursos Internos" (arts. 46.1, 46.2.a y 46.2.b Convención Americana sobre Derechos Humanos). Opinión Consultiva OC-11/ 90, 10 August 1990.

"Informe Anual 2008, Capítulo IV, Colombia". Available at: http://www.cidh.org/ annualrep/2008sp/cap4.Colombia.sp.htm (accessed 9 May 2009).

"Informe sobre el proceso de desmovilización en Colombia", Washington, 13 December 2004. Available at: http://www.cidh.org/countryrep/Colombia04sp/ indice.htm (accessed 3 September 2009).

"Informe sobre la implementación de la Ley de justicia y paz: etapas iniciales del proceso de desmovilización de las auc y primeras diligencias judiciales". Available at:http://www.cidh.org/pdf%20files/III%20Informe%20proceso%20 desmovilizacion%20Colombia%20final.pdf (accessed 5 July 2009).

"Informe sobre Terrorismo y Derechos Humanos", OEA/Ser.L//V/II.116, 22 October 2002. Available at: http://oas.org/dil/esp/informe_sobre_terrorismo_ derechos_humanos.pdf (accessed 3 September 2009).

"La CIDH se pronuncia frente a la aprobación de la Ley de justicia y paz en Colombia". Available at: http://www.cidh.org/Comunicados/Spanish/2005/26. 05.htm (accessed 3 September 2009).

"Las mujeres frente a la violencia y la discriminación derivadas del conflicto armado en Colombia". Available at: http://www.cidh.org/countryrep/Colombia Mujeres06sp/indicemujeres06sp.htm (accessed 3 September 2009).

"Lineamientos principales para una política integral de reparaciones". Available at: http://www.cidh.org/pdf%20files/Lineamientos%20principales%20para% 20una%20política%20integral%20de%20reparaciones.pdf (accessed 3 September 2009).

"Pronunciamiento de la comisión interamericana de derechos humanos sobre la aplicación y el alcance de la Ley de justicia y paz en la república de colombia". Available at: http://www.cidh.org/countryrep/Colombia2006sp/pronunciamiento. 8.1.06esp.htm (accessed 3 September 2009).

2.3.2.2 Centro de Investigación y Educación Popular

"Nombrar lo Innombrable. Reconciliación desde la perspectiva de las víctimas". Available at: http://www.cinep.org.co/pdf/libros/propaz_nombrar_lo_innombr able.pdf (accessed 3 September 2009).

2.3.2.3 Fundación Ideas para la Paz

"Boletín siguiendo el conflicto n° 45". Available at: http://www.ideaspaz.org/ secciones/publicaciones/download_boletines/boletin_conflicto45.pdf (accessed 7 June 2009).

"Conflicto y paz en Colombia". Available at: http://www.ideaspaz.org/new_site/secciones/publicaciones/download_publicaciones/conflictoypazencolombia.pdf (accessed 3 September 2009).

"Estadísticas sobre reinserción en Colombia 2002-2009." Disponible en http://www.ideaspaz.org/new_site/secciones/conflictoynegociacion/estadisticas.htm (accessed 31 January 2009).

"Justicia, verdad y reparación en medio del conflicto". Available at: http://www.ideaspaz.org/new_site/secciones/publicaciones/download_publicaciones/cuaderno_conflicto.pdf (accessed 3 September 2009).

"Reconstrucción, reinserción y región". Available at: http://www.ideaspaz.org/new_site/secciones/publicaciones/download_publicaciones/cuaderno_conflicto_2.pdf (accessed 3 September 2009).

2.3.2.4 Other documents

Amnistía Internacional. "Déjenos en Paz. La población civil, víctima del conflicto armado interno en Colombia", 2008. Available at: http://www.amnesty.org/es/for-media/press-releases/colombia-paz-conflicto-armado-datos-cifras-20081028 (accessed 3 September 2009).

Corporación Nuevo Arco Iris. "Observatorio del Conflicto Armado, los expedientes de la parapolítica." Available at: http://www.nuevoarcoiris.org.co/sac/files/oca/analisis/parapolitica_legislativa_JUNIO_2009.pdf (accessed 29 August 2009).

Declaración de Luis Moreno-Ocampo: Informal meeting of Legal Advisors of Ministries of Foreign Affairs, Nueva York, 24 October 2005.

Draft OTP Regulations, 9 October 2007.

Eight Report of the Prosecutor of the International Criminal Court, to the Security Council pursuant to UNSC 1593 (2005), 3 December 2008. Available at: http://www.icc-cpi.int/NR/rdonlyres/BBA77B57-C81C-4152-988C-D8D953471453/279075/8thUNSCreportsenttoUNENG1.pdf (accessed 3 September 2009).

Fundación Medios Para la Paz. "Los 10 temores sobre la desmovilización", en *Hechos del Callejón* n° 8, October 2005. Available at: http://www.mediosparalapaz.org/index.php?idcategoria=2601 (accessed 3 September 2009).

Human Rights Watch. "Benchmarks for assessing possible national alternatives to International Criminal Court cases against LRA leaders", May 2007, 1. Available at: www.iccnow.org/documents/icc0507web[1].pdf (accessed 3 September 2009).

Human Rights Watch, comments to the Office of the US Trade Representative concerning the US-Colombia Free Trade Agreement/, 15 September 2009, available at: http://www.hrw.org/en/news/2009/09/15/human-rights-watch-comments-office-us-trade-representative-concerning-us-colombia-fr-_ftnref4 (accessed 13 November 2009).

International Law Comission. “Draft Statute for an International Criminal Law”, 1994. Available at: http://untreaty.un.org/ilc/texts/instruments/english/commentaries/7_4_1994.pdf (accessed 3 September 2009).

MAPP-OEA. “Décimosegundo Informe Trimestral del Secretario General al Consejo Permanente sobre la Misión de Apoyo al Proceso de Paz en Colombia”, Consejo Permanente, OEA/Ser.G CP/doc. 4365/09 corr. 1, 9 February 2009. Available at: http://www.mappoea.org/sites/default/files/images/decimosegundo%20informe%20trimestral%20mapp.pdf (accessed 31 July 2009).

MAPP-OEA. “Sexto informe trimestral del secretario general al consejo permanente sobre la misión de apoyo al proceso de paz en Colombia” (MAPP/OEA), 2006. Available at: http://www.altocomisionadoparalapaz.gov.co/registro_inf/2006/SEXTO_INFORME%20DE%20LA%20OEA.pdf (accessed 3 September 2009).

Ms. Olivia Swaak-Goldman, Outlining the Three-Year Report, Session 1: Interested States, Second public hearing of the OTP, 25 September 2006; Ms. Géraldine Mattioli – HRW, Session 2: NGOs and other experts, 26 June 2006; Mr. Antoine Bernard – International Federation for Human Rights (FIDH), Session 2: NGOs and other experts, Second public hearing of the OTP, 26 June 2006; Mr. Richard Dicker, HRW, Session 4: NGOs and other experts, Second public hearing of the OTP, 18 October 2006; Helge Brunberg, Demographer, Session 3: Needs for demographic and statistical expertise at the International Criminal Court (paper), Second public hearing OTP, 25 April 2003. Available at: http://www.icc-cpi.int/Menus/ICC/Structure + of + the + Court/Office + of + the + Prosecutor/Network + with + Partners/Public + Hearings/Second + Public + Hearing/ (accessed 3 September 2009).

Oficina del Alto Comisionado Para los Derechos Humanos, “Oficina de la ONU para los Derechos Humanos lamenta hundimiento del proyecto de ley de víctimas”, 23 June 2009. Available at: http://www.hchr.org.co/publico/comunicados/2009/comunicados2009.php3?cod=17&cat=74 (accessed 27 June 2009).

OTERO, Diego Prada. Experiencias de Investigación: las cifras del conflicto, available at: http://www.indepaz.org.co/attachments/191_cifras 1964 -2007.pdf (accessed 13 November 2009).

OTP “Policy paper R. Dicker, HRW, Session 1: Transcript, First public hearing of the OTP”, 17–18 June 2003. Available at: http://www2.icc-cpi.int/Menus/ICC/Structure + of + the + Court/Office + of + the + Prosecutor/Network + with + Partners/Public + Hearings/First + Public + Hearing/Session+1 (accessed 3 September 2009).

OTP, “Criteria for Selection of Situations and Cases,” draft policy paper on file with Human Rights Watch, June 2006.

OTP, “Informal expert paper: the principle of complementarity in practice”, 2003. Available at: http://www.icc-cpi.int/iccdocs/doc/doc654724.PDF (accessed 3 September 2009).

OTP, “Iraq response, Annex to the Update on communications received by the office of the prosecutor of the ICC”, 10 February 2006. Available at: http://www.

iccnow.org/documents/OTP_letter_to_senders_re_Iraq_9_February_2006.pdf (accessed 3 September 2009).
OTP, "Report on Prosecutorial Strategy", 14 September 2006. Available at: http://www.iccnow.org/documents/ProsecutorialStrategy_06Sep14.pdf (accessed 3 September 2009).
OTP, "Report on the activities performed during the first three years" (June 2003–June 2006) 12 September 2006. http://www.iccnow.org/documents/3YearReport%20_06Sep14.pdf (accessed 3 September 2009).
Regulations of the Office of The Prosecutor, ICC-BD/05-01-09, entry into force 23 April 2009. Available at: http://www.icc-cpi.int/NR/rdonlyres/FFF97111-ECD6-40B5-9CDA-792BCBE1E695/280253/ICCBD050109ENG.pdf (accessed 3 September 2009).
The Amnesty Act 2000, Laws of Uganda vol. XII Chapter 294. Available at: www.C–r.org/ourwork/accord/northernuganda/documents/2000_Jan_The_Amnesty_Act.doc (accessed 17 April 2009).
Third Report of the Prosecutor of the International Criminal Court, to the Security Council pursuant to UNSC 1593 (2005), 14 June 2006. Available at: http://www.icc-cpi.int/NR/rdonlyres/E61D7F34-7D21-44B9-8840-53B254172AF7/0/OTP_ReportUNSC_3Darfur_English.pdf (accessed 3 September 2009).
War Crimes Research Office . "The gravity threshold of the ICC", 2008. Available at: www.wcl.american.edu/warcrimes/icc/icc_reports.cfm (accessed 3 September 2009).

2.3.2.5 Unpublished documents

Ambos, Kai/Studenroth, Stefan. "Informe y recomendaciones a las consultas y observaciones realizadas en Bogotá y en la región piloto de Barranquilla (Costa)", Bogotá, GTZ-Proyecto ProFis, 2008.
Ambos, Kai/Bernal, Gloria. "Informe de visita a la región piloto", 25–26 August 2009 Guachaca, Santa Marta, Barranquilla, Cartagena, Sincelejo y Montería.
Ambos, Kai. "Stellungnahme zu den kolumbianischen Gesetzesentwürfen im Rahmen des Demobilisierungsprozesses der Regierung Uribe mit bewaffneten Gruppen". Ponencia en el coloquio de especialistas del grupo FriEnt, Bonn, 3 y 4 de noviembre de 2004. En español: "Dictamen sobre el proyecto de Ley colombiano en el marco del proceso de desmovilización de los "grupos armados" en el gobierno de Uribe". Available at: http://www.department-ambos.uni-goettingen.de/index.php?option=com_content&view=article&id=342&Itemid=181&lang=de (accessed 20 August 2009).
Comisión Colombiana de Juristas. "Gobierno quiere evadir sentencia de la Corte Constitucional sobre ley de Justicia y Paz". Available at: http://www.coljuristas.org/justicia/comprensa300806.pdf (accessed 7 June 2009).
Huber, Florian, "¿Qué quieren las víctimas como reparación y qué pueden esperar de los mecanismos de reparación diseñados por la Ley de Justicia y Paz? – Un balance crítico de la implementación de la Ley 975 de 2005 y su impacto

práctico", Presentation during the Conference "Reparación en Colombia: Qué quieren las víctimas? Retos, desafíos y alternativas para garantizar la integralidad.", organized by ProFis of GTZ, Bogotá, 8 May 2009.

ProFis-GTZ, Resumen de las conclusiones del taller "Decisión de la Corte Suprema sobre la Primera Sentencia", Bogotá, 29 August 2009.

Unidad de Justicia y Paz de la Fiscalía General de la Nación, Informe sobre la aplicación de la LJP, 15 July 2009.

2.3.3 *Press reports*

"¿Tras extradición de jefes paramilitares habrá verdad, justicia y reparación?, 14 May 2008. Available at: http://www.eltiempo.com/archivo/documento/CMS-4163130 (accessed 14 June 2009).

"'Don Berna' aseguró que financió campaña presidencial de Uribe en 2001", 22 April 2009, Available at: http://www.verdadabierta.com/web3/justicia-y-paz/extraditados/1155-don-berna-aseguro-que-financio-campana-presidencial-de-uribe-en-2001 (accessed 22 June 2009).

"'Mellizo' Mejía salpica a ex gobernador Julio Acosta y a la Fuerza Aérea", 21 January 2009. Available at: http://www.verdadabierta.com/web3/justicia-y-paz/versiones/80-versiones-seccion/765-el-mellizo-salpica-a-ex-gobernador-julio-acosta-y-a-la-fuerza-aerea (accessed 19 June 2009).

"Aprueban ley de víctimas del gobierno", 13 November 2008. Available at: http://www.verdadabierta.com/web3/la-historia/periodo4/entrega-de-bienes-de-victimarios/542-aprobada-version-gubernamental-de-la-ley-de-victimas (accessed 31 June 2009).

"Colombia: Ley de Víctimas rechazada en el Senado, Uribe no la apoyó", 18 June 2009. Available at: http://www.infolatam.com/entrada/colombia_ley_de_victi mas_rechazada_en_el-14516.html (accessed 27 June 2009).

"Colombia: Uribe pide a los legisladores no aprobar la Ley de Víctimas", 18 June 2009. Available at: http://www.infolatam.com/entrada/colombia_uribe_pide_a_los_legisladores_n-14513.html (accessed 27 June 2009).

"La estrategia 'para' en Estados Unidos", 24 April 2009. Available at: http://www.elespectador.com/impreso/articuloimpreso137748-estrategia-estados-unidos (accessed 12 May 2009).

"Ley de víctimas no es discriminatoria", 8 December 2008. Available at: http://www.elespectador.com/noticias/politica/articulo97101-ley-de-victimas-no-dis criminatoria-gobierno (accessed 27 June 2009).

"Por no confesar sus delitos, 1.600 ex 'paras', están punto de perder beneficios de Justicia y Paz". Available at: http://www.eltiempo.com/archivo/documento/CMS-5288010 (accessed 22 August 2009).

"Uribe dice que rechazó ley de víctimas porque "trataba igual a terroristas, soldados y policías"", 2 June 2009. Available at: http://www.semana.com/

noticias- conflicto-armado/uribe-dice-rechazo-ley-victimas-porque-trataba-igual-terrorisas-soldados-policias/125419.aspx (accessed 27 June 2009).

“Van 20 representantes de víctimas asesinados en tres años y la cifra podría dispararse”, 22 February 2009. Available at: http://www.eltiempo.com/archivo/documento/MAM-3328500 (accessed 31 July 2009).

Amnistía Internacional, “La ‘Ley de Víctimas’ es discriminatoria”, 25 November 2008. Available at: http://www.amnesty.org/es/news-and-updates/news/ley-victimas-colombia-discriminatoria-20081125 (accessed 27 July 2009).

Comunicado de la Presidencia de la República, 27 April 2004, http://www.altocomisionadoparalapaz.gov.co/noticias/2004/abril/abr_27_04.htm (accessed 3 August 2009).

Comunicado de Prensa N 21/08, 14 May 2008, Comisión Interamericana de Derechos Humanos expresa preocupación por extradición de paramilitares colombianos. Available at: http://www.cidh.oas.org/Comunicados/Spanish/2008/21.08sp.htm (accessed 7 March 2009).

Comunicado de Presidencia – Colombia, MPP Medios para la Paz, 24 April 2004, puntos 6 y 7. Available at: http://www.mediosparalapaz.org/index.php?idcategoria=1769 (accessed 11 May 2009).

Conferencia de Prensa del Embajador de Estados Unidos en Colombia, 13 May 2008, puntos 4 y 5, transcritos en página web de la embajada de Estados Unidos en Colombia. Available at: http://spanish.bogota.usembassy.gov/rp_001_13052008.html (accessed 11 May 2009).

In www.elcolombiano.com: “Autodefensas exigen ser excluidos de alcance de la CPI”, 18 de marzo de 2004; “Negociaciones, AUC invitan a negociar a E.U.”, 23 March 2004; “Bcb dice que no habrá más desmovilizaciones parciales”, 13 April 2004; “CPI se reservará derecho a juzgar guerrilleros y autodefensas”, 21 October 2004; “Las AUC rechazan el tribunal de la verdad”, 11 December 2004; “AUC moverán sus fichas políticas”, 20 February 2005. (accessed 10 January 2009).

In www.eltiempo.com: “sin Ley de penas, se hunde la paz con las autodefensas”, 31 August 2003; “Paras contemplan consulta popular”, 1 February 2004; “Extradición divide debate sobre Ley de alternatividad penal para facilitar negociaciones”, 24 March 2004; “Solución de extradición es política”, 26 March 2004; “Futuro del proyecto de Ley de alternatividad penal se decide este miércoles”, 4 May 2004; “El tiempo entrevistó al Estado Mayor de las AUC en pleno. Un día en el corazón de los paramilitares”, 16 May 2004; “Noticias del proceso. Por qué no estaba Baez”, 1 July 2004; “Nuevas condiciones de Salvatore Mancuso sobre presencia de jefes paramilitares en Santa Fe de Ralito”, 5 August 2004; “Gobierno advierte que no creará más ralitos. Comisionado explica ultimátum”, 7 August 2004; “críticas a proceso de Ralito”, 1 October 2004; “Álvaro Uribe dice que desmovilización de AUC facilita marco legal a la negociación”, 13 December 2004; “Paramilitares anuncian que terminó el ciclo de desmovilizaciones sin contraprestaciones”, 26 December 2004; “Se fugaron 11 ex paramilitares del Bloque Bananero, que debían permanecer en Santa Fe de Ralito”, 20 January 2005; “Paramilitares amenazan con romper proceso si no se negocian términos para su sometimiento”, 23 February 2005; “Las AUC bajan el tono de la discusión y dicen que no presionan a Gobierno, Congreso ni prensa", 24 February 2005; "El Procurador pide explicaciones al Comisionado de paz y solicita eliminar el llamado narcomico", 13 March 2004. (accessed 10 January 2009).

Entrevista exclusiva a 'Mellizo Mejía', "Todos tenemos que pedir perdón", 22 January 2009. Available at: http://www.verdadabierta.com/web3/victimarios/los-jefes/783-entrevista-con-miguel-angel-mejia-munera-alias-pablo-arauca (accessed 19 June 2009).

Extradición de paramilitares estancó sus procesos judiciales en Colombia, 13 May 2009. Available at: http://www.caracol.com.co/nota.aspx?id=811096 (accessed 18 August 2009).

Informe de prensa en IPS Noticias, "La Otra Historia", 13 May 2008. Available at: http://ipsnoticias.net/print.asp?idnews=88403 (accessed 25 May 2009).

Palabras del director de la UNFJP, Luis González de León. "Justicia y Paz a los ojos de su guardián", in *El Espectador,* Bogotá, 1 March 2009. Available at: http://www.elespectador.com (accessed 20 May 2009).

Secretaría de Prensa, Noticias, "Comunicado", 18 June 2009. Available at: http://web.presidencia.gov.co/sp/2009/junio/18/05182009.html (accessed 27 June 2009).

Secretaría de Prensa, Noticias, "Palabras del Presidente Álvaro Uribe en el seminario 'Pobreza, Desarrollo y ODM', en la Universidad de la Salle", 18 June 2009. Available at: http://web.presidencia.gov.co/sp/2009/junio/18/07182009.html (accessed 31 June 2009).

Secretaría de Prensa, Presidencia de la República de Colombia, "Arrancó Programa de Restitución de Bienes." Available at: http://web.presidencia.gov.co/sp/2009/julio/10/05102009.html (accessed 28 July 2009).

Secretaría de Prensa, Presidencia de la República, "Colombia envió nota a Comisión Interamericana de Derechos Humanos", 15 May 2008. Available at: http://web.presidencia.gov.co/sp/2008/mayo/15/13152008.html (accessed 3 August 2009).

Secretaría de Prensa, Presidencia República de Colombia, 14 May 2008. Available at: http://oacp.presidencia.gov.co/snerss/detalleNota.aspx?id=15233 (accessed 9 May 2009).

2.4 (Further) BIBLIOGRAPHY

2.4.1 Monographs/Books

2.4.1.1 International criminal law, transitional justice, peace process, demobilisations and related topics

Alonso Espinal, Manuel *et al. Estudio sobre el proceso de desmovilización, desarme y reinserción en Antioquia: anotaciones desde lo local,* Medellín, Comisión Departamental de seguimiento y acompañamiento al Proceso de Desmovilización, Desarme y Reinserción en Antioquia, 2007.

Ambos, Kai. *Internationales Strafrecht*, 2ª ed., Múnich, C-.H. Beck, 2008.

Ambos, Kai. *Principios e imputación en el derecho penal internacional*, Barce lona, Atelier, 2008.

Ambos, Kai. *¿Cómo imputar a los superiores crímenes de los subordinados en el Derecho penal internacional?* Bogotá, Universidad Externado de Colombia, Centro de Investigación Filosofía y Derecho, Colección de Estudios No. 37, 2008.

Ambos, Kai/Malarino Ezequiel/ELSNER, Gisela (eds.). *Justicia transicional. Informes de América Latina, Alemanía, Italia y España,* Montevideo, Georg August Universität-Göttingen y Konrad Adenauer Stiftung, 2009.

Aponte Cardona, Alejandro. *El desplazamiento forzado como crimen internacional en Colombia. Reglas, principios de interpretación y fórmulas de imputación,* Bogotá, Observatorio internacional DDR-Ley de justicia y paz/Centro internacional de Toledo para la paz, 81 pp.

Aponte Cardona, Alejandro. *Protocolo para el reconocimiento de casos de violaciones a los derechos humanos, con éngasis en el homicidio en persona protegida,* Bogotá, Programa de lucha contra la impunidad, Vicepresidencia de la República, 2008, s.n.

Botero, Catalina. *Ley de alternatividad y justicia transicional: documento de recomendaciones,* Bogotá, ICTJ-Fundación Social, 2004.

Cárdenas Sarrias, José Armando. *Los parias de la guerra: análisis del proceso de desmovilización individual,* Bogotá, Ediciones Aurora, 2005.

Ceballos, Marcela. *El papel de las comisiones extrajudiciales de investigación y de las comisiones de verdad en los procesos de paz – aspectos teóricos y experiencia internacional-,* Bogotá, Departamento Naciona de planeación, 2002.

Centro Internacional Para la Justicia Transicional. *Ensayos sobre la justicia transicional*, New York, 2003.

Chernick, Marcw. *Acuerdo posible: solución negociada al conflicto armado colombiano: seis décadas de violencia, veinticinco años de proceso de paz,* Bogotá, Aurora, 2008.

Chichon Álvarez, Javier. *Derecho internacional y transiciones a la democracia y la paz: hacia un modelo para el castigo de los crímenes pasados a través de la experiencia latinoamericana*, Madrid, Ediciones Parthenon, 2007.

Cinep *et al. Seminario Internacional. Verdad y Justicia,* Bogotá, CINEP, 2003.

Comisión Colombiana de Juristas. *Principios internacionales sobre impunidad y reparaciones,* Bogotá, 2007.

Comisión Colombiana de Juristas. *Verdad, justicia y reparación. Algunas preguntas y respuestas,* Bogotá, 2007.

Cortés Castillo, Carlos Eduardo (Editor). *Desaparición forzada, política criminal y procesos restaurativos. Dilemas y desafios de la verdad, la justicia y la reparación en el contexto colombiano,* Bogotá, 2006.

Duncan, Gustavo. *Los señores de la guerra: de paramilitares, mafiosos y autodefensas en Colombia*, Bogotá, Planeta, 2006.

El Zeidy, Mohamed. *The principle of complementarity in international criminal law*, Leiden-Boston, Martinus Nijhoff, 2008.

Elster, Jon. *Transitional justice in historical perspective,* Cambridge, CUP, 2004.

Elster, Jon. *Seminario Internacional Justicia Transicional en la resolución de conflictos y secuestro: memorias*, Bogotá, Vicepresidencia de la República, Universidad Nacional de Colombia, 2007.

Fundación Social. *Los derechos de la vícitimas en los procesos de justicia transicional*, Bogotá, Ed. Geminis, 2005.

Gamboa Tapias, Camila de (ed.). *Justicia transicional: teoría y praxis*, Bogotá, Universidad del Rosario, 2006.

Gaviria, José Obdulio. *Parapolítica. Verdades y mentiras,* Bogotá, Ed. Planeta, 2008, 363.

Giraldo, Jorge/Riaza Restrepo, William. *Análisis del desempeño de la seguridad en Medellín 2000–2006,* Medellín, Alcaldía de Medellín, 2007.

Gleichmann, Colin. *Desarme, Desmovilización y Reintegración. Guia teórica y práctica*, Frankfurt am, El Colegio Sueco para la Defensa Nacional (FHS), el Centro Noruego para la Defensa Internacional (FSS), el Centro Canadiense para el mantenimiento de la Paz (PPC) y la Cooperación Técnica Alemana (GTZ), 2004.

Gómez Méndez, María Paula. *Verdad, justicia y reparación. Colombia ante la Corte Interamericana de Derechos Humanos,* Bogotá, Instituto Interamericano de Derechos Humanos, 2006.

Guerrero Peralta, Óscar Julián. *Fundamentos teórico constitucionales del nuevo proceso penal,* 2ª ed., Bogotá, Ediciones nueva jurídica, 2007.

Human Rights Watch. *¿Rompiendo el control? Obstáculos de la justicia en las investigaciones de la mafia paramilitar en Colombia,* Nueva York, The author, 2008.

Human Rights Watch. *Selling Justice Short. Why Accountability Matters for Peace,* New York, HRW, July 2009.

Instituto Popular de Capacitación. *Píldoras para la memoria. Violaciones de los derechos humanos y crimenes de lesa humanidad en el Valle de Aburra y el oriente Antioqueño (2000–2004),* Medellín, The author, 2006.

Junod, Sylvie-Stoyanka *et al. Comentario del Protocolo del 8 de junio de 1977 adicional a los Convenios de Ginebra del 12 de agosto de 1949 relativo a la protección de las víctimas de los conflictos armados sin carácter internacional (Protocolo II) y del artículo 3 de estos convenios*, Bogotá, Comité Internacional de la Cruz Roja – Plaza y Janés Editores Colombia S.A, 1998.

Kleffner, Jean K. *Complementarity in the Rome Statute and National Criminal Jurisdictions*, Nueva York et al., Oxford University Press, 2008.

Lovaton, David *et al. La justicia de paz en los Andes: estudio regional,* Lima, Instituto de Defensa Legal, 2005.

Martínez Ortiz, Astrid/Ramírez Gómez, Claudia/Borda Medina, Ernesto. *Persistir en la paz negociada: análisis del contexto socioeconómico y político del conflicto en Colombia*, Bogotá, Editorial Antropos, 2003.

Mockus Sivickas, Antanas/Cante, Freddy (Coords). *Acción colectiva, racionalidad y compromisos previos*, Bogotá, UNAL, 2006.

Najar Moreno, Esperanza. *Derecho a la verdad y justicia transicional en el marco de aplicación de la Ley de justicia y paz,* Bogotá, Grupo editorial Ibáñez, 2009.

Nasi L., Carlo. *Cuando callan los fusiles. Impacto de la paz negociada en Colombia y en Centroamerica,* Bogotá, Ed. Norma, 2007.

Oficina del Alto Comisionado Para la Paz. *Desmovilización de las Autodefensas,* Bogotá, 2007.

Olásolo, Héctor. *The criminal responsability of senior political and military leaders as principales to international crimes*, Oxford, Hart Publishing, 2009.

Orozco Abad, Iván. *Sobre los límites de la conciencia humanitaria: dilemas de la paz y de la justicia en América Latina,* Bogotá, Ed. Temis, 2005.

Orozco Abad, Iván. *Justicia transicional en tiempos del deber de memoria,* Bogotá, Universidad de los Andes – Temis S.A., 2009.

Palacio Cepeda, Marisol. *Justicia, paz y tratamiento de víctimas en el sistema penal,* Bogotá, Grupo Editorial Ibáñez, 2008.

Palou, Juan Carlos/Llorente, María Victoria. *Reintegración y Seguridad Ciudadana en Medellín: un balance del Programa de Paz y Reconciliación (2004–2008)* Bogotá, Fundación ideas para la paz, 2009.

Pardo Rueda, Rafael. *Fin del paramilitarismo ¿es posible su desmonte?*, Bogotá, Ediciones B, 2007.

Pastor, Daniel. *El plazo razonable en el proceso del estado de derecho*: *una investigación acera del problema de la excesiva duración del proceso penal y sus posibles soluciones*, Buenos Aires, Ad Hoc, 2002.

Pecaut, Daniel. *Orden y violencia: evolución socio-política de colombia entre 1930 y 1953*, Bogotá, Editorial Norma, 2001.

Procuraduría General de la Nación. *Seguimiento a políticas públicas en materia de desmovilización y reinserción. Derecho a la verdad, memoria histórica y protección de archivos - Tomo I, II, II, IV –*, Bogotá, USAID, 2008.

Rangel, Alfredo. *El poder paramilitar,* Bogotá, Fundación Seguridad y Democracia-Planeta, 2005.

Rangel, Alfredo (ed.). *Justicia y paz. Cuál es el precio que debemos pagar?,* Bogotá, Fundación seguridad y democracia, 2009.

Rettberg, Angélika. *Entre el perdón y el paredón: preguntas y dilemas de la justicia transicional,* Bogotá, Universidad de los Andes, 2005.

Rettberg, Angélika. *Buscar la paz en medio del conflicto: un propósito que no da tregua. Un estudio de las iniciativas de paz en Colombia (desde los años 90 hasta hoy),* Bogotá, Universidad de los Andes, 2006.

Rettberg, Angélika. *Reparación en Colombia. ¿Qué quieren las vícitimas?*, Bogotá, GTZ-Fiscalía General de la Nación-Universidad de los Andes-Embajada de la República Federal de Alemania, 2008.

Romero, Mauricio/Valencia, León (ed.). *Parapolítica: la ruta de la expansión paramilitar y los acuerdos políticos*, Bogotá, Intermedio, 2008

Springer, Natalia María. *Desactivar la guerra: alternativas audaces para consolidar la paz*, Bogotá, Aguilar, 2005.
Uprimny Yepes, Rodrigo. *Justicia transicional sin transición?: Verdad justicia y reparación en Colombia,* Bogotá, Centro de Estudios de Derecho, Justicia y Sociedad, 2006.
Uprimny Yepes, Rodrigo/Rodríguez Garavito, César Augusto/García Villegas, Mauricio. *¿Justicia para todos? Sistema judicial, derechos sociales y democracia en Colombia*, Bogotá, Grupo Editorial Norma, 2006.
Valencia, León. *Parapolítica: la ruta de la expansión paramilitar y los acuerdos políticos,* Bogotá, Corporación Nuevo Arco Iris, 2007.
Velásquez Velásquez, Fernando. *Derecho Penal, Parte General*, 4ª ed., Bogotá, Librería Jurídica Comlibros, 2009.

2.4.1.2 Law 975 of 2005

Arango Rivanedeira, Rodolfo. *Derechos Humanos como límite a la democracia. Análisis de la Ley de justicia y paz,* Bogotá, Norma – Universidad de los Andes, 2008.
Centro Internacional de Toledo Para la Paz (CITPAX), "Observatorio sobre DDR y la Ley de Justicia y Paz, Informe Primera Fase" – Diciembre 2008. Available at: http://www.citpaxobservatorio.org/archivos/CITpax_Informe_de_Primera_Fase_Observatorio_DDR_y_LJP.pdf (accessed 10 November 2009).
Centro Internacional de Toledo Para la Paz (CITPAX), "Observatorio Internacional sobre el proceso de DDR y la aplicación de la Ley de Justicia y Paz en Colombia", Área de Justicia, *2° informe sobre las fórmulas de imputación de crímenes internacionales en el marco de Justicia y Paz*, July 2009.
Comisión Colombiana de Juristas. *Anotaciones sobre la Ley de justicia y paz: Una mirada desde los derechos de las víctimas,* Bogotá, The author, 2007.
Comisión Colombiana de Juristas. *Colombia: el espejismo de la justicia y la paz. Balance sobre la aplicación de la Ley 975 de 2005,* Bogotá, The author, 2008.
Cuervo Restrepo, Jorge Iván *et al. Justicia transicional: modelos y experiencias internacionales: a propósito de la Ley de justicia y paz*, Bogotá, Universidad Externado de Colombia, 2007.
Deutsche Gesellschaft Für Technische Zusammenarbeit GmbH (GTZ-Proyecto Profis). *Manual de procedimientos para Ley de justicia y paz*, Bogotá, GTZ-Embajada de la República Federal de Alemania en Colombia, 2009.
Deutsche Gesellschaft Für Technische Zusammenarbeit GmbH (GTZ-Proyecto ProFis)/Embajada de la República Federal de Alemania/ Fiscalía General de la Nación. *Guía de procedimientos de la unidad nacional de Fiscalías para justicia y paz. Ley 975 de 2005,* Bogotá, The authors, 2009.
González Medina, Diego Andres/Perdomo Torres, Jorge Fernando/Mariño Rojas, Cielo. *Reparación judicial, principio de oportunidad e infancia en la Ley de justicia y paz,* Bogotá, GTZ-Embajada de la República Federal de Alemania en Colombia, 2009.

2.4.2 *Articles in journals/books*

2.4.2.1 International criminal law, transitional justice, peace process, demobilisation and related topics

Ambos, Kai. "Joint Criminal Enterprise and Command Responsibility", en *JICJ* 5(1), 2007, pp. 159–183.

Ambos, Kai. "El principio acusatorio y el proceso acusatorio: un intento de comprender su significado actual desde la perspectiva histórica", en Bachmaier Winter (ed.). *Proceso penal y sistemas acusatorios*, Madrid, Marcial Pons, 2008, pp. 49–52; versión revisada publicado en *Derecho Penal Contemporáneo*, Editorial Legis S.A., N° 28, Julio-Septiembre de 2009, Bogotá, 5–36.

Ambos, Kai. "Vorbemerkung zu §§ 8 ff.", en *Münchner Kommentar Strafgesetzbuch. Nebenstrafrecht III Völkerstrafgesetzbuch,* Múnich, Beck, 2009, pp. 620–649.

Ambos, Kai/Woischnik, Jan. "Resumen comparativo de los informes nacionales", en Maier/Ambos/Woischnik (Coords.) *Las reformas procesales penales en América Latina*, Buenos Aires, Ad-hoc, 2000, pp. 835–896.

Aponte Cardona, Alejandro. "Colombia", en Ambos/Malarino (eds.) *Jurisprudencia latinoamericana sobre derecho penal internacional,* Montevideo, Konrad Adenauer Stiftung-Temis S.A., 2008, pp. 159–212.

Aponte Cardona, Alejandro. "Colombia", en Ambos/Malarino/Elsner (eds.) *Justicia de Transición*, Berlín, Konrad Adenauer Stiftung, 2009, pp. 235–300.

Berdall, Mats R. "Disarmament and Demobilization after civil wars", en *Adelphi Paper, 303,* London, The International Institute for Strategic Studies, 1996, pp. 1–88.

Bergsmo, Morten. "The Jurisdictional Regime of the International Criminal Court (Part. II, Art. 11–19)" en *Eur. J.Cr., Cr. L. & Cr. J.* 6, 1998, pp. 29–47.

Bickford, Louis. "Transitional Justice", en Shelton (ed.). *Encyclopedia of Genocide and Crimes Against Humanity,* vol. 3, Nueva York, Macmillan Reference, 2004, pp. 1045–1047.

Burke-White, William. "Proactive complementarity: The International Criminal Court and national courts in the Rome system of international justice", en *Harvard International Law Journal* 49, 2008, pp. 53–108.

Chaves, Juan. "La justicia transicional: de la razón a la racionalidad y de la racionalidad a la razón", en *Antípoda* N 4, Bogotá, Ene–Jun 2007, pp. 225–242.

Chichon Álvarez, Javier. "Transición española y justicia transicional: ¿qué papel juega el ordenamiento jurídico internacional en un proceso de transición? A propósito de la coherencia, buena fe y otros principios de derecho internacional postergados en la transición política de España", en *Entelequia, Revista Insterdisciplinar: Monográfico N° 7,* Madrid, Sep. 2008, pp. 331–354.

Cinep. "Alternativas a la Guerra. Iniciativas y procesos de paz en Colombia", en *Controversia n° 181 Especial.* Available at: http://www.cinep.org.co/controversia.

htm?AA_SL_Session=35aff6547ed9b0d5c8521e3f02cb5c50&x=820 (accessed 3 September 2009).

Cortés Rodas, Francisco. "Realistas versus idealistas en el proceso de paz con los grupos paramilitares", en *Debates N. 40,* Medellín, En–Abr 2005, pp. 3–6.

Cortés Rodas, Francisco. "Los derechos de las víctimas de la violencia política a la verdad, la reparación y la justicia : reflexiones sobre cuatro casos en América Latina", en *Estudios Políticos N. 31,* Medellín, Jul–Dic 2007, pp. 61–86.

de la Calle Lombana, Humberto. "Castigo y perdón en el proceso de justicia y paz con los paramilitares en Colombia", en Rangel Suárez (ed.). *Justicia y paz. ¿Cuál es el precio que debemos pagar?*, Bogotá, Fundación seguridad y democracia, 2009, pp. 75–158.

Dudley, Steven. "Investigación, Usos y Abusos de la Extradición en la Lucha contra las Drogas, Extradición: ¿Un obstáculo para la justicia?, Fundación Ideas para la Paz", en *Policy Brief* 1/20, abril, 2009. Available at: http://www.verdadabierta.com/web3/justicia-y-paz/extraditados/1180-extradicion-iun-obstaculo-para-las-victimas (accessed 11 May 2009).

El Zeidy, Mohamed. "The gravity threshold under the Statute of the International Criminal Court", en *CLF* 19, 2008, pp. 35–57.

Franco Restrepo, Vilma Liliana. "Justicia retributiva y responsabilidad política: una respuesta al dilema transicional", en *Debates* N. 45, Medellín, Sep–Dec 2006, pp. 10–24.

Gil Ramírez, Max Yuri. "Los derechos de las víctimas en el marco del proceso de negociación entre el gobierno colombiano y los grupos paramilitares, 2002–2007", en *Controversia* n° 189, CINEP. Available at: http://www.cinep.org.co/revistas/controversia/controversia189/189_art4.pdf (accessed 3 September 2009).

González Zapata, Julio. "La justicia transicional o la relegitimación del derecho penal", en *Estudios Políticos N° 31,* Medellín, Jul–Dec 2007, pp. 23–42.

Herrera Jaramillo, Carlos José/Torres Pacheco, Silvano. "Reconciliación y justicia transicional: opciones de justicia, verdad, reparación y perdón", en *Papel Político N. 18,* Dec. 2005, pp. 79–112.

Holá, Barbora/Smeulers, Alette/Bijlevled, Catrien. "Is ICTY sentencing predictable? An empirical analysis of ICTY sentencing practice", in *LJIL* 22, 2009, pp. 79–97.

Jiménez Ocampo, Sandro/Munera, Leidis. "La autonomia del Estado en sociedades afectadas por conflictos armados internos: una lectura de la configuracion del Estado entre la transnacionalizacion y la transicionalidad", en *Revista de Antropologia y Arqueología N. 04,* Bogotá, Ene–Jun 2007, pp. 188–206.

Martínez E., Martha Lucía. "Tres años en la ruta hacia la reparación y la verdad", in *Boletín CNRR* n° 6, Bogotá, July 2008, pp. 4–5.

McAuliffe deGuzman, Margaret. "Gravity and the legitimacy of the ICC", en *Yale Law School Student Scholarship Series*, 2008 (paper 69), 30 http://lsr.nellco.org/yale/student/papers/69 (accessed 3 September 2009).

Medina Arbeláez, Camila. "La relación excombatientes - estado en el marco del proceso de desarme, desmovilización y reintegración en Colombia. Un debate permanente sobre participación política, ciudadanía y garantía de derechos". Available at: http://www.institut-gouvernance.org/fr/analyse/fiche-analyse-284.html (visitado por última vez el 10 de marzo de 2009).

Modolell González, Juan Luis. "La justicia de transición en América Latina y Europa, y la jurisprudencia de la Corte Penal Internacional. Informe del VI seminario del Grupo Latinoamericano de Estudios sobre Derecho Penal Internacional", en *Zeitschrift für Internationale Strafrechtsdogmatik* 2/2009, pp. 82–87. Available at: www.zis-online.com (accessed 10 November 2009).

Murphy, Ray. "Gravity issues and the International Criminal Court", en *CLF* 17, 2006, pp. 281–315.

Orozco Abad, Iván. "Apuntes para una historia comparada de la justicia transicional. El papel de las ONG de derechos humanos en los procesos de justicia transicional: los casos del Cono Sur y El Salvador", en *Análisis Político n° 48,* Bogotá, Ene–Abr 2003, pp. 52–76.

Pérez Toro, William Fredy. "Orden Jurídico, negociación, paz y reinserción: la constante imbricación entre guerra, política y derecho en Colombia", en *Estudios Políticos N. 27,* Medellín, Jul–Dic 2005, pp. 67–100.

Pérez Toro, William Fredy. "La dificial aproximación al delito político", en *Estudios Políticos N. 31*, Jul–Dic 2007, pp. 43–60.

Ramírez Barat, Clara. "Javier Chinchón A., Derecho internacional y transiciones a la democracia y la paz : hacia un modelo para el castigo de los crímenes pasados a través de la experiencia latinoamericana", en *Revista de Estudios Políticos N° 139,* Madrid, Ene–Mar 2008, 241–251.

Posada Carbo, Eduardo. "La paz y sus principios". Available at: http://www.ideaspaz.org/new_site/secciones/publicaciones/download_publicaciones/la_paz_y_sus_principios.pdf (accessed 3 September 2009).

Prittwitz, Cornelius. "La relación entre justicia y la pena privativa de la libertad", en *Cuadernos del Conflicto,* Bogotá, Legis S.A. – Semana – Fundación Ideas para la Paz, April 2005, pp. 30–31.

Schabas, William. "Prosecutorial discretion v. judicial activism at the International Criminal Court", en *JICJ* 6, 2008, pp. 731–761.

Schabas, William. "Prosecutorial discretion and gravity", in Stahn/Sluiter (eds.), *The emerging practice of the International Criminal Court*, Leiden – Boston, Martinus Nijhoff, 2009, pp. 229–246.

Stahn, Carsten. "Judicial review of prosecutorial discretion: Five years on", in C-. Stahn/G. Sluiter (eds.) *The emerging practice of the International Criminal Court*, Leiden – Boston, Martinus Nijhoff, 2009, pp. 247–279.

Stegmiller, Ignaz. "The gravity threshold under the ICC Statute: gravity back and forth in Lubanga and Ntaganda", in *ICLR* 9, 2009, pp. 547–565.

Uprimny Yepes, Rodrigo. "Justicia transicional en Colombia: algunas herramientas conceptuales para el análisis del caso Colombiano", en *Revista Foro N° 53,* Bogotá, May 2005, pp. 45–57.

Uprimny, Rodrigo/Lasso, Luis Manuel. "Verdad, reparación y justicia para Colombia: Algunas reflexiones y recomendaciones", en *Conflicto y Seguridad Democratica. Temas Críticos y propuestas,* Bogotá, Fundación Social, Fescol, Embajada de la República Alemana en Colombia, 2004, pp. 101–188.

Uprimny, Rodrigo/Saffon, María Paula. "Transitional Justice, Restaurative Justice and Reconciliation. Some Insights from the Colombian case", 2005. Available at: http://www.dejusticia.org/interna.php?id_tipo_publicacion=5?id_tipo_publicacion=5?id_tipo_publicacion=5?id_tipo_publicacion=5&id_publicacion=348 (last accessed 13 July 2009).

Uprimny, Rodrigo/Saffon, María Paula. "Usos y abusos de la justicia transicional en Colombia", 2007. Available at: www.dejusticia.org (accessed 3 August 2009).

Uribe de Hincapié, María Teresa. "Notas preliminares sobre resistencias de la sociedad civil en un contexto de guerras y transacciones", in *Estudios Políticos* N. 29, Medellín, Jul–Dec 2006, pp. 63–78.

Valencia Villa, Hernando. "Introducción a la justicia transicional", en *Claves de la Razón Práctica N. 180,* March 2008, pp. 76–82.

Vargas, Alejo/Rubio, Rocío. "Desmovilización y reinserción de ex – combatientes=¿transición hacia...?", in *Conflicto y Seguridad Democrática. Temas Críticos y propuestas,* Bogotá, Fundación Social, Fescol, Embajada de la República Alemana en Colombia, 2004, pp. 189–258.

Waugaman, Adele. "Five minutes with Luis Moreno-Ocampo: An interview with the ICC Prosecutor", en XV International Affairs Review 2, 2006, 1. Available at: http://www.gwu.edu/~iar/articles/2006/S2006_Web_Special.pdf (accessed 3 September 2009).

2.4.2.2 Law 975 of 2005

Görzig, Carolin/Planta, Katrin. "Das kolumbianische" Ley de Justicia y Paz, "Wendepunkt oder Fallstrick?" en *HuV-I* 22, February 2009, pp. 94–100.

2.5 FIELD WORK: INTERVIEWS AND MEETINGS

2.5.1 Interviews

Acosta, Jairo. Procuraduría General de la Nación. Bogotá, 11 August 2009. With: Kai Ambos/John Zuluaga.

Aponte, Alejandro. Observatorio Internacional sobre el proceso de DDR y la aplicación de la Ley de Justicia y Paz en Colombia. Bogotá, 12 August 2009. With: Kai Ambos/John Zuluaga.

Balosea, Heydi/Aza, Fernando. Units of Public Council of Defense for Demobilized Persons and Legal Representation for Victims. Defensoría del Pueblo. Bogotá, 12 August 2009. With: Kai Ambos/John Zuluaga.

Bernal, Camilo. International Center for Transitional Justice (ICTJ), Bogotá, 14 August 2009. With: John Zuluaga.

Castro, Sandra y Peña, Miriam. National Unit for Human Rights and International Humanitarian Law' Fiscalía General de la Nación. Bogotá, 11 August 2009. With: Kai Ambos/John Zuluaga.

Ceballos, Camilo/Roncal, Juan Carlos. MAPP-OEA. Bogotá, 13 August 2009. With: Kai Ambos/John Zuluaga.

Eslava Mojica, Luz Amira. CNRR. Bogotá, 14 August 2009. With: John Zuluaga.

Gonzalez León, Luis/Encinales, John. Special Unit for Justice and Peace, Fiscalia General de la Nación. Bogotá, 13 August 2009. With: Kai Ambos/John Zuluaga.

Guerrero, Óscar Julián. Procuraduría General de la Nación. Bogotá, 15 August 2009. With: Kai Ambos/John Zuluaga.

Gutierrez, María Viviana. Acción Social. Bogotá, 14 August 2009. With: John Zuluaga.

López, Zeneida. Prosecutor, Coordinator of the Special Unit for Justice and Peace in Barranquilla. Barranquilla, 19 August 2009. With: Kai Ambos.

Orozco Abad, Iván. Group of Historial Memory, CNRR. Bogotá, 12 August 2009. With: Kai Ambos/John Zuluaga.

Porras, Eduardo. Magistrado de Control de Garantías. Barranquilla, 19 August 2009. With: Kai Ambos.

Posada Orrego, John Jaime. Coordinator of the Special Unit for Justice and Peace of the Procuraduría General de la Nacion, Office of Medellín. Medellín, 5 August 2009. With: John Zuluaga.

Ramírez Meneses, Bladimir. Corporación Jurídica Libertad (NGO). Medellín, 6 August 2009. With: John Zuluaga.

Uprimny, Rodrigo. Dejusticia (NGO). Bogotá, 11 August 2009. With: Kai Ambos/John Zuluaga.

2.5.2 Meetings

Corte Suprema de Justicia, Sala Penal. Participants: Assistant judges of the Justices Yesid Ramirez Bastidas and María del Rosario González de Lemos, Bogotá, 29 October 2009, Universidad de los Andes. With: Kai Ambos.

Corte Suprema de Justicia, Sala Penal. Participants: Justices and assistant judges. Bogotá, 10 August 2009. With: Kai Ambos/Andreas Forer/John Zuluaga.

Tribunal de Distrito Judicial, Bogotá, Justicia y Paz, Judges of the Chamber for Justice and Peace. Higher Court of Bogotá. Participants: Julio Ospina, Uldi Teresa Jiménez, Lester María González. 10 August 2009. With: Kai Ambos/John Zuluaga.

Fiscalía General de la Nación, Unidad de Justicia y Paz, Bogotá. Participants: León González (director of the Special Unit for Justice and Peace), Myriam Consuelo Méndez Christancho. 30 October 2009. With: Kai Ambos/Andreas Forer.

Fiscalía General de la Nación, Prosecutors and investigators of the Special Unit for Justice and Peace of Barranquilla. Participants: delegated Prosecutor for Justice and Peace, three prosecutors of the regional office and two investigators. Barranquilla, 19 August 2009. With: Kai Ambos.

Fiscalía General de la Nación, Special Unit for Justice and Peace, Office of the Prosecutor, Regional Office of Montería. Participants: two prosecutors, twoassistant prosecutors, delegated prosecutor for excavations of disappeared persons and 12 investigators. 20 August 2009. With: Kai Ambos.

Defensoría del Pueblo, Bogotá. Patricia Luna, Coordinator of the Victims Assistance Unit "Unidad de Atención Integral a las Victimas" of the Defensoría del Pueblo; Pedro David Berdugo, councel, legal representative of victims; Mónica Suárez Moscoso, Coordinator of the Office of Support of the Defensoría del Pueblo, Bogotá, 30 October 2009. With: Kai Ambos/Andreas Forer.

Defensoría del Pueblo, Office of Legal Representation for Victims, Bogotá, 13 August 2009. With: Kai Ambos/John Zuluaga.

Defensoría del Pueblo, Councels of Defense of the Defensoría del Pueblo in Barranquilla. Participants: aprox. 100 councels of the regional office of the Defensoría. Barranquilla, 19 August 2009. With: Kai Ambos.

CNRR, National Office of the CNRR. Participants: José Hernandez, coordinator of the legal department; Ana Teresa Bernal (commissioner), Claudia Vizcaino, Luisa Lopez, Nini Johana Soto, Blanca Lucía Mora Méndez. Bogotá, 30 October 2009. With: Kai Ambos/Andreas Forer.

CNRR, Legal Department of the National Office of the CNRR. Participants: José Hernández Rueda, Claudia Vizcaíno, Luz Amira Mojica, Regulo Madero, Felipe Rodríguez, Nini Johana Soto, Luisa Fernanda López, Blanca Lucía Mora, Daniela Guzmán. Bogotá. 11 September 2009. With: Kai Ambos/John Zuluaga.

CNRR, Regional Office of the CNRR, Sincelejo. Participants: four women who form part of the "tejedoras de la memoria" network, two pschologists working with the CNRR, four officials, incluiding the coordinator, of the regional office of the CNRR in Sincelejo, assistant prosecutor of the Special Unit for Justice and Peace in Sincelejo, two members of "Pastoral Social" of Sincelejo, an official of the Office of the Vice President (Human Rights and University Professors Program). 20 August 2009. With: Kai Ambos.

Coordinating Committee, Santa Marta. Participants: 11 officials of the Fiscalía, Defensoría del Pueblo, CNRR, Alto Consejero de la Gobernación, the coordinator and two assistants of the Victims Assistance Unit "Unidad de Atención Integral a las Victimas" of the Defensoría del Pueblo.18 August 2009. With: Kai Ambos.

Inter-institutional coordinating committee, Cartagena. Participants: Delegates of the Office of the Prosecutor General, Office of the Vice President, Procuraduría General de la Nación, Personería Distrital, Gobernación de Bolívar, Defensoría del Pueblo, Cuerpo Técnico de Investigaciones (CTI) and Zeneida Lopez (coordinator of the Special Unit for Justice and Peace of the Office of the Prosecutor General in Barranquilla). 20 August 2009. With: Kai Ambos.

Inmates of the Picota Prison – "Justice and Peace" Wing (ERE 3). Bogotá. Participants: Jorge Rojas (Spokesman of the demobilized inmates of the AUC in Bogotá), Germán Senna, Walter Ochoa Guisao "aka el Gurre". 12 August 2009. With: Kai Ambos/Andreas Forer/John Zuluaga.

3. LAW NO. 975, 25 JULY 2005 (English translation)*

ISSUING PROVISIONS FOR THE REINCORPORATION OF MEMBERS OF ILLEGAL ARMED GROUPS WHO EFFECTIVELY CONTRIBUTE TO THE ATTAINMENT OF NATIONAL PEACE, AND OTHER PROVISIONS FOR HUMANITARIAN ACCORDS ARE ISSUED.

THE CONGRESS OF COLOMBIA

DECREES:

CHAPTER I

Principles and definitions

Article 1. *Purpose of this law.* The purpose of this law is to facilitate the processes of peace and individual or collective reincorporation into civilian life of the members of illegal armed groups, guaranteeing the victims' rights to truth, justice, and reparation.

An illegal armed group is understood to be a guerrilla or self-defense group, or a significant and integral part of them such as blocks, fronts, or other modalities of these same organizations, which are the subject of Law 782 of 2002.

Article 2. *Scope of the law, interpretation, and normative application.* This law regulates matters of investigation, prosecution, punishment, and judicial benefits with respect to those persons linked to illegal armed groups as perpetrators or participants in criminal acts committed during and on occasion of their membership

*The original translation is available at http://www.globaljusticecenter.net/projects/colombia/Law%20975.pdf. It has been updated with regard to the fundamental judgment of the Colombian Constitutional Court C-370-06 of 18 May 2006. The parts of the text which are crossed out have been declared unconstitutional (*inexequible*) by the Court; the parts which are underlined have been declared "conditionally constitutional" (*condicionalmente exequible*).

in those groups, who have decided to demobilize and contribute decisively to national reconciliation.

The provisions of this law shall be interpreted and applied in keeping with the Constitution and the international treaties ratified by Colombia. The incorporation of some international provisions in this law should not be understood as negating other international provisions that regulate this same subject matter.

The reinsertion into civilian life of those persons who may be able to benefit from an amnesty, pardon, or any other benefit established in Law 782 of 2002 shall be governed by the provisions of that law.

Article 3. *Alternative sentencing.* Alternative sentencing is a benefit consisting of suspending execution of the sentence determined in the respective judgment, replacing it with an alternative sentence that is granted for the beneficiary's contribution to the attainment of national peace, collaboration with the justice system, reparation for the victims, and the person's adequate re-socialization. This benefit is granted in accordance with the conditions established in this law.

Article 4. *Right to truth, justice, and reparations and due process.* The process of national reconciliation made possible by this law should promote, in every case, the right of the victims to the truth, justice, and reparations, and respect the rights to due process and judicial guarantees of those persons who are prosecuted.

Article 5. *Definition of victim.* For the purposes of this law, the victim is understood to be a person who individually or collectively has suffered direct harm such as temporary or permanent injuries that cause some type of physical, psychological, or sensory disability (visual and/or hearing), emotional suffering, financial loss, or infringement of his or her fundamental rights. The harm must be the consequence of actions that were in violation of the criminal law, by illegal armed groups.

In addition, the victim shall be understood to refer to the spouse, or common-law spouse, and relatives in the first degree of consanguinity, or first civil, of the direct victim, when the victim was killed or is disappeared.

The status of victim is acquired independent of whether the perpetrator of the criminal conduct has been identified, apprehended, prosecuted, or convicted, and without consideration of any family relationship between the perpetrator and the victim.

In addition, victims shall also include the members of the armed forces and National Police who have suffered temporary or permanent injuries that cause some type of physical, psychological and/or sensory disability (visual or hearing), or infringement of his or her fundamental rights, as a consequence of the actions of a member or members of the illegal armed groups.

In addition, victims shall include the spouse, common-law spouse, and relatives within the first degree of consanguinity, of the members of the armed forces and National Police who have lost their lives in undertaking acts in service, that were service-related, or outside of service, as a result of the acts carried out by a member or members of the illegal groups.

Article 6. *Right to Justice.* Under existing legal provisions, the State has the duty to undertake an effective investigation that leads to the identification, capture, and punishment of persons responsible for crimes committed by the members of illegal armed groups; to ensure the victims of such conduct access to effective remedies to make reparation for the harm inflicted; and to adopt measures aimed at preventing the recurrence of such violations.

The public authorities who are involved in the proceedings that take place pursuant to this law should give special attention to the duty addressed in this article.

Article 7. *Right to the truth.* The society, and especially the victims, have the inalienable, full, and effective right to learn the truth about the crimes committed by illegal armed groups, and to know the whereabouts of the victims of kidnapping and forced disappearance.

The investigations and judicial proceedings to which this law applies should promote an investigation into what happened to the victims of such conduct, and inform the family members of the relevant findings.

The judicial proceedings instituted as of the entry into force of this law shall not preclude the future application of other non-judicial mechanisms for reconstructing the truth.

Article 8. *Right to reparation.* The victims' right to reparation includes the actions taken for restitution, compensation, rehabilitation, satisfaction, and guarantees of non-repetition.

Restitution is defined as actions that seek to return the victim to the situation prior to the crime.

Indemnity is defined as compensation for the damages caused by the crime.

Rehabilitation is defined as actions aimed at the recovery of victims who suffer physical and psychological traumas as a result of the crime.

Satisfaction or moral compensation is defined as actions aimed at reestablishing the dignity of the victim and disseminating the truth about what happened.

Guarantees of non-repetition include, among others, the demobilization and dismantling of the illegal armed groups.

Symbolic reparation is understood to mean any benefit granted the victims or the community in general aimed at ensuring the preservation of the historical memory, the non-repetition of the victimizing acts, the public acceptance of the acts, public forgiveness, and reestablishing the victims' dignity.

Collective reparation should be geared to the psychosocial rebuilding of the populations affected by the violence. This mechanism is established especially for the communities affected by the occurrence of acts of systematic violence.

The competent judicial authorities shall set the individual, collective, or symbolic reparations as appropriate, in the terms of this law.

Article 9. *Demobilization.* Demobilization is understood to be the individual or collective act of laying down arms and abandoning the illegal armed group, before the competent authority.

The demobilization of the illegal armed group shall be carried out in keeping with the provisions of Law 782 of 2002.

CHAPTER II

Preliminary aspects

Article 10. *Eligibility requirements for collective demobilization.* Members of an illegal armed group who have been or may be indicted, accused, or convicted as perpetrators of or participants in criminal acts committed during and on occasion of their membership in those groups may accede to the benefits established in this law, when they cannot be beneficiaries of any of the mechanisms established in Law 782 of 2002, so long as they are included in the list that the National Government provides to the Office of the Attorney General, and also meet the following conditions:

10.1 That the organized armed group in question has demobilized and dismantled, in accordance with an agreement with the National Government.
10.2 That the assets obtained as a result of the illegal activity be surrendered.
10.3 That the group place at the disposal of the Instituto Colombiano de Bienestar Familiar (Colombian Family Welfare Institute) all minors who have been recruited.
10.4 That the group cease all interference with the free exercise of political rights and public freedoms and any other illegal activity.
10.5 That the group was not organized for the purposes of drugs trafficking or illicit enrichment.
10.6 That the persons kidnapped who are under their control be released.

Paragraph. The members of the illegal armed group who are deprived of liberty may accede to the benefits contained in this law and those established in Law 782 of 2002, so long as their membership in the respective group is determined in the respective judicial rulings.

Article 11. *Eligibility requirements for individual demobilization.* Those members of the illegal armed groups who have demobilized individually and who contribute to the attainment of national peace may accede to the benefits established in this law, so long as they meet the following requirements:

11.1 That they provide information or collaborate in the dismantling of the group to which they belonged.
11.2 That they have signed an act of commitment with the National Government.
11.3 That they have demobilized and laid down their arms in the terms established by the National Government to that end.
11.4 That they cease all illegal activity.
11.5 That the assets obtained as a result of illegal activities be surrendered, so as to make reparation to the victim, ~~when these become available~~.
11.6 That their activity not have had as its purpose narcotics trafficking or illicit enrichment.

Only those persons whose names and identities are presented by the National Government to the Office of the Attorney General may accede to the benefits provided for in this law.

CHAPTER III

Procedural principles

Article 12. *Oral procedure*. The procedure shall be oral, and suitable technical means shall be used to ensure it is faithfully reproduced.

It shall be up to the Secretary of the National Prosecutorial Unit for Justice and Peace, (Unidad Nacional de Fiscalía para la Justicia y la Paz) created by this law, and the Chamber of the Superior Judicial District Court that sits in judgment, as the case may be, to keep the records.

Article 13. *Speedy process*. The matters debated in the hearing shall be resolved within the same hearing. Notice of the decisions shall be considered made when posted on the court notice board.

The preliminary hearings shall take place before the Judge for Control of Guarantees (Magistrado de Control de Garantías) designated by the respective Court.

The following matters shall be addressed in the preliminary hearing:

1. The early collection of evidence which for well-founded reasons and extreme necessity is required to prevent the loss or alteration of the evidence in question.
2. The adoption of means to protect victims and witnesses.
3. The request for and decision to impose a measure to ensure appearance of the accused.
4. The request for and decision to impose precautionary measures on ~~illegally-obtained~~ assets.
5. The arraignment.
6. The indictment.
7. Those that resolve situations similar to the foregoing.

The decisions that resolve substantive matters and the judgments should set forth the factual, evidentiary, and legal grounds, and indicate the motives for accepting or rejecting the parties' claims.

The assignment of the matters referred to by this law should be done the same day as the record is received in the corresponding judicial office.

Article 14. *Defense*. The defense shall be entrusted to the defense counsel of trust freely designated by the indicted or accused person, or, alternatively, to the one assigned by the National System of Public Defenders.

Article 15. *Clarification of the truth*. Within the procedure established by this law, public servants shall rule as necessary to ensure clarification of the truth as to the facts subject of investigation, and to guarantee the defense of those who are prosecuted.

The National Prosecutorial Unit for Justice and Peace established by this law shall investigate, through the prosecutor delegate for the case, with the support of the specialized judicial police group, the circumstances of time, manner, and place in which the criminal conduct was committed; the living conditions, social conditions, and family and individual situation of the indicted or accused person and his or her prior conduct; the judicial and police records; and the harm that he or she, individually or collectively, may have directly caused the victims, such as physical or psychological injuries, emotional suffering, financial loss or substantial infringement of fundamental rights.

With the collaboration of the demobilized persons, the judicial police shall investigate the whereabouts of persons kidnapped or disappeared, and shall report the results of such investigations to the next-of-kin in timely fashion.

The Office of the Attorney General shall see to the protection of the victims, witnesses, and expert witnesses it intends to present at trial. Protecting the witnesses and expert witnesses the defense intends to present shall be entrusted to the Office of the Human Rights Ombudsperson. Protecting the judges who sit on the Superior Judicial District Courts that are to preside over the trials shall be a responsibility of the Superior Council of the Judiciary.

CHAPTER IV

Investigation and prosecution

Article 16. *Jurisdiction.* Once the name or names of the members of illegal armed groups willing to make an effective contribution to the attainment of national peace has or have been received by the National Prosecutorial Unit for Justice and Peace, the corresponding prosecutor delegate shall immediately assume jurisdiction to:

16.1 Take cognizance of the investigations of the criminal acts committed during and on occasion of their membership in the illegal armed group.
16.2 Take cognizance of the investigations under way against their members.
16.3 Take cognizance of the investigations that are to be initiated and those of which there is knowledge at the time of or subsequent to demobilization.

The Superior Judicial District Court determined by the Superior Council of the Judiciary, by decision issued prior to initiating any proceeding, shall have jurisdiction to sit in judgment of the criminal conduct referred to in this law.

There may not be any conflict or clash of jurisdiction between the Superior Judicial District Courts that hear the cases referred to in this law and any other judicial authority.

Article 17. *Spontaneous declaration and confession.* The members of the illegal armed group whose names are submitted by the National Government for the consideration of the Office of the Attorney General, who expressly avail themselves of the procedure and benefits of this law, shall make a spontaneous declaration before the prosecutor delegate assigned to the process of demobilization, who will question them about all the facts of which they have knowledge.

In the presence of their defense counsel they shall describe the circumstances of time, manner, and place in which they have participated in the criminal acts committed on occasion of their membership in these groups, prior to their demobilizing, and in respect of which they avail themselves of this law. In that procedure they shall indicate the assets that are surrendered for making reparation to the victims, if they have any, and the date of their entry in the group.

The declaration given by the demobilized person and all other records produced in the demobilization process shall be placed immediately at the disposition of the National Prosecutorial Unit for Justice and Peace so that the prosecutor delegate and the Judicial Police assigned to the case may prepare and develop the methodological program for initiating the investigation, verifying the truthfulness of the information provided, and clarifying those facts and all those that come to its attention within the scope of its authority.

The demobilized person shall ~~immediately~~ be placed at the disposal of the judge who performs the function of controlling guarantees ~~in one of the places of detention determined by the National Government pursuant to Article 31 of this law~~, who within the subsequent thirty-six (36) hours shall schedule and hold an arraignment hearing, pending a prior request by the prosecutor handling the case.

Article 18. *Arraignment.* When, based on the material evidence, physical evidence, information lawfully obtained, or the spontaneous declaration, one may reasonably infer that the demobilized person is a perpetrator of or participant in one or several crimes being investigated, the prosecutor delegate for the case shall ask the judge who performs the function of controlling guarantees to schedule a preliminary arraignment hearing.

At this hearing, the prosecutor shall make the factual indictment of the charges investigated and shall ask the judge to order the pre-trial detention of the accused in the appropriate detention center as provided for in this law. In addition, the prosecutor shall ask that precautionary measures be adopted with respect to ~~illegally obtained assets that have been surrendered~~ for the purpose of making reparation to the victims.

Within sixty (60) days of this hearing, the National Prosecutorial Unit for Justice and Peace, with the support of its group of judicial police, will undertake the investigation and verification of the facts admitted by the accused, and all those that may come to its attention within the scope of its jurisdiction. Upon the conclusion of this term, or earlier if possible, the prosecutor assigned to the case shall ask the judge who performs the function of controlling guarantees to schedule an indictment hearing, within ten (10) days following the request, if there is to be one.

The statute of limitations on the criminal action is interrupted by the arraignment.

Article 19. *Acceptance of charges.* In the indictment hearing the accused may accept the charges presented by the Office of the Attorney General, as a result of the spontaneous declaration or the investigations under way at the time of the demobilization.

In order for it to be valid, he or she must do so freely, voluntarily, spontaneously, and with the assistance of defense counsel. In this case the judge who performs the function of controlling guarantees shall immediately send the record to the Office of the Clerk of the Chamber of the Superior Judicial District Court that is to hear the matter.

Once the record is received, the corresponding Chamber shall schedule a public hearing, within ten (10) days, to determine whether the acceptance of charges was free, voluntary, spontaneous, and with the assistance of defense counsel. If it is found to be according to law, within the following ten (10) days it will schedule a hearing for sentencing and imposition of the individual penalty.

Paragraph 1. If in this hearing the accused does not accept the charges, or retracts those admitted to in the spontaneous declaration, the National Prosecutorial Unit for Justice and Peace shall refer the record to the government officer with jurisdiction, pursuant to the law in force at the time the conduct investigated was committed.

Paragraph 2. When there is a request for comprehensive reparation, the provisions of Article 23 of this law shall be implemented first.

Article 20. *Joinder of proceedings and accumulation of sentences.* For the procedural purposes of this law, any proceedings already under way for criminal acts committed during and on occasion of membership of the demobilized person in an illegal armed group shall be joined. In no case shall there be joinder for criminal conduct committed prior to membership of the demobilized person in an illegal armed group.

When the demobilized person has been previously convicted of criminal conduct committed during and on occasion of his or her membership in an illegal armed group, the provisions of the Criminal Code on serving sentences concurrently (acumulación jurídica de penas) shall be taken into account, ~~but in no case may the alternative sentence be greater than that provided for in this law~~.

Article 21. *Rupture of procedural unity.* If the indicted or accused person accepts the charges in part, the procedural unity will be broken with respect to those not admitted to. In that case, the investigation and prosecution of the charges not accepted shall be handled by the competent authorities and pursuant to the procedural laws in force at the time they were committed. With respect to the charges accepted, the benefits that are addressed in this law shall be granted.

Article 22. *Investigations and indictments prior to the demobilization.* If at the time a demobilized person avails himself or herself of this law, the Office of the Attorney General is undertaking investigations or has formally indicted him or her, the indicted or accused person, with the assistance of defense counsel, may orally or in writing accept the charges set forth in the order that imposed the measure to ensure appearance, or in the arraignment, or in the resolution or brief of accusation, as the case may be. Such acceptance shall be before the judge who is performing the function of control of guarantees in t*he* conditions provided for by this law.

Article 23. *Interlocutory proceeding for comprehensive reparation.* In the same hearing in which the respective Chamber of the Superior Judicial District Court finds that the acceptance of the charges is lawful, after an express request made by the victim, or by the prosecutor handling the case or by the Public Ministry upon request of the victim, the judge writing for the court shall immediately open the interlocutory proceeding for comprehensive reparation of the harm caused by the criminal conduct, and shall call a public hearing within five (5) days.

That hearing shall begin with a statement by the victim or his or her legal representative or public defender, to state specifically the type of reparation sought, and to indicate the evidence that he or she will introduce to support his or her claims.

The Chamber shall examine the claim, and shall dismiss it if the person filing it is not the victim or if actual payment of the damages is shown and if this were the only claim made; said decision may be challenged in the terms of this law.

Once the claim is admitted, the Chamber shall inform the accused that it has accepted the charges, and will then invite the parties involved to conciliate. If they reach agreement, it shall be incorporated in the ruling in the interlocutory proceeding; otherwise, it shall order that the evidence offered by the parties be produced, it shall hear the arguments in support of their respective claims, and in the same act it shall rule on the interlocutory proceeding. A decision either way shall be incorporated into the guilty verdict.

Paragraph 1. Exclusively for the purposes of the conciliation provided for in this article, the victim, the accused or defense counsel, the prosecutor handling the case, or the Public Ministry may ask that the Director of the Social Solidarity Network (Red de Solidaridad Social) be subpoenaed in his capacity as controller of expenditures of the Fund for the Reparation of Victims.

Paragraph 2. The granting of an alternative penalty may not be denied if the victim fails to exercise his or her right in the interlocutory proceeding for comprehensive reparation.

Article 24. *Content of the verdict.* In keeping with the criteria established in the law, the guilty verdict shall set the principal sentence and the accessory penalties. It shall also include the alternative sentence provided for in this law, the commitments with respect to conduct for the term ordered by the Court, the obligations with respect to moral and economic reparation to the victims, and forfeiture of the assets that are to be earmarked for reparation.

The respective Chamber shall be responsible for evaluating compliance with the requirements provided for in this law to be eligible for the alternative penalty.

Article 25. *Facts that come to be known after the verdict or the pardon.* If the members of illegal armed groups who received the benefits of Law 782 of 2002, or who benefitted from the alternative sentence under this law, subsequently come to be accused of crimes committed during and on occasion of their membership in these groups and prior to their demobilization, that conduct shall be investigated and judged by the competent authorities and the laws in force at the time of such conduct, ~~without prejudice to the granting of the alternative sentence in the event that they collaborate effectively in clarifying or accept, orally or in writing, freely,~~

~~voluntarily, expressly, and spontaneously, having been duly advised by their defense counsel, their participation in their commission, and so long as the omission was not intentional. In this case, the convicted person may benefit from the alternative sentence. The alternative sentences shall be served concurrently, without exceeding the maximum terms established in this law~~.

~~Taking into account the seriousness of the new facts judged, the judicial authority shall impose an increase of twenty percent of the alternative penalty imposed, and a similar increase of the time on probation~~.

Article 26. *Remedies.* Except for the judgment, a motion for annulment may be brought against all the decisions, and it is argued and resolved orally and immediately in the respective hearing.

Appeals may be brought against those orders that resolve merits issues that are adopted in the course of the hearings, and against the verdicts. They are to be raised in the same hearing in which the decision is handed down, and when granted have the effect of staying the decision challenged pending decision by the Criminal Chamber of the Supreme Court of Justice.

The judge writing the decision shall summon the parties and participants to a hearing for oral arguments that shall be held within ten (10) days once the record is received at the Office of the Clerk of Criminal Cassation. Once the appellant has argued the grounds for the appeal, and all other parties and participants have been heard from, the Chamber may decree a recess of up to two (2) hours to issue its decision. If the appellant is not present or no argument is presented in support of the appeal, it shall be declared to have been abandoned.

Paragraph 1. The processing of the remedies of appeal addressed in this law shall have priority over all other matters under the jurisdiction of the Criminal Chamber of the Supreme Court of Justice, except matters relating to writs of protection of fundamental rights (acciones de tutela).

Paragraph 2. The Plenary Chamber of the Supreme Court of Justice shall hear special motions for reconsideration provided for in the Code of Criminal Procedure in force.

Paragraph 3. No motion for cassation may be brought against the judgment on appeal.

Article 27. *Archive of the proceedings.* If, in relation to the facts admitted or not admitted by the demobilized person in his spontaneous declaration or in a later procedure, as the case may be, before the arraignment hearing, the prosecutor delegate should come to find that there are no motives or factual circumstances that allow them to be characterized as a crime, or that indicate their possible existence, he or she shall immediately archive the record. Nonetheless, if new evidence arises the inquiry will be reopened in keeping with the procedure established in this law, so long as the criminal action has not extinguished.

Article 28. *Intervention of the Public Ministry.* In the terms of Article 277 of the Constitution, the Public Ministry shall intervene as necessary in the defense of the legal order, public property, and fundamental rights and guarantees.

CHAPTER V

Alternative Sentence

Article 29. *Alternative sentence*. The Chamber with jurisdiction of the Superior Judicial District Court shall determine the sentence that corresponds to the crimes committed, in keeping with the rules of the Criminal Code.

In the event that the convicted person has met the conditions provided for in this law, the Chamber shall impose an alternative sentence that consists of deprivation of liberty for a term of at least five (5) years and not greater than eight (8) years, to be set based on the seriousness of the crimes and his or her effective collaboration in their clarification.

To have the right to an alternative sentence, the beneficiary will be required to commit himself or herself to contribute to his or her re-socialization through work, study, or teaching during the time that he or she is deprived of liberty, and to promote activities geared to the demobilization of the illegal armed group of which he or she was a member.

Once the alternative sentence has been served and the conditions imposed in the judgment have been met, the beneficiary shall be released on probation for a term equal to half the alternative sentence imposed, during which time the beneficiary undertakes not to commit ~~the~~ crimes ~~for which he was convicted in the framework of this law~~, to come before the corresponding Superior Judicial District Court periodically, and to report any change in residence.

Once these obligations have been met and after the probation period has lapsed, the principal penalty shall be declared to have extinguished. Otherwise, the probation shall be revoked and the penalty initially determined shall be served, without prejudice to any of the benefits for the reduction of penalties provided for in the Criminal Code that may apply.

Paragraph. In no case shall benefits for the reduction of penalties, additional benefits, or reductions complementary to the alternative sentence be applied.

CHAPTER VI

Regime for the deprivation of liberty

Article 30. *Place of detention*. The National Government shall determine the place of detention where the effective sentence should be served.

The places of detention should meet the conditions of security and austerity typical of the centers run by the INPEC (Instituto Nacional Penitenciario y Carcelario, National Penitentiary and Prison Institute).

The penalty may be served abroad.

Article 31. *Time spent in the zones of concentration.* ~~The time that the members of illegal armed groups linked to processes for collective reincorporation into civilian life have remained in a zone of concentration decreed by the National Government pursuant to Law 782 of 2002 shall be computed as time served on the alternative sentence, without this period exceeding eighteen (18) months~~.

~~The official designated by the National Government, in collaboration with the local authorities when appropriate, shall be responsible for certifying the time that the members of the armed groups addressed in this law have been in the zone of concentration~~.

CHAPTER VII

Institutions for the execution of this law

Article 32. *Scope of jurisdiction of the Superior Judicial District Courts for Justice and Peace Matters.* In addition to the jurisdiction established in other laws, the Superior Judicial District Courts designated by the Superior Council of the Judiciary shall have jurisdiction to judge the proceedings addressed in this law, and oversee compliance with the penalties and with the obligations imposed on the convicted persons.

It shall be up to the Office of the Clerk of the respective Court to organize, systematize, and conserve the files on the facts and circumstances related to the conduct of the persons subject to any of the measures addressed in this law, in order to guarantee the rights of the victims to the truth and to preserve the collective memory. In addition, it should guarantee public access to the records of the cases in which there has been final judgment, and have a Communications Office to disseminate the truth of what happened.

Article 33. *National Prosecutorial Unit for Justice and Peace.* The National Prosecutorial Unit for Justice and Peace, delegated before the Superior Judicial District Courts, with national scope of authority and made up as indicated in this law, is hereby created.

This unit shall be responsible for performing those acts which by reason of its jurisdiction, are to be undertaken by the Office of the Attorney General in the proceedings established in this law.

The National Prosecutorial Unit for Justice and Peace shall have the permanent support of a special judicial police unit, made up of members of the appropriate authorities, assigned exclusively and permanently, and with jurisdiction throughout the national territory.

Add to the staff of positions in the Office of the Attorney General for 2005, established in transitory article 1 of Law 938 of 2004, the following positions:

150 criminal investigators VII
15 clerks IV
15 judicial assistants IV
20 drivers III
40 bodyguards III
15 assistant criminal investigators IV
20 prosecutors' assistants II

Paragraph. The Office of the Attorney General shall assign from its staff, to constitute the National Prosecutorial Unit for Justice and Peace, the following positions: 20 Prosecutors Delegate before the Court

Article 34. *Public Defender Service.* The State shall guarantee to those indicted, accused, and convicted the ability to exercise the right to defense through the mechanisms of the Public Defender Service, and in the terms indicated in the law.

The Office of the Human Rights Ombudsperson shall assist the victims in exercising their rights, and in the framework of ~~this~~ law.

Article 35. *Procurator General's Judicial Office for Justice and Peace.* The Office of the Procurator General shall create, for the purposes of this law, a Procurator General's's Judicial Office for Justice and Peace (Procuraduría Judicial para la Justicia y la Paz), with national jurisdiction. To this end, the Procurator General's Judicial Office for Justice and Peace may participate in the relevant judicial and administrative proceedings.

Article 36. *Participation of social organizations that provide assistance to victims.* In order to carry out the provisions of this law, the Office of the Procurator General shall promote mechanisms for the participation of the social organizations that assist victims.

CHAPTER VIII

Rights of victims with respect to the Administration of Justice

Article 37. *Rights of the victims.* The State shall guarantee victims' access to the administration of justice. In developing the foregoing, the victims shall have the right:

37.1 To receive dignified human treatment throughout the procedure.
37.2 To the protection of their privacy and guarantee of their security and that of their family members and witnesses, whenever they are threatened.
37.3 To prompt and comprehensive reparation for the harm suffered; <u>the perpetrator or participant in the crime shall be responsible for making such reparation.</u>

37.4 To be heard and to receive facilitation for contributing evidence.

37.5 To receive information relevant to protecting their interests from the first contact with the authorities and in the terms established in the Code of Criminal Procedure; and to know the truth of the facts that constitute the circumstances of the crime of which they have been the victims.

37.6 To be informed of the final decision in the criminal prosecution and to pursue remedies when they are available.

37.7 To be assisted during the trial by an attorney of one's trust, or by the Procurator General's Judicial Office addressed in this law.

37.8 To receive comprehensive assistance for their recovery.

37.9 To be assisted at no cost by a translator or interpreter, in the event of not knowing the language, or not being able to perceive language through the sensory organs.

Article 38. *Protection of victims and witnesses*. The government officers to which this law refers shall adopt the appropriate measures and all relevant actions for protecting the security, physical and psychological well-being, dignity, and private life of the victims and witnesses, and of all other parties in the proceeding.

To this end, all relevant factors will be borne in mind, including age, gender, and health, as well as the nature of the crime, in particular when it entails sexual violence, disrespect for gender equality, or violence against children.

Special training will be given to the government officers who work with such victims.

These measures may not redound to the detriment of the rights of the accused or the right to a fair and impartial trial, nor shall they be incompatible with such rights.

Article 39. *Exception to public trials*. As an exception to the principle that the hearings that constitute the trial should be public, the Superior Judicial District Court, in order to protect the victims, witnesses, or an accused, may order that part of the trial be held in camera. It may order that testimony be taken through an audio/video system to allow it to be controverted and confronted by the parties.

In particular, these measures shall be applied to victims of sexual assault or assault of children and adolescents who may be victims or witnesses.

Article 40. *Other measures of protection during the trial*. When public disclosure of evidentiary material elements, physical evidence, or information lawfully obtained would entail grave danger to the security of the witness or his or her family, the Prosecutor shall refrain from presenting them in any procedure prior to the trial. Instead, he or she shall prepare a summary of that information. In no case may these measures redound to the detriment of the rights of the accused or of a fair and impartial trial, nor shall they be incompatible with such rights.

Article 41. *Attention to special needs*. The judicial organs as well as the technical support agencies and the Procurator General's Judicial Office for Justice and Peace shall be mindful of the special needs of women, children, the elderly, and the disabled to ensure their participation in the proceeding.

CHAPTER IX

Right to reparation for the victims

Article 42. *General duty to make reparation.* The members of the armed groups who benefit from the provisions of this law are under a duty to make reparation to the victims of said criminal conduct for which they were convicted by judicial verdict.

In addition, when the perpetrator is not identified, but the harm and causal nexus with the activities of the Illegal Armed Group Beneficiary of the provisions of this law are proven, the Court, directly or by referral to the Prosecutorial Unit, shall order reparations, to be paid from the Fund for Reparations.

Article 43. *Reparation.* The Superior Judicial District Court, on proffering its verdict, shall order reparation for the victims and shall set the pertinent measures.

Article 44. *Acts of reparation.* The reparation for the victims addressed in this law entails the duties of restitution, compensation, rehabilitation, and satisfaction.

To have a right to enjoy the benefit of release on probation, the convicted person must provide to the Fund for the Reparation of Victims the assets, ~~if he or she has any~~, earmarked for that purpose; satisfactorily undertake the actions of reparation that have been imposed on him or her; collaborate with the National Committee for Reparation and Reconciliation, or sign an agreement with the Superior Judicial District Court that ensures the performance of his or her duties of reparation.

The following are acts of comprehensive reparation:

44.1 Surrendering to the State ~~illegally obtained~~ assets for making reparation to the victims.

44.2 A public statement that reestablishes the dignity of the victim and of the persons closest to him or her.

44.3 Public recognition of having caused harm to the victims, the public statement of repentance, the request for forgiveness directed to the victims, and the promise not to repeat such criminal conduct.

44.4 Effective collaboration in locating persons kidnapped or disappeared and in locating the victims' remains.

44.5 The search for the disappeared and for the remains of dead persons, and help in identifying them and burying them again, in keeping with family and community traditions.

Article 45. *Request for reparation.* The victims of the illegal armed groups may obtain reparation by petitioning the Superior Judicial District Court in relation to the facts of which they have knowledge.

No one may receive reparation twice for the same harm.

Article 46. *Restitution.* Restitution implies undertaking acts that aim to return the victim to the situation prior to the violation of his or her rights. It includes releasing the person if deprived of liberty, return to one's place of residence, and the return of his or her property, ~~if possible~~.

Article 47. *Rehabilitation.* Rehabilitation should include medical and psychological care for the victims or their relatives within the first degree of consanguinity in keeping with the Budget of the Fund for the Reparation of Victims.

~~The social services provided by the government to the victims, in keeping with the provisions and laws in force, are part of reparation and rehabilitation~~.

Article 48. *Measures of satisfaction and guarantees of non-repetition.* The measures of satisfaction and guarantees of non-repetition adopted by the various authorities directly involved in the process of national reconciliation should include:

48.1 Verification of the facts and the public and complete dissemination of the judicial truth, to the extent that it will not provoke more unnecessary harm to the victim, witnesses, or other persons, or create a danger to security.

48.2 The search for persons who were disappeared or killed, and assistance in identifying them and burying them anew in keeping with family and community traditions. This task is mainly entrusted to the National Prosecutorial Unit for Justice and Peace.

48.3 The judicial decision that reestablishes the dignity, reputation, and rights of the victim, and those of the victim's relatives within the first degree of consanguinity.

48.4 The apology, which includes public recognition of the facts and acceptance of responsibilities.

48.5 The application of sanctions to those responsible for the violations, all of which will be entrusted to the judicial organs that are involved in the proceedings addressed in this law.

48.6 The competent chamber of the Superior Judicial District Court may order commemorations, tributes, and acts of recognition of the victims of the illegal armed groups. In addition, the National Commission on Reconciliation and Reparations may recommend to the political or government bodies at the various levels that they adopt such measures.

48.7 Preventing human rights violations.

48.8 Attendance by the persons responsible for violations at training courses on human rights. This measure may be imposed on the convicted persons by the competent chamber of the Superior Judicial District Court.

Article 49. *Programs for Collective Reparations.* The Government, following the recommendations of the National Commission on Reconciliation and Reparations, should implement an institutional program of collective reparations that includes actions directly aimed at recovering the institutional framework intrinsic to the Social State under the Rule of Law, particularly in the areas hardest hit by the violence; to recover and promote the rights of the citizens negatively affected by the acts of violence, and to recognize and dignify the victims of the violence.

Article 50. *National Commission on Reparation and Reconciliation.* The National Commission on Reparation and Reconciliation is hereby established, made up of the Vice-President of the Republic or his delegate, who shall chair its sessions; the Procurator General or his delegate; the Minister of Interior and Justice or his delegate; the Minister of Finance or his delegate; the Human Rights Ombudsperson, two Representatives of Victims' Organizations, and the Director of the Social Solidarity Network, which shall serve as the Technical Secretariat.

The President of the Republic shall designate five notables to serve as members of this Commission; of least two of them must be women.

This Commission shall have a duration of eight years.

Article 51. *Functions of the National Commission on Reparation and Reconciliation.* The National Commission on Reparation and Reconciliation shall perform the following functions:

51.1 Guaranteeing the victims their participation in proceedings for judicial clarification and the realization of their rights.
51.2 Submitting a public report on the reasons for the rise and development of the illegal armed groups.
51.3 Monitoring and verifying the processes of reincorporation, and the work of the local authorities to ensure the full demobilization of the members of illegal armed groups, and the proper functioning of the institutions in those territories. For those purposes, the National Commission on Reparation and Reconciliation may invite the participation of foreign entities and notables.
51.4 Monitoring and periodically evaluating the reparations provided for in this law, and making recommendations to ensure they are made properly.
51.5 Submitting, within two years of the date of the entry into force of this law, to the National Government and the Committees on Peace of the Senate and the House of Representatives, a report on the process of making reparation to the victims of the illegal armed groups.
51.6 Recommending the criteria for reparations addressed by this law, charged to the Fund for the Reparation of Victims.
51.7 Coordinating the activity of the Regional Commissions for the Restitution of Assets.
51.8 Carrying out national actions of reconciliation that seek to impede the recurrence of new acts of violence that disturb the national peace.
51.9 Adopting its own rules.

Article 52. *Regional commissions for the restitution of assets.* The regional commissions shall be responsible for giving impetus to the procedures related to claims over property and possession of goods in the framework of the process established in this law.

Article 53. *Composition.* The Regional Commissions shall be made up of one (1) representative of the National Commission on Reparation and Reconciliation, who shall chair it; one delegate of the Procurator General's Judicial Office for Justice and Peace; one (1) delegate of the Office of the Municipal or District

Ombudsperson (personería); one (1) delegate of the Human Rights Ombudsperson (Defensoría del Pueblo); and one delegate of the Ministry of Interior and Justice.

The National Government shall have the authority to designate a representative of the religious communities and shall determine the functioning and territorial distribution of the commissions based on the needs of the process.

Article 54. *Fund for the Reparation of Victims*. The Fund for the Reparation of Victims is hereby created as a special account without juridical personality whose controller of expenditure shall be the Director of the Social Solidarity Network. The resources of the Fund shall be executed in keeping with the rules of private law.

The Fund shall be made up of all the assets or resources that under any guise may be surrendered by the persons or illegal armed groups to which this law refers, resources from the national budget, and donations in cash and in kind, both national and foreign.

The resources administered by this Fund shall be under the oversight of the Office of the Comptroller-General of the Republic.

Paragraph. The assets to which reference is made in Articles 10 and 11 shall be surrendered directly to the Fund for the Reparation of Victims created by this law. The same procedure shall be observed with respect to the assets linked to criminal investigations and forfeiture proceedings in course at the time of the demobilization, as long as the conduct was carried out on occasion of their membership in the illegal armed group and before the entry into force of this law.

The Government shall regulate the functioning of this Fund and, in particular, everything concerning the claims for and surrender of assets with respect to good-faith third party holders.

Article 55. *Functions of the Social Solidarity Network*. The Social Solidarity Network, through the Fund addressed in this law, shall be in charge, in keeping with the budget allocated to the Fund, of the following functions:

55.1 Liquidating and paying the judicial compensation addressed in this law ~~within the limits authorized in the national budget~~.
55.2 Administering the Fund for the Reparation of Victims.
55.3 Undertaking other actions for reparation, when appropriate.
55.4 All others indicated in the regulations.

CHAPTER X

Conservation of archives

Article 56. *Duty of memory*. The knowledge of the history of the causes, developments, and consequences of the actions of the illegal armed group should be maintained by the use of adequate procedures, pursuant to the State's duty to preserve the historical memory.

Article 57. *Measures for preserving the archives.* The right to the truth implies that the archives must be preserved. To this end, the judicial organs that are in charge of them, and the Office of the Procurator General, shall adopt measures to prevent any removal, destruction, or falsification of the archives aimed at imposing impunity. The foregoing is without prejudice to the application of the relevant criminal statutes.

Article 58. *Measures for facilitating access to the archives.* Access to the archives should be facilitated in the interest of ensuring that the victims and their next-of-kin are able to assert their rights.

When access is requested in the interest of historical research, the formal requirements for authorization shall be aimed merely at controlling access, custody, and adequate maintenance of the materials, and shall not be used for censorship.

In any event, the necessary measures should be adopted to safeguard the right to privacy of the victims of sexual violence and of children and adolescents who are victims of the illegal armed groups, and so as not to provoke more unnecessary harm to the victim, the witnesses, or other persons, or endanger their security.

CHAPTER XI

Humanitarian Accords

Article 59. It is an obligation of the Government to guarantee the right to peace pursuant to Articles 2, 22, 93, and 189 of the Constitution, in view of the public order situation in the country and the threat to the civilian population and the legally constituted institutions.

Article 60. To carry out the provisions of Article 60 of this law, the President of the Republic may authorize his representatives or spokespersons to pursue contacts that make it possible to reach humanitarian accords with the illegal armed groups.

Article 61. The President of the Republic shall have the power to request of the competent authority, for the purposes and in the terms of this law, that it conditionally suspend the sentence and bestow the benefit of the alternative sentence on the members of illegal armed groups with whom humanitarian accords are reached.

The National Government may demand such conditions as it deems pertinent for these decisions to contribute effectively to the search for and attainment of peace.

CHAPTER XII

Entry into force and complementary provisions

Article 62. *Complementarity.* For all matters not provided for in this law, Law 782 of 2002 and the Code of Criminal Procedure shall apply.

Article 63. *More favorable future law.* If subsequent to the promulgation of this law, laws are issued that grant members of illegal armed groups benefits more favorable than those established in this one, the persons who have been subject to the alternative mechanism may avail themselves of the conditions established in such subsequent laws.

Article 64. *Surrender of minors.* The surrender of minors by members of illegal armed groups shall not be grounds for the loss of the benefits referred to by this law and Law 782 of 2002.

Article 65. The National Government, the Superior Council of the Judiciary, and the Office of the Attorney General shall appropriate sufficient resources essential to the proper and timely application of the asset forfeiture law.

Article 66. In keeping with the Program on Reincorporation into Civilian Life, the National Government shall seek to link the demobilized persons to productive projects or training or education programs so as to facilitate their access to productive employment.

Simultaneously, and in keeping with the same program, it shall seek their support for entering adequate psychological care programs that facilitate their social reinsertion and their adaptation to normal day-to-day life.

Article 67. The Judges of the Superior Judicial District Courts that are created pursuant to this law shall be elected by the Plenary Chamber of the Supreme Court of Justice from lists forwarded by the Administrative Chamber of the Superior Council of the Judiciary.

The requirements to serve as a member of these courts shall be the same as those required for serving as a judge on the current Superior Judicial District Courts.

The Administrative Chamber of the National Council of the Judiciary may establish the administrative and social support groups for these Courts. The appointment of employees shall be up to the judges of the Courts created by this law.

Article 68. The motions addressed in this law and which are processed before the Supreme Court of Justice shall have priority over all other matters under that Court's jurisdiction, and shall be resolved within thirty days.

Article 69. The persons who have demobilized under the framework of Law 782 of 2002 and who have been certified by the National Government may be beneficiaries of a motion to dismiss (resolución inhibitoria), preclusion of the investigation, or cessation of proceedings, as the case may be, for the crimes of conspiracy to engage in criminal conduct in the terms of section 1 of article 340 of the Criminal Code; illegal use of uniforms and insignia; instigation to criminal conduct in the terms of section 1 of article 348 of the Criminal Code, manufacturing, trafficking, and bearing arms and munitions.

The persons convicted of the same crimes and who meet the conditions established in this article may also access the legal benefits for them enshrined in Law 782 of 2002.

Article 70. *Reduction of sentences*. ~~The persons who at the time of the entry into force of this law are serving sentences after final judgments shall have the right to a reduction in the sentence imposed by one-tenth, except for those convicted of sexual offenses, crimes against humanity, and drug-trafficking~~.

~~For the granting and setting of the benefit, the judge of enforcement of sentences and security measures shall take into account the convict's good conduct, his or her commitment not to repeat the criminal acts, his or her cooperation with the justice system and actions to make reparation to the victims~~.

Article 71. *Sedition*. ~~Add to Article 468 of the Criminal Code a section that reads as follows: "Those who form or are a part of guerrilla or self-defense groups whose action interferes with the normal operations of the constitution and legal order shall have committed the crime of sedition. In that case, the sentence shall be the same as provided for the crime of rebellion~~.

~~Article 3(10) of the United Nations Convention Against Illicit Trafficking in Narcotic and Psychotropic Substances, signed in Vienna on December 20, 1988, and incorporated into the national legislation by Law 67 of 1993 shall remain in full force~~."

Article 72. *Entry into force and repeals*. The present law repeals all provisions contrary to it. It shall only be applied to acts that occurred prior to its entry into force, and it governs as of the date of its promulgation.

4. Schematic Overview of the Procedure Under Law 975

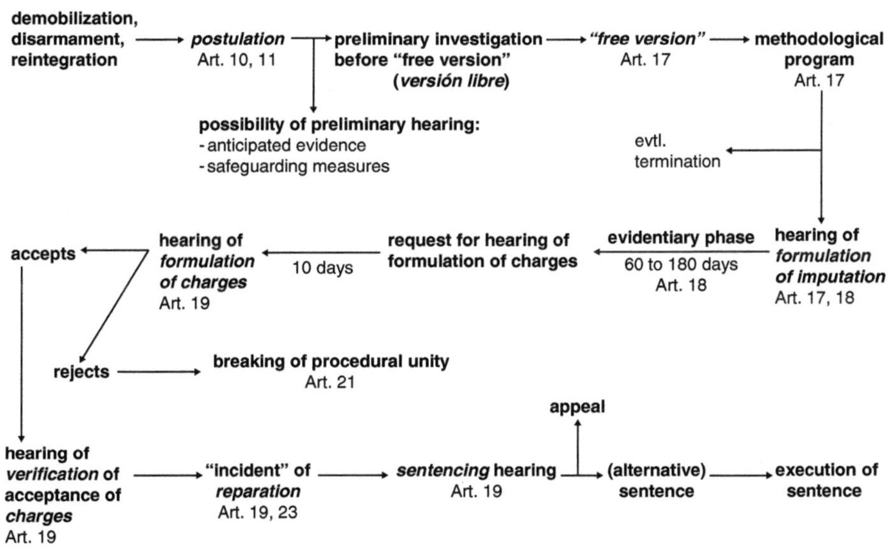

MIX
Papier aus verantwortungsvollen Quellen
Paper from responsible sources
FSC® C105338

If you have any concerns about our products,
you can contact us on
ProductSafety@springernature.com

In case Publisher is established outside the EU,
the EU authorized representative is:
Springer Nature Customer Service Center GmbH
Europaplatz 3, 69115 Heidelberg, Germany

Printed by Libri Plureos GmbH
in Hamburg, Germany